Vera Matarese
The Metaphysics of Bohmian Mechanics

Epistemic Studies

Philosophy of Science, Cognition and Mind

Edited by
Michael Esfeld, Stephan Hartmann, Albert Newen

Editorial Advisory Board:
Katalin Balog, Claus Beisbart, Craig Callender, Tim Crane, Katja Crone,
Ophelia Deroy, Mauro Dorato, Alison Fernandes, Jens Harbecke,
Vera Hoffmann-Kolss, Max Kistler, Beate Krickel, Anna Marmodoro, Alyssa Ney,
Hans Rott, Wolfgang Spohn, Gottfried Vosgerau

Volume 51

Vera Matarese

The Metaphysics of Bohmian Mechanics

—

A Comprehensive Guide to the Different Interpretations of Bohmian Ontology

DE GRUYTER

ISBN 978-3-11-162727-4
e-ISBN (PDF) 978-3-11-079387-1
e-ISBN (EPUB) 978-3-11-079423-6
ISSN 2512-5168

Library of Congress Control Number: 2023930647

Bibliographic information published by the Deutsche Nationalbibliothek
The Deutsche Nationalbibliothek lists this publication in the Deutsche Nationalbibliografie; detailed bibliographic data are available on the internet at http://dnb.dnb.de.

© 2024 Walter de Gruyter GmbH, Berlin/Boston
This volume is text- and page-identical with the hardback published in 2023.
Typesetting: Integra Software Services Pvt. Ltd.

www.degruyter.com

To all my academic mentors

Acknowledgments

This book is based on research conducted during my Ph.D. studies at the University of Hong Kong. Section 3.6 draws on material from my paper "On The Methodological Arguments for Wave–Function Realism", published in *International Studies in the Philosophy of Science*, 34:2, pp. 63–80.

The development of the ideas contained in this book greatly benefited from the interactions that I had in the past years with my mentors and colleagues. In particular, I am very grateful to Jo Wolff, Claus Beisbart, Dan Marshall, Davide Romano, Casey McCoy, Michael Esfeld, Eddy Keming Chen, Guido Bacciagaluppi, Jill North, Valia Allori, Jack Yip, Jamin Asay, Paolo Beltrame, Detlef Dürr, Shelly Goldstein, Nino Zanghì, Jonas Werner, Matthias Rolff, Vincent Lam, Matthias Egg, Cristian Lopez, Dustin Lazarovici, Mario Hubert, Antonio Vassallo, Matthias Lienert, Andrea Oldofredi, for helping me develop and sharp my views on Bohmian mechanics through long conversations, insightful suggestions, or challenging questions.

I thank Renato Pettoello for encouraging me to publish this work, and Michael Esfeld for his willingness and readiness to help me achieve this goal. I also thank Christoph Schirmer and Mara Weber for their professional assistance during the publication process.

Finally, this book is dedicated to all my academic mentors, who have been a constant source of inspiration and support for the past ten years, and who kept me going and helped me grow intellectually.

Bern, 30 October 2022,
Vera Matarese

Contents

Acknowledgments —— VII

Illustrations —— XV

Abbreviations —— XVII

Introduction —— 1

I The Bohmian System

1 **Bohmian Mechanics: The Fundamentals** —— 9
1.1 The Particles —— 9
1.2 The Wave-function —— 11
1.3 The Wave-function and the Particles —— 12
1.4 The Dynamics —— 13
1.4.1 The Schrödinger Equation —— 13
1.4.2 The Guiding Equation —— 15
1.5 Non-locality —— 17
1.6 Non-locality, Non-separability or Universality, and Entanglement —— 19
1.7 Subsystems —— 20
1.8 Determinism —— 23
1.9 Probabilities —— 24
1.10 The Rutgers-Munich-Genova Group: Quantum Equilibrium, Equivariance and Absolute Uncertainty —— 25
1.11 Valentini's Quantum Non-equilibrium —— 29
1.12 Summing up: The Bohmian Postulates —— 30
1.13 The Questions We Shall Ask —— 30

II The Status of the Particles

2 **Bohmian Particles and Bohmian Properties** —— 35
2.1 Particles —— 35
2.2 The Dependence of Bohmian Properties on Positions —— 41
2.3 Contextual Properties, Particles and the Wave-function —— 46
2.4 Mass and Charge —— 48
2.5 The Principle of Generosity —— 49

2.6	The Principle of Parsimony —— 50	
2.7	A Case of Underdetermination —— 52	
2.8	The Primitive Ontology Approach and Bohmian Mechanics —— 53	
2.9	The Super-Humeanism Approach by the Lausanne School —— 57	
2.10	Many Particles or Just One Particle? The Marvelous and the Miserable Particle View —— 59	

III The Status of the Wave-function

3	A Realist Interpretation for the Wave-function —— 63	
3.1	Wave-function Realism —— 63	
3.2	The Centrality of the Quantum Wave-function —— 63	
3.2.1	The Hamiltonian-Jacobi Equation and the Guiding Law —— 64	
3.2.2	The Bohmian Dynamics. From Newtonian to Bohmian Mechanics —— 67	
3.3	A Metaphysical Analysis of the Wave-function Realist Ontological Picture —— 70	
3.3.1	Field Theory —— 71	
3.3.2	Causality and Properties —— 72	
3.4	The Problems with the Resulting Ontology —— 74	
3.4.1	A Strange Field Theory —— 74	
3.4.2	Problems: The Violations of the Criteria for Physicality —— 81	
3.4.3	Problems with Causality —— 86	
3.4.4	Valentini's Responses —— 88	
3.5	Summary: The Realist View Is Bad for Ontological Results —— 93	
3.6	The Methodology of the Realist View —— 94	
3.6.1	The Wave-function as a *physical field* in Configuration Space: A Problem of Reification —— 94	
3.6.2	A First Reply from the Realist —— 97	
3.6.3	High-dimensional Space? —— 99	
3.6.4	The First Principle —— 100	
3.6.5	The Second Principle —— 107	
3.7	The Multi-field View —— 112	
4	A Nomological Interpretation for the Wave-function —— 114	
4.1	The Guiding Equation —— 114	
4.1.1	Simplicity and Symmetries —— 114	
4.1.2	Probability Current —— 118	
4.1.3	The De Broglie Equation —— 119	

4.2	The Resulting Ontology —— 122	
4.2.1	The Wave-function as a Law —— 122	
4.2.2	The Defense —— 125	
4.2.3	The Wave-function as a Part of the Law —— 127	
4.3	How to Understand Nomological Entities, and Thus the Wave-function: Different Metaphysical Scenarios —— 129	
4.3.1	The Realist View on Nomological Entities: Primitivism —— 130	
4.3.2	Problems —— 133	
4.3.3	Anti-realism and the Humean View: No Gap, No Explanation —— 134	
4.3.4	The Supervenience Problem —— 137	
4.3.5	The Non-locality Problem —— 138	
4.3.6	Simplicity and Informativeness —— 139	
4.3.7	The Unsatisfactory Humean View —— 141	
4.4	The Dispositional Interpretation —— 142	
4.4.1	The Dispositional Property of Motion —— 147	
4.4.2	The Mumford Dilemma —— 147	
4.5	Esfeld's Super-Humeanism —— 149	
4.6	General Problems of the Nomological View —— 150	
4.6.1	The Problem of Underdetermination —— 150	
4.6.2	The Physicality of the Wave-function: The Wave-function Can Kill! —— 150	
4.7	The Methodology —— 153	

IV The Structuralist View

5	**Ontic Structural Realism: The State of the Art —— 161**	
5.1	Introduction —— 161	
5.2	The State of the Art —— 163	
5.2.1	Structural Realism —— 163	
5.2.2	Ontic Structural Realism —— 166	
5.3	Ontic Structural Realism: The Methodological Program —— 170	
5.3.1	Ontic Structural Realism: An Anti-armchair-metaphysics Program —— 171	
5.3.2	Summing up: The 'Danglers' —— 176	
5.3.3	An Example: The Aether —— 177	

6	**Bohmian Mechanics and Ontic Structural Realism —— 178**
6.1	The Problem of Underdetermination Given by the Wave-function —— 178
6.2	Is the Wave-function a Dangler? —— 179
6.3	The Problem of Invariance and Objectivity: What the Wave-function Represents Cannot Be in 3ND —— 180
6.4	What the Laws Reveal —— 183
6.5	Modality —— 186
6.6	Particles, Properties and Structure —— 190
6.7	The Individuality of Particles —— 193
6.8	The Bohmian Ontology and Moderate Ontic Structural Realism —— 194
6.9	Particle Positions: Extrinsic or Intrinsic Properties? —— 197
6.10	Position as Extrinsic and a Relational Space —— 198
6.10.1	A Speculative Relational Bohmian Mechanics —— 198
6.11	Position as Intrinsic and a Substantival Space —— 201
6.12	Position as Extrinsic and a Substantival Space —— 203
6.13	Example: Singlet and Triplet States —— 205
7	**Conclusive Remarks —— 207**
7.1	The Best of Both Worlds: A Structuralist Ontology for Bohmian Mechanics —— 207
7.1.1	The Status of the Wave-function —— 207
7.1.2	Balance between Parsimony and Explanatory Power —— 208
7.1.3	Underdetermination —— 208
7.1.4	Compatibility with Different Mathematical Formulations —— 209
7.1.5	Experiments – Empty Trajectories —— 209
7.2	A Structuralist Reconciliation of the Realist and Nomological Views in Bohmian Mechanics —— 210
7.2.1	The Status of the Wave-function —— 210
7.2.2	The Determination of the Dynamics —— 211
7.3	A Final Defense of the Structuralist Reading of the Wave-function —— 212
7.4	Open Questions for Future Research —— 214
7.4.1	A Possible Threat: Circularity and Non-supervenience —— 214
7.4.2	A Possible Threat: The Wave-function as a Background Structure – A Case of Underdetermination? —— 217
7.4.3	A Possible Threat: The Single Particle Case —— 219
7.4.4	A Possible Threat: Is Bohmian Mechanics with Property-less Particles Possible? —— 220

7.5	Possible Objections —— **225**	
7.5.1	The Unobservability and Underdetermination of the Dynamical Structure —— **225**	
7.5.2	It Is Not a Structuralist 'Reconciliation', Rather It Is a Structuralist 'Rejection' —— **226**	

Conclusion —— 228

Bibliography —— 231

Index —— 241

Illustrations

Figure 1 A two-dimensional configuration space —— **10**
Figure 2 A two-dimensional configuration space —— **11**
Figure 3 The Stern-Gerlach device —— **41**
Figure 4 The spin property —— **42**
Figure 5 Flipping the box —— **43**
Figure 6 Spin-entanglement —— **44**
Figure 7 Ensemble of particle trajectories varying position and momentum —— **65**
Figure 8 Retarded action at a distance —— **77**
Figure 9 Entanglement in one-dimensional space —— **108**
Figure 10 Entanglement in two-dimensional configuration space —— **109**
Figure 11 The dispositional interpretation of the wave-function —— **145**
Figure 12 The reduced configuration space —— **222**

Abbreviations

BM	Bohmian Mechanics
BT	Bundle Theory
DESR	Direct Epistemic Structural Realism
DGZ	Dürr, Goldstein, Zanghì
EOSR	Eliminative Ontic Structural Realism
ESR	Epistemic Structural Realism
IESR	Indirect Epistemic Structural Realism
IOSR	Intermediate Ontic Structural Realism
LLT	Localizability Thesis
MOSR	Moderate Ontic Structural Realism
MRL	Mill, Ramsey, Lewis
OOEOW	Obvious ontology evolving in an obvious way
OSR	Ontic Structural Realism
PO	Primitive Ontology
QM	Quantum Mechanics
ROSR	Radical Ontic Structural Realism
SR	Structural Realism

Introduction

Preamble

In physics, any complete scientific theory consists of two important components: a formalism and an interpretation. The formalism, which takes the form of a set of equations and some computational rules, is essential for the empirical adequacy of the theory and for a formal explanation. The interpretation provides a clear understanding of the ontological structure underlying the theory, since it answers the question of what there is at the fundamental level of reality.[1] Therefore, we can say that every scientific theory in physics is supposed to fulfill three different roles:
(i) it is expected to successfully predict certain events;
(ii) it is expected to provide a mathematical explanation of why they occur, by appealing to mathematical rules or mathematical objects;
(iii) it is expected to provide an understanding of the ontology, i. e. of what exists in the world according to the theory.

While physicists are more concerned with the empirical adequacy of the theory and the formal explanation, philosophers of physics are more inclined towards the ontological interpretation.

The aim of this book is to present and elaborate on the diverse ontological interpretations of Bohmian mechanics, which have been developed to answer the question of how the two main elements that constitute the Bohmian theory, the Bohmian particles and the Bohmian wave-function, should be ontologically interpreted. What are the properties of the Bohmian particles? How can we characterize their individuality? And what is the wave-function?

Why Bohmian Mechanics?

Bohmian mechanics is not the standard quantum theory normally endorsed by the scientific community. It is therefore important to briefly alert the reader of the difference between the orthodox theory of quantum mechanics, also called the Copenhagen interpretation, and how it differs from Bohmian mechanics. The Copenhagen interpretation is based on two elements: a wave-function Ψ and some

---

[1] For the definitions of formalism and interpretation I use here, refer to Cushing, 1994, chapter 2.

macroscopic variables Λ corresponding to the outcomes of certain experiments. A few important points need to be made about this theory:

- The microscopic level is described only by the mathematical object called the wave-function. The wave-function provides epistemic and subjective knowledge of the microscopic domain and successfully demonstrates predictive power and usefulness. However, this object also presents some mathematical features that, if regarded as revealing the nature of the microscopic ontology, would imply the existence of a very vague world. In such a world, microscopic entities are in a superposition of incompatible states, particles do not have continuous trajectories and so on. The consequence of this is that most defenders of the Copenhagen interpretation claim that we should not commit to a quantum reality that goes beyond the quantum description, maintaining that there is nothing there beyond the wave-function. But if this is so – if there is no microscopic world that we can be knowledgeable about – then it is not exactly clear what quantum mechanics describes at the microscopic level.
- The macroscopic level consists of our familiar objects and the outcomes of experiments (identified with variables Λ) that we perform in our laboratories. In such a world, our experimental results are definite (for instance, cats are either dead or alive) and macroscopic objects always have precise positions. The wave-function is salient in our macroscopic world only because it gives us the right probabilities of the outcomes of our experiments.
- The key problem that the Copenhagen interpretation has to face is how it can bridge the fuzziness of the microscopic 'domain' or 'world' and the definite character of our classical world. In order to do this, many philosophers of physics introduced the role of observers, which have the power to create definite outcomes. This is often presented with the simplistic expression that, in quantum mechanics, 'observers create reality'.

All of this is murky and obscure. The Copenhagen interpretation, in sum, faces a dilemma: either it gives up the role of providing an understanding of what exists at the fundamental level of reality and remains only as an epistemic (and incomplete) theory, or it takes up this role but provides a very problematic and unsatisfactory ontological picture.

I take it that many may be happy with the belief that observers create reality or that at the most fundamental level physical entities are in a superposition of states. But this book aims to discuss another proposal, the theory called 'Bohmian mechanics', which I consider to be much clearer and more straightforward. Bohmian mechanics offers a formalism that is based on two elements: the wave-function Ψ (which is the same as the one in the Copenhagen interpretation) and the position of particles Q. The theory consists of the following:

- At the microscopic level, we have particles that follow continuous trajectories that are determined by the wave-function via the guiding law of motion for the particles.
- At the macroscopic level, all the objects consist of conglomerates of these particles, and all the measurement outcomes of our laboratories consist in particles' positions.

Bohmian mechanics takes the most natural ontological elements we know of – the particles – and, with them, it implements standard quantum mechanics in order to answer the question of what exists in the world. In other words, it completes standard quantum mechanics by presupposing an 'obvious ontology evolving in an obvious way'[2] (which the Bohmians refer to with the acronym OOEOW) at the microscopic level.[3]

This characterization of Bohmian mechanics, however, is not enough for us to acquire a clear ontological interpretation. Indeed, it is only the first step. In order to fully understand the theory, we also need to be able to metaphysically characterize this ontology. The fact that we have particles and a wave-function in Bohmian mechanics offers us a stable ground on which we can build a sound discussion of what exists in the world, but several questions are still at stake. First of all, we need to investigate the status of the particles – that is, whether they instantiate properties, and how they can be metaphysically characterized. Secondly, and most importantly, we need to understand the ontological status of the wave-function. We said that in Bohmian mechanics the wave-function has a dynamical role: it determines the dynamics of the particles. But it is not clear how this determination occurs, and, consequently, it is not clear how the wave-function should be interpreted ontologically. Moreover, what I aim to show is that ontological interpretations are always intertwined with metaphysical considerations about the kinds of entities that our ontology deals with. In this book, there will be plenty of examples: for instance, it will not be enough to characterize the wave-function as a field or as a law, for we also need to spell out what being a 'field' or a 'law' metaphysically amounts to. Indeed, questions arise concerning the nature of fields (i. e. whether fields are only a collection of intrinsic properties of space or are concrete particulars) and of laws (i. e. whether laws are only descriptions of the world or have modal power). Another example is concerned with the status of particles and what we mean when we define particles as 'point-like' objects. In

---

2 See Goldstein, 1996.
3 In chapter 2, I will show why particles are taken to be the most obvious constituents of the ontology, while in chapters 3 and 4 I will show why the law of motion that dictates their behavior is 'obvious'.

most cases, it seems that we need to endorse a particular metaphysical position regarding how to characterize the ontology of the world.

The Methodology

While developing an ontological interpretation of these two elements, the problem of the relation between formalism and interpretation will inevitably arise. In the literature, there are two main approaches to understanding the constitution of the Bohmian ontology. Sometimes, the characterization of the ontology is mainly determined by our metaphysical presuppositions of what the world should be like. For example, in the discussion of the particles, we will see that it is usually presupposed that Bohmian particles are impenetrable. But this presupposition is more determined by our metaphysical concerns and not by the formalism, which in fact allows particles to share the same position at the same time, even though this, contingently, never happens. Other times, the metaphysical characterization of the ontology is mainly determined by the formalism. For example, we will see that the realists interpret the wave-function as a physical field in configuration space because they rely on a process of reification of mathematical entities.

In this book, I discuss and evaluate both approaches. Most of the time, my approach will navigate between the 'Scylla' of our metaphysical presuppositions of what exists in the world and the 'Charybdis' of the mathematical formalism. My methodology will involve a back-and-forth approach between mathematical and metaphysical considerations, so that the former can shape the latter and vice-versa.

Guidelines to the Reader

This book is situated at the intersection of metaphysics and physics. And like most works in this area, it is difficult to adopt a language that can reach both academic communities equally well at the same time. The language used here is tailored for scholars who are already accustomed to philosophical jargon but not necessarily to the physical one. For this reason, I take great care in explaining mathematical aspects of the theory that for a physicist may sound quite obvious and not worth explaining. In particular, I wrote this book imagining that the hypothetical reader was any graduate student in philosophy, who is unfamiliar with the quantum physics. Moreover, I tried to keep the mathematical presentations and the philosophical discussions as separate as possible so that the reader can follow the philosophical discussion without knowing the details of the formalism.

Furthermore, I have adopted jargon that is normally used in the philosophy of science academic literature. Trying to transpose this kind of language into metaphysical debates may lead to some misunderstandings. For example, whenever we say that an entity 'exists' in the philosophy of physics, it is clear that we mean that it is a physical entity. Unless otherwise specified (for example in chapter 4), in this book terms like 'ontology' or 'reality' denote a physical existence. Another important example is the term 'nomological', which should not be understood to mean 'part of the ideology', but as part of the 'laws of nature'. I have always specified the different meanings most commonly used in the literature I deal with in order to avoid any confusion, but it is hard to provide a clarification for all of them.

The structure of this book is as follows.

The first part (chapter 1) is a formal and conceptual presentation of the fundamentals of Bohmian mechanics. It does not aim to be a complete description of the theory, but it does aim to provide a complete presentation of all the aspects of Bohmian mechanics that are important for understanding the interpretational work that will follow.

The second part (chapter 2) offers a discussion of the particles and of the properties of the Bohmian system. Here I will introduce the problem of particle impenetrability, and the problem of the instantiation of scientific properties in the Bohmian system. This chapter will also present the so-called 'primitive ontology' approach, which is normally regarded as providing the best understanding of particles in Bohmian mechanics.

The most important contribution to the debate in Bohmian mechanics is in part three (chapters 3 and 4), and in part four (chapters 5, 6, 7).

The third part (chapters 3 and 4) constitutes the main body of the book and is entirely dedicated to the ontological status of the wave-function. In this part, I will provide a discussion of the two most famous views on the status of the wave-function: the realist view (chapter 3) and the nomological view (chapter 4). Concerning the realist view, I will mainly focus on how Valentini on the one hand, and Albert on the other hand, developed the view. Concerning the nomological view, I will mainly concentrate on the version developed by the Rutgers-Munich-Genova group (also referred to as 'DGZ' since the members of the group are Dürr, Goldstein and Zanghì), but I will also take into consideration other contributions, in particular the metaphysical characterization of the Bohmian ontology recently presented by the Lausanne school, led by Esfeld. In both chapters, I will proceed as follows. First, I will show why there are two different ontological interpretations of the wave-function. I will suggest that the difference in the ontology may partially rely on the particular formalism adopted to express the equation of motion of the particles and on its interpretation. While the realist view, within Valentini's account, is supported by a certain formalism in which the law of motion is regarded as a dynamical law (which implies the existence of a cause), the nomological view regards the law of motion for the particles as a kinematic law (i. e. there is no causal connection involved). After spelling out this link, I will discuss the ontology of both views and analyze why they are not satisfactory from a metaphysical perspective. Finally, in the last section of both chapters I will evaluate the methodological program that grounds and justifies the two views. I will show that both views not only offer unsatisfactory ontological results, but they also rely on problematic methodologies.

The last part of the book (chapters 5, 6, 7) will be entirely dedicated to the presentation of the metaphysical framework provided by ontic structural realism and its application to Bohmian mechanics. I will argue that a moderate version of structural realism provides a very natural metaphysical characterization of the Bohmian ontology concerning both the status of the wave-function and the status of the particles. Moreover, it fares better than the realist and nomological views with regard to its resulting ontology and methodological aspects. Finally, it can be considered as a reconciliation of the two competing camps given that it takes on features of both views.

I The Bohmian System

1 Bohmian Mechanics: The Fundamentals

Bohmian mechanics is a quantum theory that postulates the existence of particles whose trajectories are determined by a function called 'the wave-function'. Therefore, according to Bohmian mechanics, two elements are needed in order to fully specify the state of the physical system: the particle positions, also called the 'particle configuration', and the wave-function. In this book, we will use Q to refer to the particle configuration and Ψ to refer to the wave-function.

1.1 The Particles

The particle configuration Q is fully specified by listing all the different particles' positions at one time. Given an instant of time,

$$Q = q_1, q_2, q_3 \ldots q_N$$

where capital Q refers to all the positions of all the existing particles,[4] while each non-capital 'q' refers to the position that each particle occupies at that time.[5]

The particles inhabit our space (or space-time), hence a three-dimensional space (or four-dimensional space), and continuously follow definite trajectories for all times. In this regard, we can imagine the Bohmian particles to be much like the Newtonian particles.

Even though the particles live in a three-dimensional space R^3, normally represented by a Euclidean three-axis space, their positions can be represented in a much more convenient way as a single point in another space that is high-dimensional. This way, our Q is just a point in this high-dimensional space. We call this new high-dimensional space the 'configuration space'. The configuration space is constructed in such a way that each of its dimensions represents a degree of freedom of the particle system. Given that each particle has three degrees of freedom because of the three-dimensionality of the space where they live, we can construct the dimensionality of the configuration space by multiplying the number of the particles (N) by three. The dimensions of our configuration space thus become: 3N. Hence, we can refer to our configuration space with: R^{3N}. Each degree of freedom of the particle

---

[4] Note that here and in the following, I am implicitly endorsing the view that, strictly speaking, the Bohmian system is, at the fundamental level, the totality of our universe (Dürr et al., 1992, 2013). For this reason, here Q refers to the positions of all existing particles. In a more technical language, Q refers to the positions of all the particles of the Bohmian system.

[5] q_k refers to the position of the kth- particle belonging to Q.

configuration is represented by one axis of the configuration space, and all the axes are orthogonal to each other.

It would be impossible to draw this space on a sheet of paper! Given that the number of the particles in the universe is around 10^{80}, the number of dimensions of the configuration space would be 30^{80}! But in order to show how we can pinpoint all the particles' positions with one single point Q in our R^{3N}, let me provide a very idealized example.

Consider that our Bohmian universe consists of two particles in one-dimensional space:

$$Q = q_1, q_2$$

Then, our configuration space, whose dimensions are given by the number of degrees of freedom of our particles (in this case, 1) multiplied by the number of particles, is a two-dimensional space. It can thus be easily drawn as demonstrated in Figure 1.

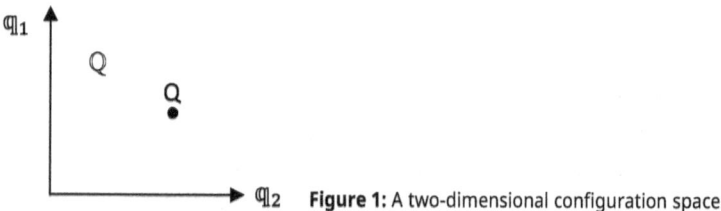

Figure 1: A two-dimensional configuration space.

Each axis represents all the possible positions that each particle could take in their physical one-dimensional space, and we denote them with ꟼ. Each point of the configuration space represents a possible particle configuration, or, in other words, a possible 'Q': a possible arrangement of the different particle positions, while ℚ refers to a 'possible' but non-actual Q.

We can suppose in our example that while the first particle position is $q_1 = 2$, the second particle position is $q_2 = 5$. These two positions in one-dimensional space are identified uniquely by a single point in our R^{1N} (our configuration space), as can be seen in Figure 2.

We have also seen that the Bohmian particles move, following definite and continuous trajectories all the time. Given that we can represent all the particles' positions of the universe with one single point in our configuration space, we can easily represent the trajectories of all the particles of the universe in our configuration space with one single trajectory by adding the axis for time.

Note that we have not yet added any new elements that are not already present in classical mechanics. In classical mechanics as well, we have point-like particles

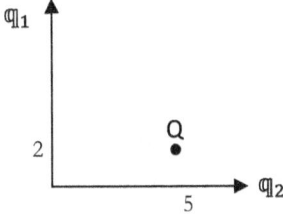

Figure 2: A two-dimensional configuration space.

moving along definite trajectories, and while they live in a three-dimensional space (our physical space), they can be represented as a single point in configuration space.

1.2 The Wave-function

The second element of Bohmian mechanics, which demonstrates the quantum character of the theory, is the so-called 'wave-function':[6]

$$\Psi(x)$$

The wave-function is a complex-valued function that maps each point of the configuration space, at each time, to a complex number. One can think of it as a decoration of our configuration space, or, more precisely, as a continuous distribution of complex numbers. The wave-function is defined for the whole configuration space, which means that it is defined for all possible points in the configuration space (all 'x's). Given that our space is three-dimensional, the configuration space is 3N-dimensional, and the wave-function has 3N degrees of freedom:[7]

$$\Psi(x_1, x_2, x_3, \ldots x_{3N}, t)$$

Since in Bohmian mechanics the points of the configuration space represent all the possible particle configurations $\mathbb{Q}$, mathematically, we can describe the wave-function as the function whose domain is all the possible particle configurations

---

[6] The Bohmian wave-function is exactly the same wave-function we find in standard quantum mechanics.

[7] Here and in the rest of this book, I assume that it is methodologically correct to infer the dimensions of the wave-function from the number and the degrees of freedom of the particles in three-dimensional space. However, this is controversial if one regards our three-dimensional space as derivative and the configuration space where the wave-function lives as fundamental. For a discussion of this topic, see for example Albert, 1996; Lewis, 2006.

(all $\mathbb{Q}$s) and whose co-domain is constituted by the complex numbers. This would amount to:[8]

$$\exists \Psi \, (\Psi(\mathbb{Q}_1, t_1) = C_1 \, \& \, \Psi(\mathbb{Q}_2, t_2) = C_2 \, \& \ldots)$$

Given that the wave-function attributes values (represented by the complex numbers) to a space – that is, the configuration space – then it is a complex-valued 'field'. As such, we can also think of the wave-function as a mapping from a base space (our configuration space R^{3N}) to a target space (in this case $\mathbb{C}$). Each point of the space consists of a spatial point with a complex number.

Since our wave-function is complex-valued, it can be written in 'polar' form, which means that it can be split into two different parts, the modulus (or amplitude) $R(x,t)$ and the phase $S(x,t)$, which are two different real functions of x and t (the time):

$$\Psi(x,t) = R(x,t) e^{\frac{iS}{\hbar}(x,t)}$$

where $\hbar = h/2\pi$ and h is the Planck's constant. We need to be aware that we should not think of the 'modulus' as the real part of the wave-function, nor should we think of the 'phase' as the complex part.[9]

1.3 The Wave-function and the Particles

Now that we have introduced both the wave-function and the particles, we can go back to our first claim that, in Bohmian mechanics, any system is defined by specifying two elements: the wave-function and the particle configuration. It is useful to put all the pieces of information described above concerning the particles and the wave-function together. As hinted in the last section, the wave-function is defined for the whole configuration space, and for this reason it is specified for any possible 'Q', which we represent with a generic 'x'. In Bohmian mechanics, each x of the wave-function configuration space corresponds to a possible 'Q', which we denoted with $\mathbb{Q}$. We take Q to be the actual configuration of all the particles taken together, while each 'x' corresponds to each $\mathbb{Q}$. Whenever we want to talk about the generic wave-function, we will use $\Psi(x)$, but whenever we want to evaluate the wave-function of the actual system or find the value that the wave-function attributes to the actual configuration of all the particles, we will use $\Psi(Q)$. In the

---

[8] This representation of the role of the wave-function is taken from Ted Sider's lecture notes (Rutgers, Philosophy of Physics Graduate Seminar, Winter 2016).
[9] For clarifications, see Bowman, 2008, chapter 10.

following equations, sometimes we will also use 'q' to denote a generic position variable in configuration space. Indeed, the 'q' is useful to remind the reader that the wavefunction in Bohmian mechanics a complex function on the space of possible particle configurations q of the system. If we want to evaluate the wavefunction of one single particle position q_1, then we use $\psi(q_1)$. I use the capital Ψ to represent the universal wave-function, while the non-capital ψ represents different wave-functions, one for each subsystem.[10]

1.4 The Dynamics

Neither the particles nor the wave-function is static; rather, they evolve over time in a deterministic way. Two different equations dictate their evolution.

1.4.1 The Schrödinger Equation

The temporal development of the wave-function is given by the famous Schrödinger equation, which is a linear unity differential equation:

$$i\hbar \frac{d\Psi}{dt} = \hat{H}\Psi$$

or, for a system with many degrees of freedom:

$$i\hbar \frac{\partial \Psi(x_1, x_2, \ldots, t)}{\partial t} = \hat{H}\Psi(x_1, x_2, \ldots, t)$$

where $\hbar$ is a constant, and $\hat{H}$ is a quantum operator called the Hamiltonian.[11] Classically, the Hamiltonian is a function that expresses the total energy of the system. The energy of a system can take different forms (there are different forms of

---

[10] In this section, I have tried to explain the formal apparatus of the theory in a very intuitive and conceptual way for readers who are not familiar with mathematical formalism. I am aware that without formal and rigorous definitions, the notation of this book may appear sloppy to mathematicians. For a precise use of the notation of the equations present in this book, refer to the beautiful book by Dürr and Lazarovici (2020).

[11] Technically, if I write the Hamiltonian as an operator, I should write the wave-function as a "ket" (a vector). Operators only act on vectors, not on scalar functions. However, here, for the sake of clarity and simplicity, I adopt this formulation, which can be also found in standard textbooks on Bohmian mechanics (Oriolis & Mompart, 2012; Sanz & Miret-Artés, 2013). Thanks to Dr. Romano for raising this point.

energy); however, generally, we can define the Hamiltonian as the sum of the kinetic K and the potential energy of the system V:

$$H = K + V$$

given that

$$K = \frac{p^2}{2m}$$

then:

$$H = \frac{p^2}{2m} + V$$

where 'p' is the momentum, and 'm' is the mass of the particle.

We just spelled out the Hamiltonian in classical mechanics. In quantum mechanics, as we have seen, the Hamiltonian is an operator, and in order to transform the classical Hamiltonian into a quantum operator, we just need to replace the classical momentum with the quantum one:

$$p \to \hat{p} = -i\hbar \frac{\partial}{\partial x}$$

This way, the quantum Hamiltonian becomes:

$$\hat{H} = \frac{-\hbar^2}{2m} \frac{\partial^2}{\partial x^2} + V$$

and the Schrödinger equation becomes:[12]

$$i\hbar \frac{\partial \Psi(x_1, x_2, \ldots, t)}{\partial t} = \frac{-\hbar^2}{2m} \frac{\partial^2}{\partial x^2} \Psi(x_1, x_2, \ldots, t) + V\Psi(x_1, x_2, \ldots, t)$$

And given that the partial derivative $\frac{\partial}{\partial x}$ is the gradient ∇:[13]

---

[12] For a multi-particle system, we could rewrite the Schrödinger equation with a summation, where N is the number of all the particles:

$$i\hbar \frac{\partial \Psi(x,t)}{\partial t} = \left(\sum_{k=1}^{N} -\frac{\hbar^2}{2m} \frac{\partial^2}{\partial_k^2} + V(x,t) \right) \Psi(x,t)$$

[13] Technically, the gradient is the 'gradient-vector' defined: $\nabla = \begin{pmatrix} \nabla_1 \\ \nabla_2 \\ \nabla_{\ldots} \\ \nabla_N \end{pmatrix}$

$$i\hbar \frac{\partial \Psi(x_1, x_2, \ldots, t)}{\partial t} = \frac{-\hbar^2}{2m} \nabla^2 \Psi(x_1, x_2, \ldots, t) + V\Psi(x_1, x_2, \ldots, t)$$

The Schrödinger equation shows that the temporal evolution of the wave-function is generated or determined by the Hamiltonian; hence, the solutions of the Schrödinger equation depend on the form of the Hamiltonian. The form of the Hamiltonian depends on the physical interactions within the system it describes and on the physical interactions that the system entertains with the environment.

1.4.2 The Guiding Equation

The law of motion for the particles can be written as a first or second-time derivative of their position. On the one hand, the second-time derivative guiding law has the same structure as our familiar Newtonian dynamical law, since they are both based on the acceleration of the particles.

$$\frac{d}{dt}(m\dot{x}) = -\nabla(V + Q)$$

where Q

$$Q(x, t) = -\frac{\hbar^2}{2m} \frac{\nabla^2 R}{R}$$

is the quantum potential energy, which is also called 'quantum potential'. This equation describes the dynamics of a particle subject to a force, which is generated by both the classical and the quantum potential energy:

$$F = -\nabla(V + Q)$$

The first-order equation, on the other hand, given that it is the first-time derivative of the Bohmian position, is based on velocity. Specifically, the velocity of the particles is given by the gradient of the phase of the wave-function:

$$v^\Psi(Q) = \frac{dQ}{dt} = \frac{\nabla S}{m}$$

Given that the momentum is equal to:

$$p = mv$$

we can also re-write:

$$m\frac{dQ}{dt} = p = \nabla S$$

The velocity of the particles is determined by the wave-function through its phase. In the equations above, we are evaluating the velocity of Q (hence of the single point in configuration space), but we can use the same equation to find the velocity of one single particle in our space. Suppose that our universe consists of only one single particle in one-dimensional space. Our guiding equation would then simply be:

$$v^{\Psi}(q_1) = \frac{dq_1}{dt} = \frac{\nabla S(q_1, t)}{m}$$

where the super-script Ψ is there just as a reminder that, given that S is the phase of the wave-function, the velocity is generated by the wave-function (through its phase).[14] Suppose now that we want to find the velocity of two different particles that are non-interacting.

$$v^{\Psi}(q_1) = \frac{dq_1}{dt} = \frac{\nabla S(q_1, t)}{m}$$

$$v^{\Psi}(q_2) = \frac{dq_2}{dt} = \frac{\nabla S(q_2, t)}{m}$$

From a 'wave-function perspective', it does not make any difference whether our system consists of two particles in one-dimensional space or one particle in two-dimensional space. Indeed, as we have already seen, it is constructed on the number of degrees of freedom of the particle system, and it treats all the degrees of freedom 'equally', on an equal footing. What the wave-function takes into consideration is simply the number of degrees of freedom of the system and not what kinds of degrees of freedom we are dealing with. For this reason, we can reformulate the two equations above without committing to 'particle positions' but only to generic coordinates:

$$v^{\Psi}{}_1 = \frac{\nabla S_1(x, t)}{m}$$

$$v^{\Psi}{}_2 = \frac{\nabla S_2(y, t)}{m}$$

From the wave-function perspective, the two coordinates follow two independent equations. When two equations are independent of each other, we call them

---

[14] Also here, the formulation is simplified. To be precise, it would be:

$$v^{\Psi}_k = \frac{\partial S(q, t)}{\partial x_k}$$

where k identifies the coordinates of the particle under investigation.

'decoupled' equations, which means that the phase of the total wave-function representing both particles (or both coordinates) is simply the sum of each phase corresponding to each particle:

$$S(x,y,t) = S(x,t) + S(y,t)$$

Whenever we know that the total phase is constructed in this way, by summing all the single independent phases, we can construct the total wave-function of the system as the result of the product of single wave-functions, one for each particle:

$$\Psi(q_1, q_2, t) = \psi(q_1, t)\psi(q_2, t)$$

1.5 Non-locality

However, there is a problem: when I introduced the two decoupled equations in order to derive their independent velocities, I actually misrepresented the nature of Bohmian mechanics. These independent equations were the result of a process of extreme idealization, where we imagine that the two particles are non-interacting. But this is not what normally happens in Bohmian mechanics. In fact, in Bohmian mechanics, the real and faithful guiding equation for one particle with position q_k is:

$$v^\Psi(q_k) = \frac{dq_k}{dt} = \frac{\nabla_k S(Q)}{m_k}$$

Looking closer at this equation, we can see that the velocity of particle 1 depends on the phase of all the particles' positions (i. e. on the many-particle configuration). Given that the equation does not take into consideration the distance between particle 1 and the other particles (rather, it takes all the positions together), we can also see that this dependence is simultaneous. The temporal development of each particle depends on where all the other particles are at that moment, regardless of whether the other particles are far away from the particle we are considering or very near. For this reason, the Bohmian system is said to be non-local.

Now let us consider exactly where the non-local dynamics comes from. The non-local dynamics comes from the fact that the wave-function is a function that lives in configuration space, which means that it assigns a *single value* to all the particles' positions taken together. We said that the configuration space consists of different 'xs', which in Bohmian mechanics correspond to different possible ℚs. The wave-function assigns *one single* value to each possible ℚ and determines, through the guiding law of motion, a temporal development for each of them. But each $\mathbb{Q}$ actually consists of all the positions of all the particles of this universe. For this reason, if we want to know the velocity of one single particle, we first need to know where all the other particles are, and only then we can know where our particle will be. If we did not know where all the other particles were, then we would not be able to know to which '$\mathbb{Q}$' our particle belongs to; hence, we would not be able to know which trajectory the wave-function dictates for our system.

In order to better visualize the situation, suppose that our system consists of two particles, which we shall call 'Jim' and 'Bill'. And suppose that we want to know where Bill will move in the future. In order to know this, we have to know the position of particle Jim *and* the (actual) position of particle Bill. This way, we can pick out the '$\mathbb{Q}$' by which they are represented in configuration space, and we can know what the value of the wave-function at that point is. Only with this information at hand is it possible to predict the future evolution of the particle under investigation.

Not only does the non-local character of the system imply that the velocity of one particle is determined by the position of all the other particles, but it also implies that the position that one particle takes simultaneously influences all the other particles of the universe! This also means that the motion of one particle instantaneously influences all the other particles' trajectories. This is because, even if only one particle's position changes in three-dimensional space, the respective Q in configuration space changes accordingly, and in turn a different value of Ψ will determine the future evolution of the system.

But this does not really tell us anything special. In the Newtonian gravitation theory, for example, if we want to compute the trajectory of one particle, we first need to know where the other particles are. However, an obvious difference between the two cases is that, while in the Newtonian case we need to know where the other particles are because the intensity of the gravitational force depends on the distance between the particles, in Bohmian mechanics the non-local effects do not fade away as the distance increases.[15] Indeed, what is truly special here is that non-locality is given by the fact that the wave-function lives in configuration space.[16] The reason why the particles are non-locally correlated is given by the wave-function Ψ, which is strictly speaking a non-factorizable function; hence, it

---

[15] For a discussion about this, refer to chapter 3.
[16] Note that here I am not proposing any ontological explanation of the non-local effects in Bohmian mechanics. Ontologically, the explanation of non-locality is controversial, and we will discuss it in chapters 3, 4 and 6. Here, I just would like to claim that, mathematically, non-locality comes from the fact that the wave-function is defined in configuration space (the wave-function provides the formal explanation for the non-local dynamics).

cannot be written as the product of different single wave-functions, one for each particle.

$$\Psi(q_1, q_2, t) \neq \psi(q_1, t)\psi(q_2, t)$$

1.6 Non-locality, Non-separability or Universality, and Entanglement

Here I will briefly clarify the meanings of non-locality, non-separability, universality and entanglement in Bohmian mechanics. Even though all these concepts are very much interrelated, it is methodologically important to differentiate them.

Entanglement is a physical phenomenon that concerns both the wave-function and the particles. An entangled wave-function is any wave-function that cannot be factorized into different wave-functions:

$$\Psi(q_1, q_2, t) \neq \psi(q_1, t)\psi(q_2, t)$$

Two (or more) entangled particles are two particles that are interrelated in such a way that each particle state is not independent of the other.[17] Given the primary role of position in Bohmian mechanics, we can say that the position of each particle depends on the positions of all the other particles via the wave-function.

The entanglement effect has one dynamical implication and two ontological implications. The dynamical implication is that the Bohmian system is non-local, and we can define non-locality as the violation of locality. Locality is a feature of the dynamics of the system, in which events that occur at space-like separation from a region could have no influence on the physical state assigned to that region (Maudlin, 2011). As such, non-locality is a feature of a dynamics in which this influence is possible, and this influence is faster than light.[18]

The first ontological implication is that the Bohmian system is non-separable, where non-separability can be defined as the violation of separability. Separability is the feature of a physical system that satisfies the following condition: if the system is situated in a region that can be divided into two disjunct parts $R1$ and $R2$, and the subsystem in $R1$ is in a physical state that is independent of the state of $R2$, then the state of $R1 \cup R2$ is a separable state.[19]

---

[17] Strictly speaking, entangled particles are particles described by entangled wave-functions.
[18] See Maudlin, 2011, for a discussion on what 'influences faster than light' amount to.
[19] For a historical discussion on the definition of separability see Howards (1985) and Ramírez (2020).

The second ontological implication is that the Bohmian system expresses 'universality', which is the strongest kind of non-separability because it involves the entire universe. Given that our universe can be divided into many disjunct parts ($R1$, $R2$, $R3$, $R4$...), if each subsystem is dependent on all the subsystems that constitute the universe, then the system is 'universal'. From a conceptual point of view, indeed, the Bohmian system is the universe, not parts of it. We have only one wave-function, which is, strictly speaking, non-separable (i. e. non-factorizable).

Bohmian mechanics, given that the entanglement phenomenon is applied to all the particles of the universe, presents a non-local, non-separable and universal system.

1.7 Subsystems

A criticism of Bohmian mechanics concerns the matter of impracticability. If it is true that the Bohmian system is fundamentally the universe, then how can Bohmian mechanics help us predict the motion of the particles in our lab? In physics, we continuously have to deal with different experiments (i. e. with parts of the universal system), which we may call 'subsystems'. Normally, these subsystems are more or less isolated from the rest of universe so that they are 'controllable' in experimental situations. Moreover, we would certainly be happy to give up our modest experiments in the lab and instead calculate the velocities of the particles of the universe. But how can we do so? We know neither the form of the universal wave-function, nor the positions of all the particles of the universe. Therefore, one may claim that Bohmian mechanics is, practically speaking, useless. It fundamentally describes a universal system (not subsystems), and it is practically impossible to concretely apply the theory at the universal level given our lack of knowledge. As such, how could we ever consider taking this theory seriously?

Fortunately, Bohmian mechanics is constructed in such a way that, even though ontologically the fundamental reality of the world is universal and completely non-local, the laws work just fine even in experimental situations. On one hand, we have a theoretical level, the level of the fundamental ontology. On the other hand, we have the practical level, where subsystems are (approximately) isolated. Hence, even though we should not forget that strictly speaking the universe is one,[20] we can compute the trajectories of a helium particle without taking into consideration all the other particles of the universe.

---

[20] This view of regarding the Bohmian system as universal and non-local is particularly stressed by the Rutgers-Munich-Genova group (Dürr et al., 1992, 2013).

Here is how we can describe Bohmian subsystems. First of all, recall that in our discussion of different Bohmian motions for different particles we introduced a mathematical element: a wave-function for each particle. We said that whenever the universal wave-function is factorizable, then it is possible to describe the system as consisting of different particle positions and different wave-functions, one for each particle. Now we are going to explain how exactly we can derive that 'small' wave-function.

First of all, imagine that we want to describe the state of an electron with position $q_1(t)$. Given that we are focusing our attention on q_1, we can 'split' the particle configuration Q into two different parts: q_1, which is of interest to us, and all the rest of the particles, which is 'the environment' of our electron state. We can refer to the 'environment' with Y, which is just composed of all the other particles' positions 'q':

$$Y(t) = q_2, q_3 \ldots q_N$$

Now, let us generalize this notion that for any particle configuration, we can write it out by splitting it into two generic variables 'x'[21] and 'y', one representing our subsystem and the other representing the environment. Given this, our actual particle configuration Q can be written as:

$$Q = (X, Y)$$

The universal wave-function can be now written as a function of the subsystem and the environment:

$$\Psi(x, y, t)$$

From this universal wave-function, we can derive the wave-function of the subsystem by simply evaluating the universal wave-function at $y = Y$ (that is, by simply replacing y with Y in the universal wave-function):

$$\psi_t = \Psi(x, Y(t))$$

This wave-function of the subsystem is called the *conditional wave-function*.[22]

However, one can see that the conditional wave-function presents exactly the same problems that had been raised by the universal wave-function: indeed, in order to define it, we need to know Y, which is the actual configuration of all the particles of the universe, except for the one we are considering! Therefore, the conditional wave-function still seems to be of no use.

---

[21] Note that this 'x' is not the same 'x' introduced before in our discussion of the configuration space.

[22] For a more technical and detailed discussion of the conditional wave-function, refer to Dürr et al., 1992, 2013.

However, this is just the first step. Bohmian mechanics predicts that if a subsystem is sufficiently well decoupled (and well isolated) from its environment, then the universal wave-function is the hypothetical wave-function we presented above, hence a factorizable wave-function:

$$\Psi = \psi(x)\Phi(y)$$

The fact that the universal wave-function consists of a product state of the two wave-functions (one for the subsystem and one for the environment) guarantees that the two systems are not interacting, i. e. that neither system influences the other. When this occurs, we get the two different equations of motion presented previously. However, this hypothetical scenario has already been ruled out as too speculative. It will always be the case that our system interacts with the environment somehow and that it is not completely isolated. For example, interaction between the subsystem and the environment occurs whenever we measure the subsystem. So how can we account for all the intricate and complex interrelations that occur between the subsystem and the environment?

It turns out that we can have a reasonably decoupled wave-function for the subsystem whenever the universal wave-function is in superposition of the product state and the other part of the universal wave-function $\Psi^\perp$, so that our subsystem wave-function is defined as obeying:

$$\Psi(x,y) = \psi(x)\Phi(y) + \Psi^\perp(x,y)$$

where Y must be in the support (or simply domain) of $\Phi(y)$, and where there must be a macroscopic difference[23] between the case where Y is in $\Phi(y)$ or in $\Psi^\perp$.

To sum up, we can say that *if* the wave-function of a very well-decoupled subsystem really existed, then by definition $\Psi^\perp(x,y)$ would be negligible and $\psi(x)$ would obey the Schrödinger equation. This wave-function is called the *effective wave-function*.[24] But that 'if' might be confusing. Aren't physicists always working with the effective wave-function rather than the universal wave-function? If so, doesn't that mean that we can have a very well-isolated and well-decoupled wave-function? The answer is that, in physics, we make use of many mathematical tools that 'work' because they are approximately exact. That physicists use the

---

23 Talking about 'macroscopic difference' is not technically precise enough, even though this term is normally employed in the Bohmian literature. Strictly speaking, the technical requirement for ensuring a 'macroscopic difference' is that the supports of the different $\Phi(y)$ must be approximately disjoint in configuration space. I should thank Dr. Romano for elucidating this to me.

24 For a more technical and more detailed explanation of the effective wave-function, refer to Dürr et al., 1992, 2013.

effective wave-function all the time is certainly true, but that the effective wave-function really exists in the world is doubtful, if not wrong, according to the universal character of Bohmian mechanics. Physicists probably use a shortcut when it comes to defining effective wave-functions: as Hubert (2016) notes, there is another more practical way to get the effective wave-function, and that is through the Schrödinger equation. Indeed, if we can compute the Hamiltonian of our subsystem, then the Schrödinger equation naturally gives us the effective wave-function as a solution (Dürr et al., 1992).

1.8 Determinism

The Bohmian theory is built on two deterministic equations, the guiding equation and the Schrödinger equation. For this reason, Bohmian mechanics is a deterministic theory: once the initial conditions of the particle configuration and the wave-function are known, the entire future evolution of the system is determined. Now I would like to invite you to think what this determinism implies in the configuration space. The universal wave-function is specified for the whole configuration space. This means that it can generate or determine, through the guiding law of motion, all the different possible particle trajectories. For each $\mathbb{Q}$, the wave-function attributes a possible particle trajectory in R^{3N}, which corresponds to possible trajectories in R^3, one for each three-dimensional particle. The deterministic character of Bohmian mechanics implies that, in R^{3N}, once we know where the actual configuration of particles Q is, we are able to determine which trajectory represents the future evolution of Q. Given that the evolution of the system is solely determined by the position of Q in the configuration space, we have to rule out any case where different trajectories can intersect one another or where the same trajectory can cross itself. Indeed, if two trajectories did cross at a certain point and time in R^{3N} (or the same trajectory did cross itself), it would mean that two particle states with the same particle positions could evolve in two different ways. However, this is ruled out by the deterministic aspect of the theory.

Hence, we can say that Bohmian mechanics, since it is a deterministic theory and[25] its dynamics is defined by a first-order equation, obeys the *no-intersection theorem*.

---

[25] This 'and' is of extreme importance: any deterministic theory that is based on acceleration and not velocity (for instance, Newtonian mechanics) violate the no-intersection theorem.

No-Intersection Theorem: Two distinct state space trajectories cannot intersect (in a finite period of time). Nor can a single trajectory cross itself at a later time (Hilborn, 2000, p. 77).

A last consideration that deserves attention is that non-locality and determinism might appear to be at odds with each other. I claimed that one particle's motion non-locally and simultaneously influences all the other particle trajectories. This influence happens deterministically, according to the law of motion; still, it might seem that the particle may be suddenly 'disturbed' by a distant event and forced to change its deterministic evolution. In order to shed light on this thought, we should note that the particle trajectory that influences all the other particles is already determined from the beginning of the universe, given its initial position. Therefore, the trajectories of the particles are, strictly speaking, already determined from the initial conditions of the universe.[26] All the history of this world was already written down and determined by the initial conditions the universe, via the Bohmian laws. This way, Bohmian mechanics is a deterministic theory of motion.

1.9 Probabilities

As we just discussed, Bohmian mechanics reveals itself to be a deterministic theory: both the temporal evolutions of the wave-function and of the particle configuration are completely determined by the Schrödinger equation and the guiding law of motion respectively. In particular, we can say that if we knew the initial values of the wave-functions and the particle configuration, then we would be in a position to predict all future values, for all times. But we also admitted that knowing their initial values is, operationally, practically impossible. Indeed, it turns out that it is even impossible for us to be in a position to know the exact initial values of the particle configuration and of the wave-function. The only thing we can achieve is a probabilistic knowledge of the initial conditions of our universe, hence a knowledge about the possible initial conditions of the system. Now, there are two very opposite and competing approaches to this problem, one developed by the Rutgers-Munich-Genova group, and the second developed by Valentini. The debate on this issue is

---

[26] One clarification is needed. All the future trajectories of the system are already determined from the initial conditions of the universe, if we know the temporal evolution of the wave-function (therefore, in order to predict the future evolution of the particles we need to know their initial positions and the evolution of the wave-function).

still open and it is very controversial. In this work, I will explain the former, while I will only briefly touch upon the latter.[27]

1.10 The Rutgers-Munich-Genova Group: Quantum Equilibrium, Equivariance and Absolute Uncertainty

From the Schrödinger equation, we can derive another equation: the local *quantum continuity equation*. This equation describes the transport of a conserved quantity, which is in this case the flow of probability. Its role is to ensure the conservation of the flow of probability by stating that the partial derivative of the probability distribution (or probability density function) ρ on configuration space plus the divergence of the quantum probability current J is zero:

$$\frac{\partial \rho}{\partial t} + \text{div } J^\psi = 0$$

where $J^\Psi = (J_1^\Psi, \ldots, J_N^\Psi)$ is defined here as:

$$J_k^\psi = \rho v_k^\Psi$$

so that we can re-write the continuity equation in this form:

$$\frac{\partial \rho}{\partial t} + \text{div } \rho v^\psi = 0$$

What should be recalled is that we do not know which initial positions the particles had when the universe began (or, in less drastic terms, we can imagine the scenario presented above in which we do not know what the initial particle positions were in our system). Imagine a swarm of possible initial positions and, accordingly, the swarm of possible final positions of the particles, and the swarm of trajectories that move from the initial positions to the final positions (Albert, 1992). Further imagine a particular set of initial positions with a particular distribution. The swarm with that particular distribution has a density in space that is preserved until the end of the universe.

Now the conceptual question is: how do we select that particular sort of swarm? Mathematically, the question is: how can we define ρ?

---

[27] Moreover, given the technicality of this topic, and given that it is not central to the philosophical discussion of this book, I will largely avoid focusing on the mathematical details and concentrate instead on the conceptual issues. For a detailed discussion of Bohmian probabilities, refer to Dürr et al., 1992, 2013; Oldofredi, forthcoming; Valentini, 1991, 1996.

Bohmian mechanics, according to the Rutgers-Munich-Genova group, makes a particular choice for ρ, namely to equate ρ with the square of the amplitude of the wave-function:

$$\rho(q,t) = |\Psi(q,t)|^2$$

This choice is grounded in a hypothesis, called the *quantum equilibrium hypothesis*.

Quantum Equilibrium Hypothesis: Whenever a system is described by a wave-function $\Psi(q,t)$, then the distribution of its configuration satisfies:

$$\rho(q,t) = |\Psi(q,t)|^2$$

This choice is also grounded in the *equivariant* feature of this particular measure.

Equivariance: In the case the probability density function is $\rho(q,t) = |\Psi(q,t)|^2$ at some time t_0, then $\rho(q,t) = |\Psi(q,t)|^2$ for all times t.

In order to justify the equivariance of the square of the amplitude of the wave-function, the Rutgers-Munich-Genova group shows that the equivariance expresses exactly the compatibility relative to ρ of the evolution of the wave-function *and* of the evolution of the particle configuration (Dürr et al., 1992, 2013). Moreover, they demonstrate that the equivariance of the Born rule is an immediate consequence of the equation of motion and of the continuity equation, given the Schrödinger equation (Dürr et al., 1992, 2013). The quantum equilibrium hypothesis and the fact that the measure is equivariant ensure that Bohmian mechanics is empirically equivalent to standard quantum mechanics, which is an intrinsically stochastic theory that predicts that the probability of any measurement outcome obeys the Born rule:

$$\rho(q,t) = |\Psi(q,t)|^2$$

The validity of the quantum equilibrium hypothesis is easily proved by substituting our ρ with the square of the amplitude of the wave-function in our continuity equation and in the definition of our probability current. We can see that both the equations are true with this replacement. However, the problem is not really the validity, but the justification. Indeed, why should we take

$$\rho(q,t) = |\Psi(q,t)|^2$$

as our chosen measure?

This is an issue that the Rutgers-Munich-Genova group has addressed with a very high level of technicality,[28] which will be bypassed here. At this point we can just say that Goldstein shows that the distribution $|\Psi(q,t)|^2$ is the only unique invariant distribution that satisfies some specific requirements (Goldstein & Struyve, 2007).

Now I will address what has been dubbed as 'the problem of quantum equilibrium'. The Born equation written above, in fact, is very murky. And it seems to show an inconsistency: it equates two very different objects. On the left-hand side, we have a probability distribution, a mathematical object of ambiguous physical significance, which is most of the time considered subjective. On the right-hand side, however, we have the wave-function of the universe, which is an objective dynamical object. How can they go together? One strategy would be to think that the wave-function is actually not the wave-function of the universe, but the wave-function of the subsystem. But we know that the behavior of the subsystem completely arises from the behavior of the universe, 'emerging' as a natural consequence. Hence, if we want to account for a local randomness, we first need to account for a 'universal' randomness. The alternative strategy would be to apply our ρ to the universe, but then we get the embarrassing question of what exactly it means to assign a probability distribution to the initial condition of the *universe*: what is the physical significance of having an ensemble of universes, given that we have only one?

The Rutgers-Munich-Genova group takes up the second challenge and better elaborates the meaning of ρ. The physical significance of the Born rule is just that it gives a measure of *typicality*. Indeed, they show that for every Ψ and for all the typical 'Qs' (i. e. the overwhelming majority of 'Q'), we always get the predictions given by the Born rule. Our ρ becomes, at the universal level, the *measure of typicality* (Dürr et al., 2013).

There is another way to explain the probabilities of Bohmian mechanics, which starts from considerations about typicality and ends up with the Born rule. Bohmian mechanics is like any other statistical classical system. Think of having, classically, a machine that contains thousands of fair coins and tosses them one after the other. In order to calculate the outcome of the tosses you should know all their initial positions, their momentum and an infinite series of other kinds of information about the environment. Physically, the interesting question is: what do typical initial states do?[29] But in order to know what 'typical' initial states do,

---

28 See for example Goldstein & Struyve, 2007.
29 This discussion of Bohmian probabilities is mainly taken from some notes prepared for didactical purpose by Florian Hoffman and Nicola Vona (from the Bohmian research group in LMU).

and in order to know in turn what the overwhelming majority of initial states do, you need to know what you mean by 'typical'. Therefore, you need to have a definition of typicality, or said in mathematical terms, you need a measure of typicality. Indeed, the only exact way to define what the overwhelming majority' is, would be for you to count all the initial states, but given that the possible states of initial conditions is a continuum, this turns out to be impossible. What we need is a measure that can evaluate the size of a subset. Imagine the same scenario in Bohmian mechanics, where electrons, all sharing the same wave-function, are continuously emitted one after the other. In order to know the behavior of the electrons we should know their exact initial conditions. But we do not have this information. Hence, the only reasonable thing to do is to ask how typical configurations would behave given the same wave-functions. As such, we need a measure of typicality on the space of possible particle configurations. And we just said that a natural notion of typicality is given by the square of the amplitude of the wave-function. And then we know that, given that this measure of typicality should be time-independent, it should obey the continuity equation explained above.

There is one last question that we should answer: what if we did know the exact particle configuration? Would it be possible to prepare a state with a definite wave-function as well as definite particle positions? The definite and ultimate answer is *no, never* (Dürr et al., 1992, 2013). Indeed, Bohmian mechanics not only agrees with standard quantum mechanics concerning the empirical predictions of the theory, but, more subtly, it also shares the claim that whatever additional knowledge we might have beyond the wave-function – which in this case is the particle configuration – does not (and cannot) increase our knowledge of the quantum state. Therefore, the Born equation represents for both Bohmian mechanics and standard quantum mechanics the limit, the boundaries of our knowledge. And this is the case despite the fact that, in Bohmian mechanics, the particle configuration is a real fact of the system that is not exhausted by the wave-function. In this respect, the statistical character of the wave-function, even though it represents our epistemic ignorance, has an objective and not subjective character. The measure certainly does represent our state of ignorance concerning the Bohmian state; however, this degree of ignorance is not dependent on our methods of investigation but on an objective feature of the system. Whenever we deal with a system through a measuring device, the interaction is only done through the wave-functions, which filter the knowledge about the particles. The

---

The handout can be found here: http://www.mathematik.uni-muenchen.de/~bohmmech/Bohm Home/files/Lecture_an_Introduction_to_BM.pdf (last accessed 17.10.2022).

knowledge of a configuration is constrained by the knowledge of the wavefunction, and since Ψ is a very definite dynamical and objective object, the uncertainty of our particle configuration remains absolute given that no further investigation can lead to an increase in knowledge (Dürr et al., 1992).

1.11 Valentini's Quantum Non-equilibrium

We saw that the Rutgers-Munich-Genova group explains the meaning of probabilities in Bohmian mechanics by appealing to typicality and by showing that most (i. e. the overwhelming majority of) initial states would lead to a state of equilibrium. Valentini (2011), on the other hand, claims that this program is controversial because, in order to do this, one has to impose some restrictions on the initial states, deciding which initial states are typical and which are not. And this choice can be only arbitrary: why should we select the initial conditions by assuming that the equilibrium probability density should be used as a measure of intrinsic likelihood? Valentini's strategy moves in another direction. According to him, the issue at stake here is not trying to prove that most initial states would yield to the observed results, but guessing what the initial state of the universe was. Think of what happens in classical mechanics, where we are used to explaining the position of an object at q_1 and t_1 by appealing to its previous position and some dynamical laws. A similar strategy is involved here: we identify a class of possible initial states and develop an evolutionary process that would lead all those initial states to a unique equilibrium. In a nutshell, the possible initial conditions of the universe must have been such as to yield the equilibrium obtaining today through a certain evolution. One obvious possibility is that the class of states were already in equilibrium, but, according to Valentini, it is a very unlikely one for two different reasons. The first reason is the violence that characterized the first seconds of life of our universe caused by the Big Bang explosion, and the second is the fact that the laws of Bohmian mechanics are for exact and definite trajectories. Indeed, if only equilibrium states were possible, then the Bohmian trajectories would be in principle untestable and quite meaningless. By contrast, Valentini (Valentini & Westman, 2005) hypothesizes that the initial state of the universe was a non-equilibrium state, and he also proves that non-equilibrium initial states yield equilibrium states.

1.12 Summing up: The Bohmian Postulates

Now I will summarize the pillars of Bohmian mechanics for a many-particle system.

The state description postulate: The description of a Bohmian state for an n-particle system is specified by (Ψ, Q), where $\Psi(x,t)$ is the wave-function with $x = x_1, x_2 \ldots x_N \in R^{3N}$, and $Q = q_1, q_1 \ldots q_N \in R^3$ is the set of the actual positions of the particles.

The dynamical postulate: The evolution of $\Psi(x,t)$ is given by the Schrödinger equation:

$$i\hbar \frac{\partial \Psi(x_1, x_2, \ldots, t)}{\partial t} = \frac{-\hbar^2}{2m} \nabla^2 \Psi(x_1, x_2, \ldots, t) + V \Psi(x_1, x_2, \ldots, t)$$

while the evolution of the particle positions is given by the guiding law (or equation of motion):

$$v^{\Psi}(q_k) = \frac{dq_k}{dt} = \frac{\nabla_k S(Q)}{m_k}$$

The quantum equilibrium postulate:[30] The quantum equilibrium configuration probability distribution ρ for an ensemble of systems each having quantum state Ψ is given by:

$$\rho(q,t) = |\Psi(q,t)|^2$$

1.13 The Questions We Shall Ask

In the preface of this book, I argued that Bohmian mechanics provides an unambiguous physical description of the quantum realm thanks to its ontological commitments. The aim of this first chapter was to provide a clear explanation of the elements of the Bohmian system. In sum, Bohmian mechanics presents particles that move along continuous trajectories determined by a universal wave-function. This very simple and straightforward theory, however, is not exempt from metaphysical problems. In particular, we do not know how this determination occurs. There are two alternatives: either the wave-function causally influences the particles by exercising a physical action on them, or it simply determines

---

[30] This is not in fact a postulate but a hypothesis.

their behavior nomically, without any physical involvement. This question, which has recently presented challenges for many philosophers of physics, reveals our ignorance concerning another more important issue. If we are unable to define univocally the kind of determination between the particles and the wave-function, it means that we are also unable to know how to best regard the wave-function, hence its ontological status. I will investigate this topic in the third chapter of this book.

In order to examine the ontological status of the wave-function, however, it is of foremost importance to have a sound understanding of the metaphysical characterization of Bohmian particles. Only after inquiring into the status of the particles, their properties and their role is it possible to evaluate the different interpretations of the ontological status of the wave-function. For this reason, I will dedicate the next chapter to the study of particles, and only after that will I inquire into the ontology of the wave-function.

II The Status of the Particles

2 Bohmian Particles and Bohmian Properties

In Bohmian mechanics, we take particles as constituents of the fundamental ontology. Given their importance, I will dedicate this chapter to their ontological status, individuation and to their alleged properties. I will also present the primitive ontology approach and the Super-Humean view, which regards the Bohmian particles as the property-less primitive stuff to which everything else can be reduced.

2.1 Particles

Our inquiry into the ontological status of the elements postulated by Bohmian mechanics will start with the least problematic area, which is the ontological status of particles. Bohmian mechanics takes the notion of particles seriously. As in Newtonian mechanics, the standard view is to regard particles as physical point-like objects located *in* space-time.[31] Indeed, we can describe particles as satisfying the following conditions (1), (2), (3a) and (3b):

(1) It is always the case that a particle has a definite location (position) in space-time.

This first characterization is important since it distinguishes Bohmian particles from the particles of standard quantum mechanics (the Copenhagen interpretation): in Bohmian mechanics particles always have a definite location, and by moving over time they 'draw' (or, perhaps more accurately, they 'create') a continuous trajectory in space-time. The continuity of the particle trajectories is guaranteed by the *local* conservation law, spelled out in the previous chapter:

$$\frac{\partial \rho}{\partial t} + \mathrm{div}\ \rho v^\psi = 0$$

According to this law, if a particle moves from one initial point to a final point, it must have gone through all the intermediate points that the trajectories define.[32]

We can define the continuity of trajectories as satisfying the following three conditions (French & Krause, 2006, pp. 19–20):

---

[31] Particles are not extended in space since they are only point-like objects. They are mereological atoms that satisfy the conditions 1 and 2 below.
[32] For a detailed explanation of how the continuity of particle trajectories follows from the conservation of probability density, see Oriolis & Mompart, 2012, chapter 1.1.1.

A. Trajectories must be spatio-temporally continuous;
B. Trajectories must be qualitatively continuous, i. e. each individual stage of the trajectory must be similar to the neighbor stage;
C. There is a sortal term S such that the trajectory is a succession of S-stages.

Secondly, particles are characterized by their position in space-time such that:

(2) For any instant of time, and for any two particles x and y, if x has position p_1 and y has position p_2, and $p_1 \neq p_2$, then $x \neq y$:

$$\forall x, \forall y(((p_1 x \& p_2 y) \& (p_1 \neq p_2)) \rightarrow (x \neq y))$$

This second condition rules out ubiquity, since it states that when 'two particles' have different positions in space, they cannot be the very same particle.

What is even more interesting to consider, however, is whether two distinct particles can share the same position, and therefore whether the 'impenetrability conditions' hold in Bohmian mechanics. These conditions are as follows:

(3a) For any instant of time, and for any two particles x and y, if at the same instant of time t_1 x is at p_1 and y is at p_2 and $p_1 = p_2$, then $x = y$:

$$\forall x, \forall y(((p_1 x \& p_2 y) \& (p_1 = p_2)) \rightarrow (x = y))$$

(3b) For any instant of time, and for any two particles x and y having position p_1 and p_2 respectively, if the two particles are distinct, then their positions must also be distinct:

$$\forall x, \forall y((p_1 x \& p_2 y) \& (x \neq y) \rightarrow (p_1 \neq p_2))$$

The impenetrability conditions above state that, whenever two particles share the same position, they must be the very same particle, and whenever two particles are distinct, they must have different positions (at the same instant of time). Two different particles cannot share the same spatio-temporal properties.

If these conditions were true, the spatio-temporal properties of a particle would uniquely identify the particle. Therefore, they would constitute a necessary (given condition 1 and 2) and sufficient criterion to characterize, distinguish and individuate one particle from the others. In metaphysical language, if these conditions were true for the Bohmian particles, they would constitute their *principium individuationis*. This means that, in the Leibnizian principle of identity of indiscernibles, we should replace the generic property 'P' with 'spatio-temporal property' so that the principle holds:[33]

$$\forall x, \forall y((\forall P(Px \leftrightarrow Py)) \rightarrow (x = y))$$

The interesting question of whether Bohmian particles actually are impenetrable is, however, not easy to answer. Unfortunately, the literature presents much confusion surrounding this issue. In the following, I will provide an elucidation.

The most common yet misplaced take on the matter states that Bohmian particles cannot share the same position in space because their trajectories cannot cross on account of the no-intersection theorem, which is in turn determined by the first-order dynamics of the guiding law (French & Rickles, 2003).[34] Hence, according to this common view, particles' trajectories cannot cross given that the equation of motion is based on velocity. But this view mistakenly applies the no-intersection theorem to space-time, while the theorem states that particles' trajectories cannot cross in *configuration space*. Since the velocity field attributes a unique velocity vector to each point of the configuration space, different trajectories cannot cross in configuration space. But this does not prohibit different particles' paths from crossing in space-time. Therefore, Bohmian physical laws do allow for different particles to share the same position. It is *nomologically* possible for different particles to share the same spatio-temporal properties. There is only one case where particles cannot cross and that is when particles are identical and live in one-dimensional space.[35] But if we hold true the notion that particles live in three-dimensional space, then there are no cases where the crossing of particles' paths is prohibited by the physical theory.

Another way is to point out that only the trajectories of bosons do actually cross in physical space, because the fermions' crossing of trajectories in physical space is of measure 0, so not logically or nomologically excluded by the theory but not happening. So, if we just restrict the 'Bohmian particles' to 'matter-particles' one might be willing to claim that Bohmian particles are impenetrable. This can certainly be the case, however, the fact that fermions do not cross in physical space seems to be more a matter of contingency rather than nomological impossibility.

---

[33] For a discussion of the principle of indiscernibles that is relevant to the discussion of this work, see Dorato & Morganti, 2013.
[34] This is what we read in French & Rickles, 2003: "Since these equations are first-order, the trajectories of two particles which are non-coincident to begin with will never coincide. In effect the impenetrability of the particles is built into the guidance equations and the singularity points remain inaccessible" (p. 224).
[35] Chen, 2017.

Another strategy to provide support for the impenetrability of Bohmian particles might be by grounding this impenetrability in other nomological features of the system. Even though it is nomologically possible for the particles to cross *according to Bohmian laws*, it may be the case that the Hamiltonian is such that it does not allow them to intersect. And if we take the Hamiltonian to be part of the law, hence as a nomological entity, then it may be *nomologically impossible* for the particles to cross, because of the form of the Hamiltonian.[36] However, we do not know what the Hamiltonian is for all the particles of the universe! It is impossible to answer this question. So, it turns out that this route does not bring us any closer to answering the question of whether Bohmian particles are impenetrable or not.

So far we have analyzed whether impenetrability is *nomologically* possible or not. Whenever the impenetrability of the particles is given by the physical laws, hence by the nomological character of the theory, we shall call it 'weak impenetrability'. The laws are such that the particles cannot cross because their trajectories are generated in such a way that they never cross. This impenetrability is due to nomological features of the theory and there is no commitment to the ontological properties of the particles themselves.[37] But we can also endorse the impenetrability of Bohmian particles by grounding it in some metaphysical features of the particles – we can call this 'strong impenetrability'. In this case, even though it is nomologically possible that particles are *not* impenetrable, Bohmian particles respect the impenetrability conditions because of their intrinsic ontological properties. Their ontological properties are such that whenever two particles meet at a certain point, they do not cross but bounce off each other. This is reminiscent of the atomistic view supported by Newton himself, who described classical particles in this way:

> It seems probable to me, that God in the beginning formed matter in solid, massy, hard, impenetrable, movable particles. (Newton, 1704/1952, Optics, query 31)

> The extension, hardness, impenetrability, mobility and force of inertia of the whole results from the extension, hardness, impenetrability, mobility and forces of inertia the parts; and hence we conclude that the least particles of all bodies to be also extended and hard and impenetrable, and movable. And this is the foundation of philosophy. (Newton, 1687/1999, Principia, Regula III)

---

36 Thanks to Eddy Chen for suggesting this point to me.
37 However, this is true only as long as we endorse a primitivist attitude towards nomological entities; if, on the contrary, we endorse, for instance, a dispositional version of properties (according to which nomological entities are grounded in the dispositions of the ontology), the impenetrability is fundamentally due to dispositional properties of the particles. Thanks to Dr. North for suggesting this consideration.

The atomistic view may motivate the impenetrability condition by appealing to a mereological criterion: if atomic particles constitute impenetrable bodies, they must be impenetrable as well. However, this is more of an armchair metaphysics principle and we should be very cautious about endorsing it if we do not want to endorse a metaphysical view at odds with our scientific theories. For example, we know for sure that atoms are almost empty even though they constitute hard bodies. Moreover, we know that Bohmian particles are point-like objects – but what does it mean for a point-like object to be impenetrable? The Newtonian picture provides a physical characterization that seems to be adequate more for infinitesimally small billiard balls than for point-like objects. Hence, it is better to first investigate whether there are other alternatives before committing to some metaphysical criteria that are not grounded in features of the theory itself.[38]

One such alternative is defended by Brown (Brown et al., 1999; Brown et al., 1996). According to Brown, Bohmian particles do cross in physical space. Brown also discusses the possibility that the particles, after meeting, may forever share the same trajectory. While in Brown (1996) this option seems contingently true, since he claims that "ideally" there will be "special situations" (p. 314) where the trajectories may coincide, in Brown (1999) it seems that this does not happen only in special situations but every time two particles cross. Indeed, he writes that "two particles trajectories will coincide forever if at all" (p. 233). Here we should clarify the following: nomologically, it is obviously true that if two particles share the same initial positions, then they will always have the same trajectories. Bohmian mechanics is a deterministic theory, which assigns trajectories to initial particle positions, and not to individual particles. So, it may be the case that Brown wants to claim that whenever different particles share the same initial position, they will also share entirely the same trajectory. And I believe that there are good reasons to support this reading, since the passage from which the citation is taken does talk about initial particle positions. However, in the literature, his claim is normally taken to mean that if different particles at a certain time cross at a particular point in space, then their trajectories will coincide forever. I am not sure whether it is possible to defend this claim from a physical point of view, since I do not think that the theory itself constrains two particles to follow the same identical trajectory after their trajectories cross.

---

[38] North (private correspondence) suggests that a way to ground the impenetrability of Bohmian particles would be to draw the attention to the classical limit. If classical particles are impenetrable and if we want to allow for an ontological continuity between the Bohmian world and the classical one, then we should reasonably endorse the impenetrability of Bohmian particles. However, I will not consider this proposal here since the classical-quantum divide in Bohmian mechanics and the impenetrability of classical particles are two very controversial topics.

However, from a metaphysical point of view, this claim may very well be motivated by the need to keep the principle of impenetrability. Indeed, according to Brown, once two particles share the same trajectories, they become the same particle. This way, the conditions of impenetrability still hold: two distinct particles cannot share the very same spatio-temporal properties because, once they do, they become the very same particle. Therefore, Brown's claim (that once particles cross, they share the same trajectory and become one) may be motivated by metaphysical concerns rather than physical ones. Hence, his view has two merits: the first is to allow for particle crossing (which is nomologically allowed by the theory), and the second is to keep the impenetrability principle. However, his view violates another Bohmian principle concerning the particle conservation number. In non-relativistic Bohmian mechanics, the number of particles is conserved from the beginning until the end of the universe. Therefore, any phenomenon of annihilation and creation of particles is prohibited by the theory. This principle is linked to the conservation equation (discussed above in section 2.1 and in chapter 1, section 1.11), which forbids the interruption of particle trajectories.

At this point, we have only two options: either we restrict the nomological possibility by arguing that what is nomologically possible (particle crossing) is not metaphysically possible given the metaphysical properties of the particles (see Esfeld, 2015), or we give up the impenetrability conditions. The question at stake is how important the conditions of impenetrability are and whether they can be justified by appealing to non-metaphysical criteria. I believe that at the roots of the impenetrability assumption are exactly the same motivations that lie at the roots of the non-ubiquity assumption. That we may have the very same particle in two different positions should be ruled out in the same way it should be ruled out that many different particles may occupy the very same trajectory. If we allowed for such scenarios, it would be absolutely impossible for us to distinguish different particles and to have any epistemic grip on the particle configuration.

Nevertheless, I do not want to develop any stance on the matter here, since my aim is just to provide a clarification of the ontological status of Bohmian particles. We will go back to this problem in the last chapter of the book. For now, it is enough to see that both options are perfectly compatible with the theory; as such, we are facing a problem of underdetermination.

After providing a clarification of what we mean by 'particles' in Bohmian mechanics, we should ask what makes a particle a *Bohmian* particle. Indeed, all the specifications provided above may also be shared by other theories (Newtonian mechanics, for example, if we accept impenetrability). So what is a Bohmian particle? Very simply, we can define a Bohmian particle as a particle that obeys the Bohmian guiding equation.

This characterization seems quite poor, and we want to dig deeper into the status of particles. We may ask, then, what are the properties of Bohmian particles?

2.2 The Dependence of Bohmian Properties on Positions

This seems a very naïve question to ask, given that its answer could be inferred directly by looking at the guiding law. But in this section, I would like to present some experiments from which we can begin to characterize Bohmian particle properties (Albert, 1992).[39] Before enjoying the curious results of these experiments, however, let me first explain the property that we will take into consideration. We will be analyzing the outcomes of spin-measurements, hence the measurements suitable for detecting the spin of the particle. Spin is a property of the Bohmian particles that is typical of the quantum world, and can be defined as a form of angular momentum. It can be tested by utilizing measurement devices called Stern-Gerlach devices. In a nutshell, the experiment involves sending a particle beam through a magnet. Suppose that the magnet is put in a box with an aperture (through which the beam goes in) and two exits (through which the beam leaves the box). What is noticeable is that the particle beam (our guiding wave-function), after entering the box, splits into two different paths, one going through one exit and the other going through the second exit. However, in a Bohmian setting, we know that the particle will follow a continuous path and will exit only through one of the two exits, depending on its properties. If our measurement setting is correct, then we should accept that the experiment measures a property of the particle. For example, if the particle goes up, then it has a 'spin-up' property; if it goes down, it has a 'spin-down' property (Figure 3).

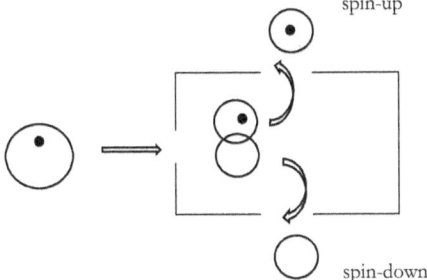

Figure 3: The Stern-Gerlach device.

---

39 In this section, I am only re-presenting the same experiments described in Albert, 1992.

Here I do not want to go over the technical details, since the presentation of three different experiments will be enough for us to draw some conclusions about the metaphysics of the property of spin. However, we can characterize our case study more specifically: I will suppose that we have a particle[40] prepared in a x-down spin, which means that we measured the spin of that particle many times by orienting the magnet along the x-axis, and that the outcome determined that the particle always had an 'down' spin (i. e. the particle took the upper exit). Now, in our experiments, we will measure the z-spin property of that particle, which means that we will measure the spin of the x-down particle along the z-axis.

The Stern-Gerlach measurement procedure is such that whenever a particle with x-spin is sent through a device that measures the z-spin, its wave-function splits, but if we re-send it through a z-spin measurement device, its wave-function will not split again. In the following, we will consider three different scenarios, all involving the measurement of the spin property.[41]

1) Suppose we take our x-down-spin particle with its own wave-function, and suppose that the particle position is in the 'upper' part of the wave-function. Given these assumptions, when we perform the experiment, the electron will always exit through the upper exit, revealing that it has a 'spin-up' property. Suppose instead that our particle's position is in the 'lower' part of the wave-function: now, the particle is always going to exit through the lower exit, showing that it has a 'spin-down' property (Figure 4). The trajectory of the particle depends exclusively on its initial position, whether it is on the 'same track' as the upper-aperture or not. Notice that this is due to the fact that trajectories cannot cross in configuration space. Here, given that we have only one particle, our configuration space is exactly

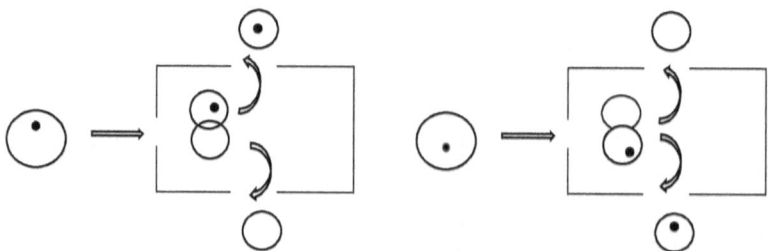

Figure 4: The spin property.

---

40 Here we can think of an electron.
41 For a detailed and complete description of these experiments refer to Albert, 1992, pp. 146 – 160.

a three-dimensional space, so it is easy to visualize. The two possible trajectories of the particle cannot intersect, hence once the electron is in the up-region, it will remain in the up-region.

2) Suppose that we perform exactly the same experiment, but that we flip the orientation of the box[42] so that the spin-up exit becomes the spin-down exit and vice-versa (Figure 5). Then, the particle will keep exactly the same path as before, depending on its initial position. The problem is that the measurement reveals the exact opposite outcomes: if the particle happens to be in the upper region, then it will exit through the upper exit, which means that the particle gets measured as a z-spin-down particle. On the other hand, if the particle is in the lower region, it will be measured as z-spin-up!

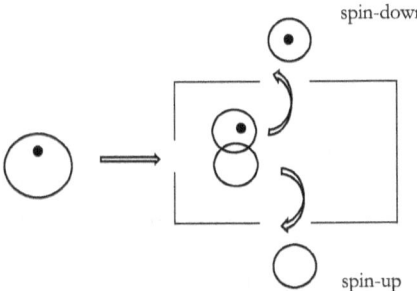

Figure 5: Flipping the box.

3) Suppose now that we perform exactly the same experiment, but with two particles. We prepare two particles together and then we send them through the Stern-Gerlach device. The trajectory of the second particle depends on the trajectory taken by the first particle. If the first particle is in the upper region of the wave-function, then it will go up, and its companion will go down, regardless of whether it had an upper or lower position. This demonstrates the entanglement of the spin, which can be written in mathematical language as follows:

$$\Psi_{AB} = \frac{1}{\sqrt{2}} | z \uparrow >_A | z \downarrow >_B - \frac{1}{\sqrt{2}} | z \downarrow >_A | z \uparrow >_B$$

---

[42] Strictly speaking, we rotate the magnet in this experiment, not the box. However, here it is more intuitive and more effective to rotate the box. Pragmatically it does not matter whether we rotate the box or the magnet. For example, Albert (1992) presents the case where we rotate the box, while Lewis (2014) and Dorato (2006) present cases where we rotate the magnet.

This equation means that if particle 'A' goes to the upper exit (along the z-axis), revealing itself to have a z-spin-up property, then particle 'B' must go down, and thus have a z-spin-down property. Similarly, if particle 'A' goes down (along the z-axis), then particle 'B' must go up (Figure 6).[43]

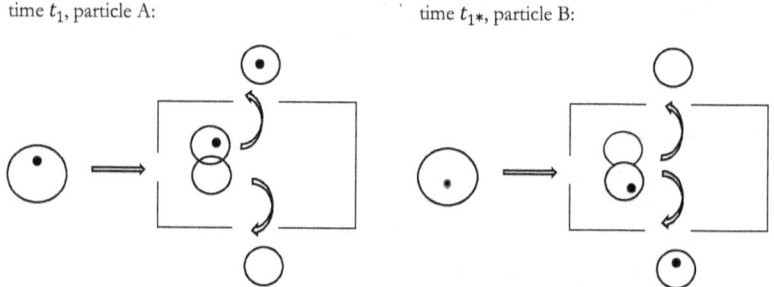

Figure 6: Spin-entanglement.

Let us try to understand, from a conceptual point of view, what is happening here. The first case tells us that position is reducible to the initial position of the particles. The measurement outcome depends exclusively on the particle position, hence on whether it is in the upper or lower region of the wave-function. Therefore, it also seems that the measurement does not reveal any particle property except for its initial position and its actual trajectory. The second case tells us that spin is reducible to the position of the particles *and* the measurement setup. The 'spin-up' result, for example, not only means that the particle's initial position was in the upper part of the wave-function, but also that the device is oriented in such a way that in the upper region there is an exit called 'spin-up'.[44] The third case tells us that in a multi-particle system, the spin depends on the positions of all the other particles that interact with it through entanglement relations. This is because the outcome measurement (which, strictly speaking, reveals the particle trajectory) depends on the wave-function, which in turns depends on all particle positions and the experiment setup (Dorato, 2006).[45] And from this we can infer some useful information regarding spin.

---

[43] The coefficients $\frac{1}{\sqrt{2}}$ reveal that there is a 50% chance that particle A goes up and particle B goes down and 50% chance that particle B goes up and particle A goes down.

[44] I understand that this is a bit tricky to say, because you might think that we cannot name the upper exit box as 'spin-down'! However, one can imagine that we rotate the magnet and not the box – then, the particle will still go up, even if the magnet is rotated.

[45] The experiment setup indeed plays a role here – one can imagine it as a collection of particles.

From this picture, it turns out that spin is not a fundamental property in Bohmian mechanics, given that it can be reduced to particle position (and this is why I did not introduce it in chapter 1, when I was presenting the fundamentals of Bohmian mechanics). Specifically, we can regard spin as a contextual property since its value depends on the 'context', which we can understand to include the other particle positions and the orientation of the box. In sum, spin is a derivative, contextual, non-local property of the particles.

It is important now to define 'contextual' properties. Lewis (2014) defines a contextual property as the property whose value depends on the context in which it is measured. However, the fact that a property is contextual makes it quite spooky. As we said, spin is a derivative property. This means that we could have told the story of the experiments without even mentioning spin, and actually the experiments would have made even more sense! The notion of spin is not only redundant and irrelevant, since the spin property can be reduced to position, but also inconsistent. In fact, if we took the spin property seriously, we would end up with an inconsistent story according to which sometimes the particle is spin-up and sometimes spin-down. It seems that now we are left with the question of whether it is right to consider spin as a property of the particle at all. In fact, we can probably rule it out from our ontology, and we should. This is stressed by Lewis (2014), Dorato (2006), Daumer et al. (1997), and Bell (1987): contextual properties are not properties at all. If the property essentially depends on the measurement setting, then was it there before even setting up the measurement? Probably not. If the value of a property essentially depends on the orientation of the device, then that is not a property at all.[46]

This does not seem very shocking. In fact, it should not surprise us that in a theory we have some contextual properties that depend on the context, cannot be intrinsically attributed to the particles as independent properties, and can therefore be ruled out from our ontology. But the problem, and what is really intriguing about the results of these experiments, is that in Bohmian mechanics almost all the properties are contextual! The only real properties of the system, whose values are independent of the orientation of the measurement device, are particle positions.

Now, this claim is supported by both Dorato (2006) and Albert (1992), who state that all the scientific properties[47] of the Bohmian particles, except for positions, are contextual. Certainly, the cases of mass and charge need to be treated

---

[46] The claim that contextual properties are not properties at all, I admit, is quite controversial and should be investigated more than I do here. However, in the literature on Bohmian mechanics, this claim is widely accepted. For a discussion on this matter, see Allori, 2005; Dorato, 2006; Lewis, 2014.
[47] By scientific properties, also referred to as 'theoretical properties', I mean all those properties whose values are measurable through scientific experiments.

separately, and, for this reason, I will ignore them here. But assume for now that Dorato and Albert's claim is correct: how can we say that particles do not have properties at all except for positions? If we did make this claim, then we would face a conceptual worry, because we would end up with an ontology of particles with positions and no other properties – let's call the particles so characterized 'property-less'.

2.3 Contextual Properties, Particles and the Wave-function

We probably reached this conclusion about the property-less nature of Bohmian particles too hastily. What we should indeed appreciate is that we were analyzing spin as a property of the particle. If we read the experiments with the assumption that spin is a property of the particle, then we end up with an uncomfortable scenario where we have contextual properties, which are no properties at all. But now consider the following set of experiments:

1) Let us take a z-up particle and then measure the z-spin several times, while rotating the box (on the same axes), so that the two exits keep flipping. All such experiments end up exactly with the same outcome: spin-up.
2) Let us now take an x-down particle and then measure its z-spin. Suppose that the particle's initial position is in the upper part of the wave-function (so that the particle will have a spin-up outcome). After that, if you keep measuring the particle z-spin, it will always have a z-spin-up outcome, no matter how you flip the exits.

Is it not the case that these experiments prove, on the contrary, that the particles do have particular spin values independently of the measuring device?

This set of experiments definitely warns us that we should be careful when handling and interpreting the results of the previous set of experiments. They seem to suggest that actually there *is* a spin property that we can attribute to the system. What we should be careful about is that earlier we ruled out that the spin is a (non-contextual) property *of the particle*. If we thought this to be true, then we would have the problems mentioned above. But we can also adjust our perspective and instead regard the spin and all the other contextual properties to be properties *of the wave-function*. In our considerations about the spin property, we focused on a hypothetical scenario in which spin is a property of the particle, and we completely forgot about the wave-function. But the wave-function is present in our experiments and plays a major role in them since it guides, it determines the motion of the particles.

If we put the wave-function back in the picture, then everything makes sense. Indeed, the wave-function, contrary to the particles, always remains faithful to a particular exit, to a particular measurement outcome. If we send an x-down wave-function into a Stern-Gerlach device that is oriented along the z-axis (given that we want to measure the x-axis), then it will split into two beams, one empty (without the particle) and one 'occupied' (with the particle). But once it chooses an exit, it remains faithful to it: if we measure it again along the z-axis, then the beam that chose the z-up exit, for example, will not split again and will choose to go through the same exit it went through previously. In this case, the particle does not have any alternative other than to follow the only beam where it is trapped, regardless of its position. If, on the contrary, the particle were in a wave-function that splits, then obviously it would choose one of the two paths, depending on the particle's position. The wave-function is always faithful to the corresponding exit, while the particle is always faithful to its position,[48] but only when the wave-function allows it to be so. The wave-function spin-up branch always goes up, the spin-down branch always goes down, forever and ever, regardless of the particles. The particle will always choose an exit depending on its position, as long as a beam can guide it there; otherwise, it will let another beam pilot it through another exit.

From this picture, it seems reasonable to claim that the spin property exists but that it belongs to the wave-function, not to the particle, since it is the wave-function (not the particle) that remains faithful to the same box exit. At this point, it would be helpful to ask what it means to attribute a spin property (or any other property, as spin is just one of many) to the wave-function. In order to answer this question adequately, however, we need a deeper treatment of the meaning of the wave-function, to which I have dedicated the third section of this book. Nevertheless, in technical terms, attributing spin to the wave-function simply amounts to attributing additional degrees of freedom to the wave-function. Once the wave-function is in our system, then the particles do not bring any additional degrees of freedom in the system except for positions.

This brings us back to the problem we left behind before: what does it mean for the particles to be property-less? Before turning to this problem, however, we still need to discuss mass and charge. If we think that mass and charge are properties of the particles, then particles do instantiate non-contextual, intrinsic properties that can characterize them.

---

[48] A particle is faithful to its own position only whenever it is in a one-particle system. Otherwise, due to entanglement, the particle's motion depends also on the other particles' positions.

2.4 Mass and Charge

In this section, we will address the problem of whether mass and charge should be attributed to the particles. First, let me clarify where these properties come from. Mass is clearly visible in the formalism of the guiding equation and is associated with a particular particle. Charge appears whenever we spell out the Hamiltonian in detail for charged particles. In both cases, the two properties are attributed to particles, and thus look like their classical counterparts. What we mean by this is that it seems that these two properties 'follow the particle wherever it goes'; they are attached to it. This is, I am aware, a very rough way to characterize these properties, but it is a powerful image that will be useful later.

In Brown et al., 1994, Brown and his collaborators presented a series of experiments that serve to clarify the status of mass and charge. Their experiments are extremely complicated, and it would be impossible to present them here with all the technical details and their associated formalism. So, instead, let me present a sketchy but true description of one experiment for mass and one experiment for charge.

Here we deal with experiments on neutron interferometry. Imagine that you have an interferometer with three plates. A neutron beam, after encountering the first plate, splits into two equal beams (one empty and one occupied with the particle), which then converge by creating an interference pattern of a certain kind. If we rotate the interferometer about the incident beam of the first plate, then in the second plate the two beams will demonstrate two different heights in the earth's gravitational field, hence two different gravitational potentials. According to Brown et al., the fact that the resulting interference patterns are shifted with a particular relative phase shift means that both the beams (the empty one and the occupied one) are affected by gravitation; thus, they must have a (passive) gravitational mass.

A similar experiment can be performed with charge. Suppose we send a charged particle with a beam through an interferometer that creates an angle such that the two beams are very far from each other (thus creating two isolated systems). If the empty beam meets a charged particle on its way, when the two beams meet again, they form an interference pattern that is different from the one they would have formed if the empty beam had not met the charged particle. This suggests that the empty beam actually interacts with the charged particle; hence, it must be charged too.

Both these experiments aim to prove that mass and charge are not localized properties (Pylkkänen et al., 2016). In other words, these results violate the Localizability Thesis (LLT).

LLT: Mass and charge are properties that are spatially localized at the position of the particle.

If we accept that mass and charge are not localized where the particle is, then we could infer that mass and charge, since they do not 'follow' the particle, are not properties of the particles but of the wave-function, just like spin. Indeed, these properties are where the empty branch of the wave-function is. But we are not forced to reach this conclusion yet. Indeed, we could infer that mass and charge are not only properties of the wave-function, but also of the particles.

It is important to note that the doubt here is not that mass and charge are properties of the particles and possibly also properties of the wave-function. Rather, they are definitely properties of the wave-function since they are detected when particles are not there; however, they might also be properties of the particles. Therefore, two are the options: either both the wave-function and the particles instantiate properties such as mass, charge, spin, or only the wave-function does, while the particles are property-less. In order to provide a clarification on the matter, I will now focus on these two alternatives and evaluate their advantages and disadvantages. In this discussion, I will not commit to any interpretation of the ontological status of 'property', since such an interpretation would really depend on the particular ontological status of the entity instantiating the particle. However, I will discuss this issue in the next chapter. For now, our focus remains on particles.

2.5 The Principle of Generosity

The first option would be to be generous, and to concede that both the wave-function and the particles instantiate properties. This generous view has the advantage of solving all the problems that the parsimonious view has to face (see the next section). But the main challenge for the principle of generosity is how to explain the 'parsimony' of the formalism of the Bohmian pillar equations; indeed, the equations present only one 'mass' and only one 'charge' rather than two, i. e. one for the particles and one for the wave-function.[49] Given that we must take into consideration the properties attributed to the wave-function in order to explain the interferometer experiments, it seems that the formalism should refer to the properties of the wave-function. Therefore, the question at stake asks why the formalism completely ignores the particles' properties (given that the principle of

---

[49] I owe this consideration to Lazarovici and Romano (private correspondence).

generosity is true). The only reasonable answer would be that the particles' properties are redundant, just as in the case of spin. At this point, it seems that not only is it meaningless to attribute properties to particles if they do not appear in the formalism, but also that it would be more methodologically correct not to postulate the existence of redundant entities unless their presence is necessary in order to avoid inconsistencies in the theory. We will explore this perspective in the next section.

2.6 The Principle of Parsimony

The parsimonious view is in line with the usual methodological criterion of Occam's razor: whatever is redundant or superfluous in an ontology should be removed. But is it really the case that the particle properties mass and charge are redundant and superfluous? Certainly, the parsimonious view seems to incur serious problems.

Firstly, it seems that if we endorse the parsimonious view and regard the Bohmian particles as property-less, we face the issue of explaining how particles inherit properties in the classical domain. The question is how and why particles suddenly become 'massive' and 'charged' whenever they undergo a transition from the quantum to the classical domain, which normally happens when some quantities of the theory approach zero. In a contrasting case where particles keep their properties in the quantum domain, the difference between the two domains is simply a matter of dynamics, not of ontological 'constitution'. Notice that this is particularly pressing in Bohmian mechanics, which is normally taken as the best guarantor of a continuity between the quantum and classical domains since it provides an ontology of particles, which is in line with the ontology of classical mechanics. If Bohmian mechanics cannot provide continuity at the level of ontology, then a big reason for its success vanishes. Therefore, it seems that keeping an ontology as similar as possible to the one in classical mechanics is the most reasonable action to take if we do not want to take away one of the biggest merits of Bohmian mechanics.

However, there are reasons to think that the classical limit should not pose a particularly dangerous threat to the parsimony principle. The first reason is that keeping an ontology of particles with properties does not really help us recover the classical limit. Indeed, we already have a very deep disruption between the two physical domains, and this is extremely hard to overcome. This disruption concerns the dynamics of the particles. One famous demonstration of this is found in the 'particle in a box' illustration. If, classically, we put a particle in a box, it moves back and forth, from one wall to the other, following continuous trajectories. Indeed, the collision between the particle (which can be equated to a bullet of 1mm) and the wall is elastic, and this causes the particle to follow a continuous and uniform trajectory, each point of which is associated with a definite position and momentum. On the other hand, if we put a Bohmian particle in a box, it remains still, as the guiding law of motion rightly predicts, because the gradient of its phase is zero. The real problem is not that there are two different behaviors (which is understandable, since the classical and quantum domains obey different sets of laws) – the problem is that classical motion cannot be recovered even in the classical limit! Hence, allowing for a disruption on an ontological level does not cause a problem for the classical limit, because the problem of the classical limit is already given by the dynamics. Indeed, it could even be claimed that an ontological discontinuity on a dynamical level would seem to be more reasonable and expected given the dynamical discontinuity.

The second reason why we should not take this objection too seriously is that the parsimonious view could also be applied to the classical case (Allori, 2017; Hubert, 2104; Esfeld, 2104). Nothing necessarily prevents us from regarding classical particles as property-less, and this seems to have become a very successful branch of research recently. More generally, it could be claimed that the challenge given by the classical limit relies on a very naïve understanding of properties, which are expected to obey the localization principle, and which are expected to be 'attached' to the particles. Certainly, the parsimonious view could in principle adopt and endorse a metaphysics of particles that rejects any ontological status of intrinsic and categorical properties (such as ontic structural realism; see chapter 5) also in classical mechanics. This way, the problem of how to recover particles in classical limit disappears.

There is, however, a second problem that the parsimonious view has to face: the problem of recognition. Suppose that we have one universal wave-function for only two different particles, which we (naïvely) categorize as a muon and an electron respectively. Suppose also that the universal wave-function can be described as two different interacting three-dimensional wave-functions, one for the 'muon' and the other for the 'electron'. Suppose further that these two wave-functions have a region of overlap, since they interfere with each other, and that the particles are in this overlap region. In this situation, it is always the case that while the 'muon-wave-function' pilots the 'muon-particle', the 'electron-wave-function' pilots the 'electron-particle'. In a certain sense, we can say that even though the two particles are in the region of overlap, the wave-functions can still 'recognize' which particle they have to 'take care of', and this is normally explained by appealing to the fact that the wave-function 'knows' which particle 'belongs' to it in virtue of the properties it instantiates. The problem of the parsimonious view is that it needs to explain what it is in virtue of that this recognition process can happen, given that both particles are property-less and are thus completely identical and without any distinctive character. Brown (Brown et al., 1996) concludes that this shows that the parsimonious view is incomplete, since it does not provide any labels that can identify the particles. But we know that this is not true: particles do in fact have labels in the form of their positions, as we saw in the opening of this chapter. The wave-function 'knows' which particle it should guide because it knows where its particle should be, given that it has guided it until that moment. This view seems to be taken into consideration by Brown, but he dismisses it by claiming that it implies temporal non-locality: "To solve this problem one must recognize that the corpuscles are recognized through (a sufficiently large part of) their history. It amounts to an admission that the interpretation is non-local in time as well as space" (Brown et al., 1996, p. 314). But I do not see why we should invoke temporal non-locality. A wave-function determines its particle velocity forever, given the deterministic character of the theory. Hence, there is a continuous involvement between the wave-function and the particle, which allows for the wave-function to remain faithful to its own particle, even when it happens to be in a region of interaction.

2.7 A Case of Underdetermination

The two different ontological interpretations of the particle properties (i. e. whether they do instantiate properties or whether they do not) constitute a case of metaphysical underdetermination, where two opposite ontologies can coexist within the same theory and with the same formalism. I hope to have shown in my previous discussion that neither the generous view nor the parsimonious view is exempt from difficulties, but also that neither of these views is knocked down by them. We might have some ontological properties in the system that are not described in the formalism only because they are 'inefficient' and too irrelevant to contribute to the explanatory power of the theory. Or, we might have a very parsimonious ontology that can still be coherent, even though it leads to an ontology completely different from what we are accustomed to. Given that I do not see any compelling reason to endorse one view instead of the other, I will not dig further into this underdetermination problem, though I will discuss it again in the final chapter of this book.

2.8 The Primitive Ontology Approach and Bohmian Mechanics

We started this chapter by underlining the centrality of particles in Bohmian mechanics. What distinguishes Bohmian mechanics from the standard quantum theory advanced by the Copenhagen interpretation is precisely its grip on physical reality, which is given by the presence of particles in the fundamental ontology.

Proponents of Bohmian mechanics have introduced a particular term to identify particles in the context of Bohmian theory – 'primitive ontology'. According to these proponents, particles constitute the 'primitive ontology' of Bohmian mechanics: "What we regard as the obvious choice of primitive ontology, the building block of everything else [. . .] should by now be clear: particles – described by their position in space, changing with time" (Dürr et al., 2013, p. 29).

The concept of primitive ontology has given rise to a particular approach in the foundations of physics called the 'primitive ontology approach', according to which all physical theories 'should'[50] describe (and be grounded in) the 'primitive ontology' (PO). PO does not have to necessarily consist in particles. Indeed, it has been applied widely in other quantum theories which do not include particles in the ontologies. The notion of PO is rather a general notion that, according to the PO proponents, should be foundational across all physical theories and act as the fundamental ontology of the theory, the ontology about which the theory is fundamentally about.

In the following paragraphs, I will provide a general description of the PO and later I will raise some concerns regarding the application of the PO to Bohmian particles. A philosophical discussion of the primitive ontology view can be found in the works by Allori (Allori, 2013; Allori et al., 2014; Allori, 2015; Allori, 2017), and by the Lausanne school (Esfeld, 2014b; Esfeld 2017; Egg & Esfeld, 2015).

The first characterization of the PO is its primitive ontological role in the constitution of physical objects. Indeed, the PO forms the building blocks of all the physical objects of the world. From this, it follows that all the physical objects of this world should be reduced to the PO. My computer, my book, my glasses are all made of the same PO. What fundamentally differentiates one object or physical state of affairs from another is the behavior of the PO and not their physical constitution. The fact that a cat meows is grounded in a certain configuration or behavior of the PO, which distinguishes the meowing cat from a silent cat. Given that physical objects live in our space-time, there are very good reasons to think that the PO

---

[50] The primitive ontology approach is normative.

lives in our space-time as well. Otherwise, it would be problematic – if not impossible – to think that the PO can constitute the objects of a space while inhabiting another space. As such, the proponents of the PO take three-dimensionality to be a necessary (but not sufficient) requirement for the PO. In this respect, we can say that the PO is different from the notion of local beables[51] introduced by Bell, since local beables can live in a multi-dimensional space.[52] The second role of the PO is explanatory. The PO provides the most primitive explanation of our manifest image and of our measurement outcomes. Its role is to provide a clear scientific image that grounds the phenomenal world (which is ultimately reducible to PO) and to provide a clear connection between the fundamental reality and our measurements. The elements of PO ground the explanatory scheme with which the theories describe and account for macroscopic physical reality and our experiences of such reality.

The Bohmian particles seem to meet all the characterizations of the PO. For example, regarding the ontological role of 'building blocks', Bell stresses the ontological role of particles as constituents of all observable matter:

> From the microscopic variables x can be constructed macroscopic variables X. Observables are constructed from the xs rather than from the wave-function. Thus, it would be appropriate to refer to the xs as the exposed variables, and to the wave-function as a hidden variable. It is ironic that in traditional terminology is the reverse of this. (Bell, 1987, p. 128)

My computer, your cat, the chair, all the concrete and physical objects of this world are physically constituted by particles, not the wave-function. For this reason, the particles should not be regarded as 'hidden' variables but as 'exposed' variables. Regarding the explanatory character of the PO, Holland (1993) reformulates the role of particles in terms of measurement: "It is precisely the positions of particles that are recorded in the experiments: they are the immediately sensed reality" (p. 21). In this case, if the pointer of our macroscopic measurement device moves to 'spin-up', we can infer that the microscopic particle just moved to the upper exit. This is intrinsically linked to the primary role of particles also from an epistemic perspective: in Bohmian mechanics, our raw 'epistemic data' are constituted by particles (Bedard, 1999). Holland (1993) claims, for example, that a psycho-physical correspondence between the physical world and our sensorial perceptions is possible only in virtue of particles; in other words, our perceptions of the world are caused exclusively by particles.

---

[51] The notion of 'beables' of a theory was introduced by Bell as "the things that exist independently of an observer" (Bell, 1987, p. 174).
[52] Bell never mentions the requirement that local beables should be in space-time (for the same consideration, see Hubert, 2016).

However, several concerns give us reason to be careful in applying such a drastic characterization of the PO to Bohmian particles. The first concern regards the role of the PO in constituting the building blocks of '*everything*'. First of all, we should take 'everything' to be reasonably applied to the 'physical' world (obviously laws and abstract mathematical entities are not constituted by physical primitive stuff). However, even if we restrict the domain of 'everything' within the domain of what is physical, it still might be not enough. If we look at the case of Bohmian mechanics, for example, we are still unsure what the wave-function is. If the wave-function turned out to be a physical field, for example, then it would be clear that the particles could not be defined as the building blocks of everything physical, because the wave-function is arguably not constituted by the particles. Given this possibility, I suggest that it is better to restrict the role of the PO even further. It would be more reasonable to regard the PO, and so the particles, as the building blocks of all the observable physical world of our space-time of our daily experience. In this way, the wave-function is not part of the 'observable world of our space-time of our daily experience' – neither is the electromagnetic field, which, despite inhabiting our space-time and being physical, is normally not considered to be an 'observable' entity. Given this restriction, we should regard the PO to be only a subset of the fundamental ontology of the world.[53] Other physical objects may exist and may not be reducible further to other entities; however, since they do not meet all the requirements of the PO (for example, they do not live in three-dimensional space, or they are not the building blocks of observable physical entities), they cannot be interpreted as the PO of the theory.

The second concern regards whether the PO is *alone* in constituting the physical world. Indeed, it seems that the supporters of the PO think that it should be the only constituent of observable matter. But in the case of Bohmian mechanics, it might be reasonable to suppose that the wave-function does as well. Bedard (1999) has developed this point very well by appealing to a case where two hydrogen atoms in a stationary state belong to two different energy levels but have the same particle configurations (i. e. both atoms are constituted by the same kind of particles with the same velocities). In this case, neither the position nor the velocity of the particles determines the essence of the entity that these two atoms constitute. A brain and a brain-shaped object are distinguished by the kind of energy bonds between the particles, which are determined by the wave-function. The nature of an object is due not to the mere positioning of the particles but to the way

---

[53] I want to stress again that this is my proposal. Most – if not all – proponents of PO consider PO as exhausting the whole ontology.

particles are bound together, hence by the properties of the wave-function. For this reason, it would seem reasonable to assume that the building blocks of our physical world are both the particles and the wave-function.

The third issue concerns the explanatory and epistemic power of the PO. It is true that, at the end of the day, measurement records the motion of the particles, yet it is the wave-function that explains why the particles move in one way instead of another. Basically, then, measurement reveals the form of the wave-function, of which the particles are just passive 'attachments'. Moreover, as Bedard (1999) points out, whenever we perceive the color that a metal acquires after being heated, we are not observing particles' positions, but the kind of bonds that the wave-function creates between the particles, which are determined by the properties of the wave-function. If we see that a glowing metal becomes red and another becomes dark, then our different perceptions are not caused by the particle configuration but by the wave-function properties.

Consider that these two last concerns might be regarded as reasonable depending on the ontological status that we attribute to the wave-function. Indeed, it might seem that the controversy regarding whether or not the particles alone are central from an epistemological and explanatory point of view depends on whether the wave-function is a physical entity. Obviously, not by chance, the proponents of the PO approach in Bohmian mechanics are those who do not regard the wave-function as a physical entity. This is true, as we will see later – however, methodologically, we should distinguish the two questions (namely, on one hand, whether the particles are the only constituents of physical matter and, on the other hand, whether the wave-function is a physical entity). Even 'wave-function realists' may think that only particles give content to our epistemic data and our measurement outcomes. It is certainly true that wave-function realists would be more inclined to endorse Bedard's argument; however, regardless of whether one is a wave-function realist or not, one can still regard the particles as constituting the PO (if one accepts the restriction according to which particles are the building blocks of all observable physical entities). I wanted to clarify this point, because Bedard's considerations have been addressed as a threat against the non-realist interpretation of the wave-function, while I believe that the issue is more subtle than this. I will try to develop this point further here.

Bedard appeals to energy bonds as the central elements for the ontological constitution of physical matter, for our epistemic grip on the world, and for providing an explanation of our measurement outcomes. However, both wave-function realists and non-realists agree that in Bohmian mechanics, concepts such as energy and momentum do not play any fundamental role. For example, Valentini (1996), who is an advocate of the realist view, makes the following claim prior to his introduction of Bohmian mechanics: "The very concepts of energy and momentum should make no appearance. We therefore seek a theory where energy and momentum make no appearance" (Valentini, 1996, p. 46). And this same view is shared by the Rutgers-Munich-Genova group (Dürr et al., 1997), which, on the contrary, rejects the realist interpretation. Valentini is definitely being misleading when he claims that concepts like energy should not appear, since potential and kinematical energies do appear in the Schrödinger equation. His claim should rather be interpreted as I suggested above, which is that energy and momentum should not be understood as fundamental concepts in Bohmian mechanics. For this reason, it would be methodologically misleading to understand the energy bonds determined by the wave-function as the fundamental content of our 'raw epistemic data' and as the fundamental 'cause' of our perceptions. But what about interpreting the wave-function as the ultimate and fundamental entity determining the bonds? Concerning measurements, our pointer shows where a particular particle goes. Even though the particle takes one trajectory because of the wave-function, the explanation of why the pointer shows a certain result is because the particle is there, and not because the wave-function is there! And that is the end of the story. The particle motion completely exhausts the need to link our macroscopic experiment outcomes with the fundamental reality of the microscopic world. On the other hand, more problematic is the example of the color of a metal after being heated, which is due to the kinds of energy bonds the particles have, and in turn to the wave-function properties. In this case, the color specifically underpins the kind of wave-function of the system – the color is directly related to the wave-function. Hence, this case shows that whether the particles can still be regarded as the PO does ultimately depend on whether we can eliminate the wave-function from the ontology and reduce the color property to the particle positions.

2.9 The Super-Humeanism Approach by the Lausanne School

The primitive ontology approach provides us with a clear recipe of how to interpret any physical theory, as the PO grounds the "architecture" of the theory. First, there are the primitive variables which are what a theory is about. Secondly, there is the dynamical structure of the theory (Esfeld, 2020) that features all the elements apt to describe the evolution of the primitive ontology. The thought is that once all the primitive variables are specified, all the other macroscopic properties are recoverable.

In the case of Bohmian mechanics, the advocates of the PO approach consider that particle positions, expressed in spatio-temporal relations (or only in spatial relations), are the only variables needed to recover all the other ones. In this sense, they fully embrace the parsimonious view, according to which particles are property-less apart from their (relational) positions.

This view, first suggested by Allori (2015), has been strongly advocated and further developed by the Lausanne school, led by Esfeld (2017, 2020). Indeed, the works by the Lausanne school combine a strong form of Humeanism, called Super-Humeanism, with the PO approach. More specifically, Esfeld's proposal is to implement Humeanism with a more radical endorsement of the parsimony principle with regard to the mosaic, by selecting only the entities strictly necessary for a minimal ontology as the PO. The Bohmian particles are property-less, in the sense that they lack intrinsic properties, and everything else supervenes on it. Super-Humeanism differs from Lewis' doctrine because it eliminates geometry, intrinsic properties and empty space-time points as substantive entities from the mosaic.

> More precisely, the proposal at hand here regards the parsimonious ontology of matter points individuated by distance relations and the change in these relations as the Humean mosaic. Hence, properties are banned from the mosaic: there are only the distance relations individuating point-objects. [. . .] This new Humeanism can be dubbed *Super-Humeanism*. (Esfeld, 2020, p. 1896)

Esfeld's way of accounting for the status of entities appearing in the laws but not in the mosaic is to endow them with a nomological status: they enter the theory not through their ontological significance but through their 'nomological role', which consists in summarizing the regularities of the mosaic in the best possible deductive system. Mass, charge, and all the other physical theoretical properties are in the laws not because particles instantiate properties other than positions, but because they allow us to build the simplest and strongest possible laws.

> The geometry as well as the dynamical parameters that figure in a physical theory [. . .] come in through the role that they play in the laws, belonging to the means that are required to achieve a representation of the overall change in the distance relations that strikes the best balance between being simple and being informative about that change. In Super-Humeanism, parameters like mass and charge are no addition to being. [. . .] Consequently, the particles are not intrinsically electrons, neutrons, etc. They can be so described because they move electronwise, neutronwise so to speak. (Esfeld, 2020, p. 1897)

As such, the Super-Humeanism foundations, like Allori's PO proposal, contain a discrepancy between the ontology and the dynamical structure of the theory. On one hand, we have a very parsimonious mosaic, the primitive ontology of the world, with only matter points and changing spatial relations. On the other hand, we have law-statements that feature 'properties' that are nothing than nomological parameters. These properties, such as mass, charge and so on, figure in the laws because they are required to achieve the best-system of laws and so should be considered as parameter rather that real properties over and above particle positions.

Interpreting the entities figuring in the dynamical laws as only part of the 'dynamical structure' of the theory and not as part of the ontology is a practice that is rather common. One notable example is the debate about the status of the quantum wave-function in Bohmian mechanics (Esfeld, 2014; Miller, 2014; Bhogal & Perry, 2017; and Chen, 2019). But this introduces the topic that will be of our next chapter, on the status of the quantum wave-function. Before moving to this new theme, we should first discuss a rather controversial question, which is whether Bohmian mechanics is about three-dimensional particles, as claimed within the standard PO approaches advocated by Allori and the Lausanne school, or just one, multi-dimensional, particle, as claimed by Albert (1996).

2.10 Many Particles or Just One Particle? The Marvelous and the Miserable Particle View

I have hitherto considered that Bohmian mechanics presents us with a fundamental ontology of particles in three-dimensional space. This is for instance the view advocated by the standard PO approach. However, this is controversial. As specified in the introduction, the wave-function is defined in the so-called configuration space, which is a high-dimensional space, whose dimensions correspond to the degrees of freedom of the particles in three-dimensional space. In this sense, there are two spaces, one where the wave-function is defined and one where the particles live. However, a possibility is that Bohmian mechanics is about one particle in configuration space. After all, what we get in the equation of motion is a variable Q that stands for all the particle positions in three-dimensional space, specified as one single point in configuration space. It is of course possible to rewrite that Q in terms of the single particle positions, which we took to be fundamental. But what if those three-dimensional particles positions are not fundamental at all, maybe even do not exist, since what simply exists is one multi-dimensional particle represented by Q in the configuration space? This view has for instance endorsed in works by David Albert and Alyssa Ney. This particle has been either considered 'the marvelous particle' that can recover all our three-dimensional world, or ridiculed as just 'a miserable particle', being completely alone, almost a speck, in the immensity of the high-dimensional configuration space.

This view has two very important benefits. The first is that it avoids the problem of having two spaces for a single theory. The second is that it avoids non-locality: once both the wave-function and 'the' particle are taken to live in the configuration space and to exhaust all the fundamental ontology, there is no fundamental entanglement. I will explain both points in detail in the next chapter.

III The Status of the Wave-function

3 A Realist Interpretation for the Wave-function

Wave-function realism regards the quantum wave-function as a high-dimensional field. This thesis has been advocated, with substantial differences, in the works by Albert and in the works by Valentini. I will present and discuss the disadvantages of such a 'realist' view in terms of its resulting ontological picture and argue that its methodology is controversial.

3.1 Wave-function Realism

The thesis that the wave-function is a high-dimensional physical field was strongly advocated by Bell (1987) and has recently defended by Albert (1996, 2013), Loewer (1996), Ney (2012a, 2012b) and North (2013). This view, now dubbed 'wave-function realism', does not simply amount to a realist commitment to the physical ontological status of the wave-function. In fact, wave-function realism endorses a specific stance on the wave-function. First of all, since the wave-function is a complex-valued function which endows, at each instant of time, every single point of the 3ND configuration space with a complex number, the quantum wave-function is a field, normally characterized as a collection of properties of space. According to the wave-function realists, the complex values, each mapped to each point of the configuration space, represent the amplitude and the phase that the field acquires at that point. Moreover, the wave-function is a high-dimensional field, because it is defined in the configuration space, which is a 3N dimensional space, where '3N' is equal to the number of degrees of freedom of the quantum system. While some supporters of wave-function realism claim that the configuration space is the only fundamental arena of the physical world, from which our space-time emerges (Albert, 1996, 2013; Ney, 2013; North, 2013), others argue for the existence of two fundamental spaces, a high-dimensional one, where the wave-function lives, and a three-dimensional one, which is where the particles live (Valentini, 1997).

3.2 The Centrality of the Quantum Wave-function

Undoubtedly, the wave-function plays a central role in Bohmian mechanics, since the Schrödinger equation rules the wave-function's temporal evolution and since it determines the particles' trajectories through the guidance equation. Given this, in order to know what Bohmian mechanics is fundamentally about, it is a priority to answer the question of what the wave-function is. Wave-function realism endorses a straightforward reading, a literal interpretation of the wave-function.

But is the wave-function ontologically significant to understand Bohmian mechanics, and how? Two different reasons for thinking in the affirmative have been offered in the literature. One concerns the central role of the wave-function in specifying the quantum system, which can be clearly seen when we compare the role of the wave-function in the classical Hamiltonian-Jacobi equation with its quantum counterpart (3.2.1). The second reason concerns the explanatory power of the wave-function in accounting for the dynamics, and rests on a particular interpretation of the guiding equation in terms of a causal law, like the Newtonian second law (3.2.2).

3.2.1 The Hamiltonian-Jacobi Equation and the Guiding Law

Apart from Newtonian mechanics, there is another way to describe a classical system, which is in terms of the Hamiltonian-Jacobi theory. This theory is built upon the Hamiltonian principle function, the action $S(q,t)$, and describes the evolution of a classical particle moving under the action of a potential V via the following partial differential equation:

$$\frac{\partial S}{\partial t} + \frac{(\nabla S)^2}{2m} + V = 0$$

The Hamiltonian principle function $S(q,t)$ generates a velocity vector field

$$v(q,t) = \frac{\nabla S}{m}$$

along which the integral curves are the possible particle trajectories of an N-particle system, such that:

$$v = \frac{dQ}{dt}$$

These equations are perfectly identical to the Bohmian equations (Valentini, 1992; Holland, 1993; Callender, 2014). Moreover, from a geometrical perspective, we can regard the action function S as defining wave-fronts that evolve over time in an extended configuration space $R^{3N} \times R^N$. As such, the classical picture described by the Hamiltonian-Jacobi formulation is equivalent to the picture we get in Bohmian mechanics: there is a wave that generates all the possible trajectories of the particle system. Once we know the initial condition of the system, it is possible to single out its trajectory.

For this reason, it is not immediately clear why in quantum mechanics we make a fuss over the ontological status of the wave-function, while in classical mechanics we simply take it as a non-physical entity that only helps us to predict the future evolution of the system. Is it not the same in Bohmian mechanics? In the following, I will explain why it is not in fact the same. Indeed, rewriting classical and Bohmian mechanics with the same mathematical language reveals a fundamental difference in the meaning of the wave-function.[54]

The Hamiltonian-Jacobi equation turns out to be extremely useful in cases where we do not know the exact initial condition of the system. In fact, its formalism allows us to compute the trajectories of an ensemble of particles with slightly different initial conditions.

Suppose, for example, that you want to find out a particle trajectory but that you do not know exactly either where this particle starts out or what its motion is. In this case, the Hamiltonian-Jacobi function provides a probabilistic description of your system, taking into consideration all the possible different initial positions and motions of the particle. The equation takes into consideration an ensemble of particle trajectories with slightly different initial conditions given the same S.

For example, if we slightly vary the initial particle positions, we get different particle trajectories, but all associated with the same S'. In the same way, if we slightly vary the momentum of the particles, we get different particle trajectories, but all associated with the same S" (Figure 7).

Figure 7: Ensemble of particle trajectories varying position and momentum.

S' and S" define two different ensembles of particle trajectories.[55] However, the same initial conditions (the same initial particle position and the same momentum) select exactly two identical trajectories in the two ensembles, regardless of whether they belong to two different Ss. This is the central point: if two particle trajectories share the same initial q (particle position) and p (the momentum),

---

54 My presentation is only a representation of what is already explained by Callender, 2014; Valentini, 1992; Holland, 1993.
55 The two images reproduced here are only a copy of the images used in Callender, 2014.

then they always have the same identical particle trajectory, regardless of which S they are associated with. If we move now to the Bohmian system, this turns out to be false. Indeed, once we have two different Ss, generated not by varying q or p but by varying the *wave-function*, the trajectories that they generate are always different, even if they share the exact same initial particle position and momentum.[56] There might be exceptions, since it may be that, contingently, two different Ss associated with two different wave-functions generate the same trajectory for particles with the same initial particle positions and same initial momenta. However, generally this is not the case. This means that in classical mechanics, in order to pick out the trajectory of our interest, we must always know the position and the momentum, regardless of S. On the other hand, in Bohmian mechanics, we need to know S (or the wave-function) and the particle position in order to pick out the right trajectory. This reveals that in classical mechanics our S (and thus our wave) is just a conventional tool built up out of fundamental quantities, useful but not necessary for representing the system; in Bohmian mechanics, however, the wave-function and the function S is a fundamental and necessary element – it is *the* element that generates the trajectories of the particles. We can go on with our discussion: in classical mechanics, our S is derived from the particle trajectories, while in Bohmian mechanics, our particle trajectories are derived from S. In the former case, S is a sort of passive element of the theory that is there only to deal with our ignorance about the system; in the latter, S is an active agent that generates the exact particle trajectories.

This difference is just a manifestation of a very simple difference between the classical and the Bohmian system: while the classical system is fully specified by p and q, the Bohmian system is fully specified by q and Ψ. This explanation about the different roles of S in describing the particle configuration clearly shows why we would be inclined to attribute a causal role to the wave-function in the quantum case. In Bohmian mechanics, S uniquely determines the motion of the particles. For this reason, it is necessary for generating the particle trajectories. This central role seems to involve a sort of ontological dependence between the particle trajectories and the wave-function. Without the (phase of the) wave-function, there would not be particle trajectories – indeed, as we know from the discussion in the previous section, the particles would be at rest.[57] The wave-function does not simply 'dictate' or 'predict' the evolution of the system, but is causally involved in it.

---

56 For a detailed discussion of this point and the following considerations, refer to Callender, 2014.
57 I am aware that this statement is inaccurate, if not wrong. But I need to keep it in order to faithfully present Valentini's realist view. For a discussion of this point, see section 3.3.3.

3.2.2 The Bohmian Dynamics. From Newtonian to Bohmian Mechanics

The second reason to regard the wave-function as a central ontological object of Bohmian mechanics is presented in the work by Valentini and concerns the interpretation of the guiding law of motion as a causal first-derivative equation.[58] Let's see how.

Our starting point will be Newtonian mechanics, in particular the second dynamical law:

$$F = ma$$

which can be rewritten as a second time derivative equation:

$$F = \frac{d\dot{x}}{dt} m = \frac{d^2 x}{dt^2} m$$

Given that the momentum can be written as:

$$p = mv$$

we can rewrite Newton's second law as:

$$F = \frac{dp}{dt}$$

We also know that in Newtonian mechanics, for any conservative force, the force is equal to the (negative) gradient of the potential energy:[59]

---

[58] In the following, I present exclusively Valentini's view, which does not represent the general realist view. Albert, for instance, would not endorse this particular interpretation of the dynamics.
[59] The relation between force and the negative of the gradient of potential energy is quite straightforward for conservative forces once we acknowledge that force and potential energy can be both written in terms of work:

$$W = -\Delta U$$

$$W = F_x(x)\Delta x$$

where Δx is just the amount of change in the x-coordinate of a physical body's position. Given the above equations, we can write:

$$F_x(x)\Delta x = -\Delta U$$

By dividing both sides by Δx we get:

$$F_x(x) = -\frac{\Delta U}{\Delta x}$$

When x approaches zero, we use the differential calculus:

$$F = m\ddot{x} = -\frac{\partial V}{\partial x} = -\nabla V$$

which determines the particle trajectory.

According to Valentini, there is a striking similarity between the Newtonian dynamical law reformulated in terms of potential and the Bohmian dynamical equation of motion, where the trajectory of the particle is given by the gradient of the phase:

$$-\frac{\partial V}{\partial x} \rightarrow classical\ trajectory;\ \frac{\partial S}{\partial x} \rightarrow Bohmian\ trajectory$$

Guided by this similarity, according to Valentini (1992, 1997), we should regard "S" as a kind of Bohmian 'potential', and we should highlight the similarity between the two dynamical equations by writing:

$$F = \frac{\partial S}{\partial x} = \nabla S$$

However, we should *not* overlook some important differences between the two equations. Indeed, while the classical dynamical equation is based on acceleration, so that any classical force causes an object to accelerate, the Bohmian dynamical law is based on velocity; as such, the Bohmian force causes the particle to have a velocity.

$$F_x(x) = -\frac{dU}{dx}$$

But here we are only considering the x-coordinate, as if our body is moving only along the x-axis. If our body is moving along different axes, then the potential energy (and the force) needs to be calculated along all the three axes. Notice that the energy calculated along one axis is independent from the energy calculated along another axis – for this reason, when we calculate the force for one axis, we consider the energy along the other two axes to be constant. Therefore, for calculus purposes we need to use the partial derivatives, which for three dimensions are going to be:

$$F_x = -\frac{\partial U}{\partial x};\ F_y = -\frac{\partial U}{\partial y};\ F_z = -\frac{\partial U}{\partial z}$$

This way, the total force in three-dimensional space becomes:

$$\vec{F} = \frac{\partial U}{\partial x}\hat{i} + \frac{\partial U}{\partial y}\hat{j} + \frac{\partial U}{\partial z}\hat{k}$$

Given that the partial derivatives of the spatial dimensions are mathematically represented by the gradient ∇, we can rewrite the force as:

$$\vec{F} = -\nabla U$$

$$F = \nabla S = mv$$

In light of this, Bohmian dynamics may be said to be 'Aristotelian' (Valentini, 1992, 1997), instead of 'Newtonian', given that the Greek philosopher considered velocity and not acceleration to be the foundation of the dynamics of rigid bodies.

This Aristotelian dynamical law naturally selects an Aristotelian kinematics and an Aristotelian space-time. The procedure to get the kinematics from the dynamics is as usual. Given that 'forces' are causes of motion, then a system is free whenever the force is set to zero:

$$0 = mv$$

Given $m \neq 0$, whenever a force is zero, the velocity must be zero as well:

$$v = 0$$

which means that the natural state of a Bohmian particle is rest and, consequently, that the space-time selects a privileged state of rest.

Notice that there is a hidden argument behind the detection of the space-time. This argument suggests that we take the guiding law as defining of the dynamics of the particles, and that from the dynamics we can infer the space-time:

Premise (1): If the dynamics is Aristotelian, then the space-time must be Aristotelian.
Premise (2): The dynamics is Aristotelian.
Conclusion: The space-time is Aristotelian.

It is the dynamics of a system that determines its own space-time (and not vice-versa). Despite this difference, which concerns the kind of dynamics and space-time of the two theories, there is a common 'story' that the Newtonian system and the Bohmian system tell: particles, which should be in a certain natural state, follow a particular 'unnatural' dynamics because of forces.

From this parallel, another ontological parallel may be stated: in both cases, the forces act as direct physical causal agents since they are the 'cause' of a certain motion, but they are supposed to have a physical source from which they are originated. The origin of the classical forces are particles (or fields); indeed, a classical force is a causal relation obtaining between different particles (or between a field and a particle). If we take the gravitational law as an example, the force causally relates two massive bodies in such a way that one is the cause of the acceleration of the other. But what about Bohmian force? Where is it generated? If we look at the guiding law as it is reformulated above, it is clear that it is generated from the wave-function through its phase. From this perspective, the wave-function is the indirect causal agent that changes the state of the particles from rest to motion by exerting a force on the particles. Given the causal role played by the wave-function, it is natural, if not necessary, to attribute physicality to it. Indeed, in order for an entity to play the causal role of physically changing the state of another entity, it needs to be physical.

Valentini's claim that the Bohmian kinematics is Aristotelian has been highly criticized, and is still been considered very controversial. However, the view that the wave-function may be a causal agent for the particles' motion is still regarded as a plausible option for wave-function realism. For this reason, I will take it into consideration in the next sections.

3.3 A Metaphysical Analysis of the Wave-function Realist Ontological Picture

According to wave-function realism, the quantum wave-function is, as we said before, a high-dimensional physical field in a high-dimensional physical space. This view, endorsed by Albert (1996), Ney (2013), North (2013), Valentini (1997), is reminiscent of Bell's famous statement:

> Note that in this compound dynamical system the wave is supposed to be just as 'real' and 'objective' as say the fields in classical Maxwell theory – although its action on the particles is rather original. No one can understand this theory until he is willing to think of ψ as a real objective field rather than just a 'probability amplitude', even though it propagates not in 3-space but in 3N space. (Bell, 1987, p. 123)

Like any other physical field, the wave-function is characterized by an assignment of values, in this case complex numbers, which represent the amplitude and the phase of the wave-function. Given the Born rule, the points are also associated with higher or lower amplitude, depending on the probabilities of the particle positions. We can thus imagine the wave-function as a gigantic wave with some peaks and some valleys, which undulates in configuration space. According to the guiding law of motion presented above, this wave is supposed to influence our small and limited universe and to cause the particles to take certain trajectories.

In order to have a complete metaphysical characterization of such a field, however, it is not sufficient to specify its high-dimensional nature. In the following, I will discuss different metaphysical options to characterize its nature as a field and its relations with the particles.

3.3.1 Field Theory

If you look at the structure of the wave-function and you take it at face value (as the realists do), Bohmian mechanics becomes a field theory. However, we are not sure how to ontologically interpret the field. Indeed, there are two common ways to understand physical fields.

The first view, which is defended by Field (1984)[60] and Albert (1996), is that a field is simply an assignment of causal and intrinsic properties to each point of space or space-region. For example, in electromagnetic theories, we attribute the property of field intensity to each space-time point, and in the case of Bohmian mechanics we assign the wave intensity to each configuration space point. This ontological interpretation of the field seems to suggest that the space where the field is spread is substantival.[61] More precisely, in the case of Bohmian mechanics, it seems to suggest that we should regard the configuration space as substantival since it implies that the configuration space is a physical space[62] whose points instantiate physical and causal properties. According to this view, however, the field almost disappears: indeed, the field is reduced to a physical space with some properties. We cannot conceive of the field independently of the space. In this respect, it would probably also be wrong to assert that the wave-function undulates in the configuration space, since the wave-function is the configuration space with the assignment of some properties. In light of this description, adding a field in the ontology simply amounts to introducing properties, not a substantive entity. Spatial points with properties exhaust the ontology of fields. It is the space "that functions as the basic substantial entity and as the basic object of prediction" (Earman, 1989, p. 155). The resulting ontological picture, however, is not always satisfactory, because it fails to account for some field-properties that are very important in a classical regime such as energy storage. Indeed, it seems quite spooky how the 'space' can actually store energy or be 'massive', since this should not be its role. Moreover, the view that the space is actually physically substantive is controversial and not widely accepted.

In contrast, the second view regards fields to be substantival entities, that is, concrete and global particulars. In this case, fields are independent of the spatial points of the configuration space. Obviously, there is a sort of correspondence between the field and the configuration space points, but this correspondence is

---

[60] Field defines a field theory as a "theory that employs causal predicates that apply to space-time points or [. . .] regions directly" (Field, 1984, p. 40).
[61] In the debate on the nature of space, a space is said to be 'substantival' if it is a physical substance.
[62] See North, 2013.

merely mathematical.[63] The field occupies space, in which it is extended, but its ontological status is independent of the ontological status of the space where it lives. Alternatively, we could say that each bit of the physical field instantiates a spatial property as well. If the Bohmian adopts this view, then the wave-function is really a substantive concrete field that floats in space. Ted Sider, for example, seems to favor this alternative in his claim that regarding the wave-function as a physical field does not entail that the space where it lives needs to be physical, given that the wave-function can live in an abstract mathematical space.[64] Horgan and Potrč (2000) have also developed an ontological account of the wave-function called 'blobjectivism', according to which the wave-function is regarded as a global particular. However, contrary to Bohmian ontology, they presuppose that the wave-function is the only physical entity in the universe.

3.3.2 Causality and Properties

The realist interpretation of the wave-function can accommodate the ontological status of properties in the same way any other field theory does. If we adopt the substantivalist view of configuration space, each point of the space instantiates a particular physical property. For instance, each point instantiates properties like amplitude and phase, but also mass and charge (see chapter 2).

If we regard the field as a substantival entity, then the wave-function itself, as a concrete individual or particular, instantiates the mass-property, the charge-property and so on, so that the wave-function can be regarded as 'massive' or as 'charged' (Holland, 1993).

But regardless of which of the two interpretations we adopt, once we endorse a realist stance, the wave-function becomes a causal agent like any other field. Within Valentini's interpretation, as we previously saw, one can accommodate the causal linkage, by expressing through the force acting between the wave-function and the particle configuration. Earlier, I briefly characterized the force

---

[63] Einstein: "Spacetime does not claim existence on its own, but only as a structural quality of the field" (Einstein, 1961, p. 155).
[64] It is not clear to me how this view can be supported. To me, it is very controversial to think that a physical multi-dimensional space can live in an 'abstract' space. Ted Sider claims that this is controversial only if we rule out 'abstract objects' like mathematical entities cannot exist. However, I do not think that this is the point of the discussion. I concede that mathematical objects exist and that the configuration space exists as a mathematical abstract object, but I do not see how a mathematical space can play the role of being the 'arena' where a physical field lives 'physically'.

as the immediate causal agency, and the wave-function as the mediate causal agent. I concede that this distinction may need explanation. I borrowed this distinction from Bigelow et al. (1988), where forces are conceived as playing 'a mediating role' between 'respectable entities in the ontology', 'between causes and effects', and in particular, between fields and their effects. In this regard, the interaction between physical entities with their own independent ontological status is mediated by forces as direct causes. In this framework, the entities from which the force is generated are mediated causes: they cause certain effects through the role of forces. Let me give you an example that draws from common experience. If I throw a ball against a window, and the window breaks, the force by which the ball hits the window is certainly the immediate cause of the window breaking. However, the ball is still regarded as the entity that caused the window to break. In light of this, the ball is a causal agent in exactly the same way the force is a causal 'agency'. However, the ball could exert its causal power only through the mediation of the physical force. In the case of Bohmian mechanics, the scenario is the same. The wave-function changes the particle configuration via the force that it generates through the gradient of its phase. Also in this case, we can regard the wave-function force as having the role of mediating between the wave-function and the particles.

Here two aspects are worth noticing. Firstly, it would be impossible to recognize the role of force without considering the wave-function as a physical entity with a mediating casual power. As Bigelow et al. state, "forces exist when and only when there exist an 'exerter' and an 'exerted upon'" (Bigelow et al., 1988, p. 618). Secondly, the fact that forces play a direct causal role does not mean that we should regard them as ontologically primary with respect to the independent entities from which they are generated. On the contrary, it is more reasonable to think that, given their merely mediating role between entities, forces should be eliminated from the theory. Why should we suppose the existence of forces in our theory if they merely express the direct interaction between entities that is already spelled out by the laws? Indeed, Bohmian mechanics can be easily understood without appealing to the reformulation given by Valentini. I agree that forces should not be regarded as ontologically fundamental by the defenders of a realist interpretation of the wave-function. Yet, the role of force seems to be important: its use is important to remark that the wave-function and the particle configuration are connected through a causal relation. Moreover, according to Valentini, this causal relation is extremely important for the detection of the natural state of the particles and for the interpretation of the wave-function. Only once we recognize that the interaction between the wave-function and the particles is causal can we deduce the Aristotelian space-time from the dynamics and understand the wave-function as a causal and real physical field.

It should be noticed that within Valentini's interpretation, there is a problematic issue at stake, namely whether the interpretation of the wave-function should come before or after the interpretation of the interaction between the wave-function and the particles. The two interpretations are, indeed, extremely connected, and once we establish one interpretation, the other naturally follows. In our earlier discussion, when I presented the parallelism between the Newtonian laws and the Bohmian laws, it was obviously the case that first we interpreted the kind of interaction, and then in light of this interpretation we further interpreted the ontological status of the wave-function. But the opposite could easily have been done. Following the discussion in our introduction, however, we wanted to infer the ontological status from the kind of dynamics presented by the law (and not vice-versa) in order to reduce to a minimum the arbitrary character of metaphysical views.

Now that we have clarified the ontology and the dynamical meaning of the wave-function, we should relate the two. In particular: how should we regard the wave-function's causal power in relation to the properties it instantiates? All the properties of the wave-function concur to its causal power, hence they can be regarded as causal properties. They all causally determine the motion of the particles in such a way that each particle's velocity just means that the wave-function has some particular intrinsic and causal property associated with the particle configuration to which that particle belongs.

3.4 The Problems with the Resulting Ontology

3.4.1 A Strange Field Theory

Is the wave-function a *field*? Even though it presents the structure of a field, its physical features do not seem to suggest that it is a field. In the following, I will present some field-features that the wave-function lacks.[65]

3.4.1.1 Source and Intensity
The first character of the wave-function that distinguishes itself in a surprising way from other physical fields (such as the electromagnetic and the gravitational fields) is that the wave-function does not have any known localized source. Normally, fields have sources from which they are generated and radiated. For example, the electromagnetic field can have two kinds of sources – either a moving

---

[65] Some of those differences are briefly mentioned in Holland, 1993.

positive charge or a negative positive charge – while the gravitational field is generated by any massive particle. Moreover, given that the wave-function does not radiate from a source, it also lacks the property of 'intensity inverse proportionality', which normally characterizes physical fields. The fact that fields normally radiate from one source gives them the property of having an intensity that is inversely proportional to the distance from the source. If we want to measure the field intensity at a particular point of space, the intensity will always be inversely proportional to the square of the distance between that point and the source. This means that, normally, fields are more intense near the source and weaker in regions that are farther away from it. Given that the wave-function does not radiate from any source, it lacks this field-property: the intensity of one field point does not depend on the region where it is located (whether it is close to the source or further away), but only on its own amplitude, which gives the probability of finding the particle at that point.

3.4.1.2 Test Particles and the Relation between Wave-function and Particles
The second peculiar characterization is that the wave-function, unlike all the other fields, does not admit any test particle. This is true because even an infinitely small particle would modify its dimension and its form. Indeed, in chapter 1, we saw that any wave-function dimensions are given by the number of the particles. This means that any particle, no matter how small it was, would bring more degrees of freedom into the system; hence, it would modify the dimension of the wave-field. Therefore, it is impossible to measure the intensity of the field from the motion of the test particle. This also shows the deep and intimate connection between Bohmian particles and the Bohmian wave-function. Strictly speaking, in Bohmian mechanics, the state of the system is not constituted by two elements (i. e. the wave-function and the particle), but by only one element – the 'particle-with-its-wave-function'. It is impossible to have a Bohmian particle without its wave-function, and it is impossible to consider the wave-function alone, without its particles. However, it is possible to consider 'empty' branches of it. Indeed, the only way we have to 'study' the wave-function without taking the particle into consideration is to 'separate' the wave-function into different beams through a beam-splitter, and consider the branches where the particle is absent.

3.4.1.3 The Force
Another differentiating aspect concerns the force generated by the wave-function. While classically the force normally depends on the intensity of the field, in Bohmian mechanics it depends on the phase, hence on the form of the field. This indicates that the force in Bohmian mechanics should be understood as causing the

motion of the particles in a completely different way from the kind of causation that occurs in classical mechanics. In classical mechanics, forces depend on intensity, hence on the distance between the two interacting entities (of which one may be the source and the other the test particle). Two close particles attract or repel each other with a much more intense force than two particles which are distant. In Bohmian mechanics, on the other hand, the distance does not have any influence on the intensity of the force. What matters is their positions, rather than their distance.

3.4.1.4 Uniformity
Classical fields normally spread continuously and uniformly in space, so that the value of each point is uniform with the values attributed to the neighbor points. In contrast, the wave-function is discontinuous since in the nodal regions where the (domain of the) wave-function is zero, the phase becomes discontinuous.[66]

3.4.1.5 Non-locality
The last peculiarity of the wave-function as a field is that it enters the theory to account not for locality but for non-locality. More precisely, within Valentini's view, it enters the theory to explain a fundamental non-locality and entanglement relations between particles; within Albert's view it enters the theory to avoid a fundamental non-locality and to account for the apparent non-locality of the world we live in.

Classical fields are normally introduced to account for why it takes time for a particle to receive information from another particle, which is a phenomenon known as 'retarded action'. Retarded action normally occurs due to the fact that the 'action' spreads from one point to another by deforming the space and thus creating a field. Retarded action can be observed in the case of the electromagnetic field.[67] Suppose that a charge is moving and that we want to calculate its force at time t_0 on a test charge located very far away (Figure 8).

In this case, the force performed by the 'source' charge on the test particle cannot be spelled out according to the usual Coulomb's law:

---

[66] Now you may wonder: what if a trajectory goes into a node? The answer is that the Bohmian trajectory would end there, because, as you should recall, the nodal regions are those where the domain of the wave-function is zero. However, it is never the case that the trajectories end, because typical trajectories would never pass through nodal areas.

[67] In order to describe the retarded action in the electromagnetic field theory, I use the same case study presented in Heaviside, 1992; Feynman, 1964; and Lange, 2002.

3.4 The Problems with the Resulting Ontology — 77

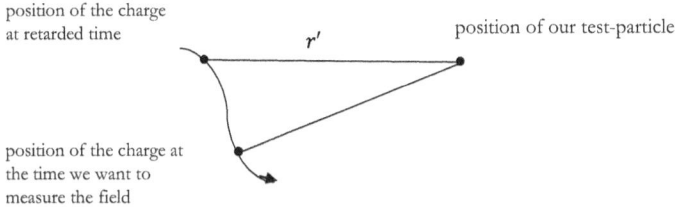

Figure 8: Retarded action at a distance.

$$F = \frac{1}{4\pi\varepsilon_0} \frac{q_1 q_2}{r^2}$$

where r is the distance at time t_0 between the moving charge and the test particle. Instead, the real value of the force felt by a charge q_2 at time t is given by the following equation:

$$F = \frac{q_1 q_2}{4\pi\varepsilon_0} \left[\frac{e_{r'}}{r'^2} + \frac{r'}{c} \frac{d}{dt}\left(\frac{e_{r'}}{r'^2}\right) + \frac{1}{c^2} \frac{d^2}{dt^2} e_{r'} \right]$$

where r' is the distance between the test particle q_2 and the moving charge q_1 at an earlier instant of time τ. The distance r' and time τ are called 'retarded distance' and 'retarded time' respectively, where the retarded time is calculated as the following:

$$\tau = t - \frac{r'}{c}$$

The first term of the equation $\frac{e_{r'}}{r'^2}$ calculates the 'retarded Coulomb force', hence the force felt by the test particle if it were at its retarded position. The force is inversely proportional to the square of the retarded distance. But obviously this term needs to be compensated by other terms in order to account for the motion of the 'source' charge and the spread of its force. Indeed, the field force felt by the test particle is not quite the same as it would be if the source particle were at its retarded position – given that the source is moving, the force spread by it changes continuously. Suppose, for example, that the source particle moves very slowly, so that the force actually changes very slowly too. In such a case we need to compensate the retarded Coulomb force, which would be almost equal to the normal instantaneous force. In order to do so, we have to add to the retarded force its velocity multiplied by the factor $\frac{r'}{c}$, which is the retardation delay. In this term, as in the first one, the value of the force at our test particle position is inversely proportional to the square of the distance between the test particle position and the source charge: $\frac{e_{r'}}{r'^2}$. This means that, if the particle trajectory and the test particle position are very far away from each other, the value of the force would not be very different regardless of whether we consider the retarded position or the actual one. The difference brought by the retarded position is hence felt only when the observational position and the trajectory of the particle are enclosed in quite a small area. However, things are different in the last term, which is inversely proportional to the distance $\frac{1}{r}$ (and not to its square!).[68] With this term, we take into account the acceleration of the charge as well, so that the calculation of the value of the force at the observational point depends on the particle retarded position, velocity and acceleration. This equation, which describes retarded action, reveals the physical existence of the electromagnetic field for the following reason: it tells us that the propagation of the force takes time. Indeed, the fact that the force at the observational point is as if the charge were still at a previous location means that the action of the field is *not* instantaneous. The reason why the force takes time to arrive at 'its destination' is easily explainable by the fact that the agent of the force, the electric field, propagates with time delay. From its source, the field propagates with finite velocity. Why? Consider the view that the field is a collection of material and causal properties: in this case, the field is a modification of the space, and this process of modification happens from one point to the next, one step after the other. The information takes time to spread; it takes time because it travels by modifying the space-time, by passing from one spatial point to another. If we consider the view that the field is a substantive entity, then we regard it as expanding in space, occupying a greater and greater portion of space with finite speed. Being a material entity, its motion may be quicker or slower depending on its physical properties. The fact that we have either a space with a collection of physical properties that propagate or a physical field that propagates itself explains why the action of the force is local instead of non-local (which was, for example, the view described by the Newtonian laws). The test particle feels the electromagnetic force when and only when the electromagnetic field reaches and 'touches' it. Given that electromagnetic fields satisfy spatio-temporal locality, we can thus arguably claim that they explain why a phenomenon presents locality instead of action at a distance (Bacciagaluppi & Valentini, 2009).

But the Bohmian case presents us with an opposite scenario. The wave-function is introduced in a many-particle system to account for the opposite phenomena; that is, non-locality. And I need to stress this point here because it will be extremely important later. In response to the question of why all the particles

---

[68] This is not clearly visible from the equation, since some calculations are needed. For a detailed explanation of how to compute the last term, refer to Feynman, 1964, vol. 2, chapter 21.

are interrelated instantaneously and are entangled, the realist introduces an entangled entity in configuration space, the wave-function. Particles are connected because they are physically connected and they are physically connected because they share the very same wave-functions (the universal wave-function); or, if we want to keep the reality of the conditional wave-functions, their wave-functions are physically interacting. So we give a physical explanation of the phenomenon and we move the explanation to a field-level in configuration space. There is a physical agent that is responsible for their non-local interaction, and that is the field. While Valentini's view ends here, Albert uses the physicality of the wave-function in high-dimensional space to explain why it seems that the world is entangled. Entanglement is not a fundamental feature of the ontology because it concerns an illusionary or at least emergent space-time, and not the fundamental physical arena of the configuration space.

3.4.1.6 Transmission of Energy

The last point I would like to draw attention to concerns the transmission of energy. Fields are normally regarded as ontological entities, because, as I mentioned above, they carry and store energy. Moreover, their role is essential for the principle of energy conservation. Suppose, for example, that one electric charge is in an electric field. If the particle moves in the same direction as the field, then the 'work' done by the field will be negative, and, for this reason, the field will release some potential energy and transmit it to the particle in the form of kinetic energy. The particle kinetic energy increase will consequently cause the particle's acceleration. In contrast, if the charged particle travels in the opposite direction, then the work done by the field is positive, and it needs to extract energy from the charge. This means that the particle releases its kinetic energy and transmits it to the field in the form of potential energy. In both cases the particle and the field exchange a certain amount of energy, in different forms, but this process of energy exchange permits the energy to always be conserved and never lost. Given the role of the field as a 'container', 'recipient' and 'transmitter' of energy, it is natural to attribute a physical status to it. More importantly, given that potential energy is normally attributed to the field, fields are regarded as physical entities. This is also discussed by Maxwell in the *Treatise*:

> Whenever energy is transmitted from one body to another in time (there is the retardation!), there must be a medium or substance in which the energy exists after it leaves one body and before it reaches the other, for energy, as Torricelli remarked, "is a quintessence of so subtle nature that it cannot be contained in any vessel except the inmost substance of material things". (Maxwell, 1954, p. 493)

But what about the wave-function? In the history of Bohmian mechanics there have been some attempts at reconstructing the dynamics of Bohmian mechanics in terms of energy, namely by revoking a sort of quantum potential energy of the wave-function. However, even though we cannot rule out the possibility that the wave-function carries energy, energy is certainly not a fundamental concept. Valentini is extremely clear in this regard, stating that "having lost their raison d'être, the very concepts of energy and momentum should make no appearance" (Valentini, 1996, p. 45), and "since nonlocality already makes them suspect, energy and momentum are the obvious culprits" (Valentini, 1996, p. 46).

This reveals the tight connection between locality and energy. Local action by contact, which is normally mediated by fields, is necessary for energy conservation.

But in Bohmian mechanics the system is, traditionally (setting aside Albert's view) already *non-local*. If the field does not mediate the action in three-dimensional space through the transmission of energy, then the energy completely loses its ontological significance. If we cannot regard energy as a quantity that is 'stored', 'transmitted' and 'conserved', then how should we think about it? The energy from ontological physical 'stuff' may become a simple computational device (in a purely instrumentalist view) or a non-physical, mathematical quantity associated with a system. The energy becomes a bookkeeping device without any ontological relevance, since any ontological relevance is inhibited by the fact that there is no medium, no field that transmits and stores it.[69]

3.4.1.7 Final Considerations

In response to the question of what the wave-function is, the realist view takes the mathematical structure of the wave-function at face value: the wave-function is a field. But as we have just discussed above, the wave-function does not look like a field at all, since it lacks the most distinctive features of classical fields. This should be enough to challenge the realist view concerning the kind of physical entity that the wave-function is. Aren't the realists mistaking the physical category of the wave-function? The question at stake is whether the realist is right to categorize the wave-function as a field. But this is not the only challenge that we want to raise. The second group of challenges comes not from the fact that the wave-function is a field, but from the fact that it is regarded as a physical entity.

---

[69] See Lange, 2002.

3.4.2 Problems: The Violations of the Criteria for Physicality

The realist view not only faces problems regarding the field character of the wave-function, but it also (and more importantly) faces problems regarding the wave-function's physicality. The realist view advocates the physicality of the wave-function (and of the configuration space, most probably[70]), but the wave-function seems to violate all the criteria that we normally use to demarcate physical entities. Moreover, even if we suppose that the wave-function is a physical entity, regardless of whether there is a violation of the criteria, it is not clear how the realist can explain the communication between the wave-function and the particles in case they endorse Valentini's view that particles live in a three-dimensional space. Below I provide a discussion of this point.

3.4.2.1 The Space-time Criterion
A common argument against the realist interpretation of the wave-function takes three-dimensionality (or four-dimensionality) to be a necessary condition for physicality. Given that the wave-function is a multi-dimensional entity, it cannot be physical. However, I suggest that this criterion only makes sense if it is grounded in the claim that only entities living in our space can be physical. But if this is true, the argument mistakenly assumes that only three-dimensional entities can live in our space. On the contrary, we know that high-dimensional entities can also live in our space, provided that their dimensions are compacted in such a way that they can live in a lower-dimensional space like ours. For example, strings are nine-dimensional entities but they still live in our space because six of their dimensions are compacted.

This cautions us to abandon the dimensionality of the entity as a criterion for demarcating physical entities from non-physical entities, and suggests that we should replace it with a space-time criterion.[71] Given that our space-time is the only arena where physical entities live, living in space-time is a necessary requirement for an entity to be physical. Here we do not want to dig into the delicate matter of whether it is also a sufficient criterion, since this would lead us to a very complicated discussion on how we should interpret the verb 'living'. Taking this criterion as necessary is already enough for the case we are examining. It is clear that the wave-function cannot live in our space-time – indeed, according to realist view, the wave-function must live in a higher-dimensional space in order to store all the information about entanglement, which is fundamental for the empirical predictive power of the theory. If we compacted the wave-function

---

[70] See note 10 for a discussion of this point.
[71] For a discussion of the criterion of space-time, see Hale, 1998.

in a three-dimensional space, then it would lose all the entanglement information about the system, and we would not know how the particles are interrelated.[72]

Given that the wave-function does not and cannot live in our space-time, the realist view violates the space-time criterion by claiming that the wave-function is a *physical* field.

3.4.2.2 The Criterion of Reciprocity

A criterion for physicality normally presented in the literature is the 'criterion of back-action/reaction', which relies on the third Newtonian dynamical law of motion. The third Newtonian law is normally taken as a guide to deciding upon the physicality of the entities presented in a physical theory. More specifically, physical entities are supposed to obey the third Newtonian law.

Third Newtonian Law: Whenever any physical object exerts a force on other physical objects, it must receive a force of equal magnitude and opposite direction back.

In light of this, we can formulate the criterion for physicality in the following terms:

Criterion for Physicality: In order for any object to be physical, it must receive a force of equal magnitude and opposite direction back whenever exerts a force on other physical objects; otherwise, it cannot be physical.

In particular, we want to take this as a sufficient and necessary criterion for physical reality: for an object to be physical, it is necessary and sufficient that it receives a back-reaction from the physical objects on which it exerts a force.

The key question here is whether the wave-function respects this criterion for physicality. In the first chapter of this book, we saw that the wave-function determines the motion of the particles, but we did not mention whether it is the case that the particles determine the evolution of the wave-function in return. If we look at the Schrödinger equation, which is the equation in which the evolution of the wave-function is described, there is no element that accounts for the interference of the particles on the wave-function. The fact that particles do not have any role in accounting for the evolution of the wave-function is actually of great importance for Bohmian mechanics. It is indeed worth noticing that the absence of the particles from any deterministic account of the evolution of the wave-function guarantees that the probabilities given by the wave-function are exactly the same

---

72 But check the multi-field view (3.7), as a valid alternative.

as the probabilities provided in standard quantum mechanics, where particles are not taken seriously in an ontological sense. The fact that the wave-function evolves as if the particles did not exist allows Bohmian mechanics to be as empirically adequate as standard quantum mechanics. Moreover, adding an interference element due to the particles' action on the wave-function may potentially break the linearity of the Schrödinger equation and also the deterministic character of the wave-evolution. In fact, there have been a few different attempts to go in this direction, but they either incur problems of empirical adequacy or lead to a very complicated and artificial construction of the Schrödinger equation.

Therefore, it seems that the wave-function violates the criterion of back-reaction:[73]

Premise (1): If any physical entity exerts a force on another physical entity, it must receive a back-action.
Premise (2): When the wave-function exerts a force on physical entities, it does not receive a back-action.
Conclusion: The wave-function is not a physical entity.

A realist of the wave-function may refute our worries by simply stating that the Newtonian laws are not supposed to apply in a quantum theory. After all, given that the first and second Newtonian laws fail to obtain in a Bohmian system, there is no reason to expect the validity of the third one. In particular, it should be noted that the Newtonian principle is based on classical intuitions, which are not supposed to hold in the quantum world. Why should the reaction be equal to the action? Why should the body that is acted upon react back? There is no reason to hold the principle true in quantum mechanics.

But it should be further noted that the third Newtonian law is intrinsically linked to a much wider principle called the principle of reciprocity. The problem is not that the wave-function violates the third Newtonian law, the problem is that the wave-function, by violating the third Newtonian law, violates the principle of reciprocity as well. Anderson states that the principle of reciprocity requires that "each element of a physical theory is influenced by every other element" (Anderson, 1964, p. 192).

Unfortunately, the way Anderson formulates this principle is very problematic on account of its vagueness and its ambiguity.

First of all, it lacks any specification of what 'each element' of a physical theory refers to. In particular, it seems that Anderson should restrict the meaning of

---

[73] Note that this criterion does not aim to be a definition of physicality.

'each element' of a physical theory to 'the dynamical physical elements' of a physical theory. Vassallo (2016), for example, points out that as long as the Lagrangian is reasonably taken to be an element of a theory, it is clear that Anderson's criterion does not apply. Hence, Anderson fails to acknowledge the difference between the descriptive elements of a theory (which arguably do not respect the principle of reciprocity) and the physical elements of a theory. Moreover, from Anderson's formulation of the principle, it seems that every satisfactory physical theory needs to be holistic. Indeed, the formulation states that each element of a physical theory is influenced by *every* other element (and not only *some*).

Without any doubt, the principle needs a more rigorous formulation, which, I suggest, should be the following:

Revised Principle of Reciprocity: Each dynamical physical element of a physical theory is influenced by some other elements.

Here, 'dynamical' refers to any element that is subject to temporal evolution. This more general formulation has also been endorsed by Einstein,[74] among others. However, in my formulation of the principle, the influence need not be reciprocal. As such, if we still want to call it the principle of '*reciprocity*', 'reciprocity' should not be understood in a strict way that implies that each element receives a back-action from the element it influences. Indeed, a physical element can influence one particular entity and be influenced back by another element that is not necessarily the one on which it exerted the influence. In this scenario, the principle is still one of 'reciprocity' in the sense that if an entity influences another one, then it is influenced as well (but not necessarily by the same entity it influenced).

Despite this generalization, I think that this principle is still too restrictive. Indeed, it could be the case that some elements are not actually influenced by other elements because of contingent reasons (but they would be in other circumstances). For example, two particles may be so far away from each other or isolated in such a way that in actuality they do not influence one another. However, we could still regard them as physical since, in different conditions, they would influence each other. Consider for example the case of a very dense fluid that permeates the universe. If an infinitely small particle is moved by the fluid along its current, the particle's size may not allow for the fluid to actually be influenced by the particle. Similarly, consider a ball in a tiny room with a highly idealized rigid

---

[74] In 1924, Einstein wrote that each physical object "influences and in general is influenced in turn by others" (Einstein, 1924, p. 15). It is "contrary to the mode of scientific thinking", he wrote earlier in 1922, "to conceive of a thing which acts itself, but which cannot be acted upon" (Einstein, 1922, pp. 55–56).

wall: the ball bounces on the wall, receives a physical action from it, and it also reacts. However, the wall, being infinitely rigid, does not change its state. In the case of Bohmian mechanics, it may also be that the particles are too small in comparison to the wave-function to act on it. But this does not mean that the wave-function is not physical.

For this reason, it would be better to apply the Leibnizian[75] formulation of the principle of 'reciprocity':

Leibnizian Principle of Reciprocity: Any physical element of a theory must be capable of acting and of being acted upon.

This further generalization of the statement reveals the real reason why the principle of reciprocity is important. Its role is not to constrain the dynamics of objects, but to forbid absolute elements in a theory. Indeed, according to the principle, any satisfactory theory should not have elements that are 'absolute' (and here I refer to the original meaning of 'absolute', which is 'freed', 'unrestricted'). All the elements of a physical theory must be in connection with each other and none should be left 'alone'. An absolute element in the theory "indicates a lack of reciprocity – it can influence the physical behaviour of the system but cannot, in turn, be influenced" (Anderson, 1964, p. 192).

But now we must address the question of why a theory should not have absolute elements. The reason why the violation of the principle of reciprocity is unreasonable lies in its arbitrariness: if we allowed some entities to be 'sensitive' to the physical phenomena around them and other entities to be 'insensitive', we would not be able to justify the difference. Why is it the case that for some entities the principle of reciprocity holds, while for others it does not? Brown & Lehmukuhl (2015) underline this point very well, by claiming that the problem of the violation of the principle of reciprocity is not really that the action must be reciprocal, but that it is arbitrary to stipulate that some physical entities are sensitive to other entities' influences while some others are insensitive and immune to such external influences.

So, in the case of Bohmian mechanics the question is not simply to ask whether the dynamics obey the third Newtonian law, but whether the wave-function is capable of being acted upon. This question is very difficult. From the Bohmian laws it

---

[75] Leibniz did not formulate the principle with the exact wording I am using here. A presentation of the principle of reciprocity by Leibniz (Leibniz, 1989) is the following: *"et onmis action sit cum reaction; nec plus minusne potentiae in effectu in causa contineatur"*, which I translate as: "an action is always with a reaction; and there is more power neither in the cause nor in the effect" (Leibniz, 1989, part I, pp. 440–441).

is clear that the particles, no matter what their sizes or their properties may be, simply do not appear to account for the evolution of the wave-function. Hence, the fact that the wave-function does not receive back-reaction is not due to contingent reasons, but to the structural character of the theory. As such, no matter how the particle configuration evolves, the wave-function is insensitive to what is happening in the three-dimensional space.

There is an obvious way in which the wave-function depends on the particles: its dimensions are given by the particle number. As we saw before, adding a particle to the configuration, no matter how small it is, brings about a huge change in the wave-function. Indeed, there is a connection between the degree of freedom of the particles and the dimensions of the wave-function. However, this dependence does not reveal that the particles can *dynamically* influence the wave-function. The dependence between the form of the wave-function and the particle configuration is only structural, and it only reflects the fact that the wave-function is a function of all the particle coordinates. Hence, the conclusion is that the wave-function, if physical, does play the role of an absolute element of the theory, thus violating the principle of reciprocity.

3.4.3 Problems with Causality

3.4.3.1 A First Problem for Causality: Spooky Communication

While the first two problems concerned two metaphysical criteria for the physicality of an entity and regard different specifications of wave-function realism, a third problem highlights the impracticability of Valentini's realist view, which, we saw, concedes the existence of two spaces: one, high-dimensional, where the wave-function lives, and one, three-dimensional, where the particles live. Indeed, a problem arises when one has to account for how this high-dimensional entity in this high-dimensional space can interact with the particles that live in our space-time. In particular, it is not clear how the wave-function can interact with the particles, given that it is unknown how the two spaces are interrelated (if they are at all). This problem, which in the literature has been addressed merely as a problem of two spaces and dubbed the problem of 'being lost in space' (Callender, 2014), has even more important implications since it touches upon the notion of physical causality that we presented above. If two physical entities do not interact 'physically', can we rightly claim, as we did in the above section, that the wave-function is a causal agent? Is it appropriate to define its influence on the particles as causal? According to the formalism introduced before, the wave-function acts on the particle via a force, which is normally regarded as a causal relation between two different entities or, more appropriately, between two different events (if a ball hits a window and breaks it, it would be more appropriate to say that the ball hitting the window caused the window to break rather than to identify the ball itself as the cause). More specifically, we can claim that the ball is the mediate causal agent, while the hitting is the immediate causal agency. From a causal view perspective, it is clear that the wave-function is the mediate causal agent, but it is not clear what the immediate causal agency should be. We know that mathematically it is expressed by a force, but it is completely unclear what this force amounts to given that the physical objects which the wave-function influences are not physically related.

To be noticed is that this problem is only present in Valentini's view, as Albert (2013) and Ney (2020) endorse the view that all the fundamental physical ontology is in 3ND-space. If we apply their view to the case of Bohmian mechanics, we can say that both the wavefunction and the particle ontology fundamentally live in a physical 3ND-space. Fundamentally, there are no particles in 3D-space, but only one marvelous high-dimensional particle living in the wavefunction high-dimensional space. This view has certainly the advantage of avoiding the problem of spooky communication. However, the pressure is to conceptually and formally reconstruct how the 3D physical world of our experience emerges from a high-dimensional reality. One well-trodden view is to adopt a functionalist strategy that aims to ground the 3D-pointers and human observers that are made out of particles via a mapping from the one Marvelous Point moving in a high-dimensional space (Albert 2013). The problem, however, is that the mapping is not unique (Chen 2017). Albert (2013) uses the dynamical structure, in particular the structure of the Hamiltonian potential term, to privilege one mapping over the other. His idea is that in the Hamiltonian potential term the fundamental degrees of freedom are grouped into triples, and this particular grouping would give rise to our 3D spatial distance. But his strategy is often criticized for being too permissive, as it would allow for the emergence of many more objects than we realize (Chen 2017). For this reason, even though Albert's view is not vulnerable to the problem of how to account for a causal physical communication between the wavefunction and particles across different spaces, there remains a sort of problem of spooky communication between the fundamental space and the manifest image.

3.4.3.2 A Second Problem for Causality: The Hydrogen Atom

Another problem seems to hinder the realist view of the wave-function. While explaining the role of the S-function in Bohmian mechanics, I said that there seems to be an *ontological* dependence between the particles' velocity and the wave-function. Indeed, without the wave-function, the particles' trajectories would not be generated. S is a fundamental and crucial element for the particles' trajectories. This claim was supported by the fact that the wave-function is supposed to cause the velocity of the particles, which would be in a state of rest without it.

However, this claim is inaccurate and reveals some reasons for being skeptical about wave-function realism. One of the most interesting features of Bohmian mechanics is how it accounts for an electron trajectory guided by the ground state wave-function of the hydrogen atom. It is physically proven that the ground state of the hydrogen atom is always real and positive everywhere.[76] This means that its imaginary part is zero, hence that the phase of the wave-function is null. It is not difficult to infer from this that Bohmian mechanics predicts that if the electron of a hydrogen atom is at rest, it does not move at all!

Still, the wave-function is there, and this situation triggers two different questions. The first is whether it would be more appropriate to regard the S-function (hence the S-field) as the causal agent for the particles' velocity – after all, in this case, the phase is null. However, interpreting the S-function rather than the wave-function as the physical field performing the action on the particles seems controversial at the least, since S is just a feature of Ψ (namely its phase). The second question is whether we are misunderstanding the role of the wave-function. Instead of revealing itself as a causal agent whose presence causes the motion of the particles, the wave-function seems to be more like a necessary but mathematical element of the theory whose value determines the velocity of the particles.

This final point seems to push us to seek out another category that would better represent the wave-function.

3.4.4 Valentini's Responses

In the section above, I discussed three different kinds of challenges. The first kind concerns the use of the field category to understand the wave-function from an ontological perspective. Indeed, we saw that, even though the wave-function has the structure of a field, it does not present typical field-properties. The second kind of challenge concerns the much broader physical character of the wave-function. Indeed, the traditional criteria that are normally used to assess the physicality of mathematical entities would all lead to the conclusion that the wave-function is not a physical entity. We also discussed the problems that the realist view has to face when it attempts to accommodate the causal relation between the wave-function and the motion of the particles. In this section, we will consider how the realists

---

[76] For a detailed explanation of this point see Dürr & Teufel, 2009, p. 154.

may defend their view by examining Valentini's responses. To be noticed is that these responses are more or less specific to Valentini's kind of realism. Albert, indeed, defends the view that the wavefunction shares the same kind of physical status as the electromagnetic field, and he endorses the view that fundamentally, the wavefunction and the particle ontology live on the very same high-dimensional space.

3.4.4.1 The Bite-the-bullet Maneuver

The response provided by Valentini (2009) to the above problems is a persistent reiteration that the wave-function is a completely new physical entity that does not correspond to any familiar ontological categories. For this reason, we should regard it as a 'new kind' of causal agent and as a 'new kind' of physical field. The wave-function is not reducible to any familiar entity and is not on the same ontological footing as other physical fields. There is no way to account for its ontological status in terms of our familiar physical understanding of the nature of the world because it requires a new conceptual 'revolution'. Given that the wave-function cannot be analyzed in more familiar terms, Valentini claims (Valentini, 2009) that it should be understood as a fundamental and primitive physical entity in no need of explanation. According to this view, it is incorrect to keep insisting that the wave-function cannot be physical because it does not live in our space or because it does not receive back-reaction, and this incorrectness arises due to the fact that the wave-function is not like the physical entities we know. We take his position to be in line with, and in some aspects similar to, the so-called primitivist approach defended by Maudlin (2013), according to which we should take the wave-function to have its own ontological category. Maudlin, however, comes to this conclusion from completely different if not opposite starting points and via a different path.[77]

Valentini supports his view by appealing to different cases in the history of physics where the physics community was forced to introduce new physical ontological categories that seemed to violate the criteria of physicality endorsed at that time or that, more generally, seemed to be completely at odds with the contemporaneous metaphysical conception of physicality. The most blatant cases of this are the introduction of force at a distance as a new physical causal agency and of fields as physical causal agents. Concerning the Newtonian gravitational force, a physical force was introduced in order to account for the interaction of

---

[77] Valentini claims that the wave-function is a physical field with a new ontological characterization; Maudlin, on the other hand, claims that we cannot know what the wave-function represents, and so it deserves its own 'primitive' ontological status (see Maudlin, 2013).

masses at a distance in the Newtonian gravitational law. That Newton found the category of physical action at a distance at odds with his familiar categories is very well shown in the following passage, where he seems not to believe his own theory (which relied on action at a distance!):

> That one body may act upon another at a distance through a vacuum, without the mediation of anything else, by and through which their action and force may be conveyed from one to another, is to me so great an absurdity, that I believe no man who has in philosophical matters a competent faculty of thinking can ever fall into it. (Newton to Bentley 1692/3, vol. 3, in Cohen, 1978, pp. 302–303)

The reason behind Newton's skepticism was that if a body feels the presence of another body at a distance and for this reason its behavior is changed, there must be something that 'carries' the information in the space. Hence, postulating a physical 'force' that travels through the void connecting different physical entities without them having a material action 'by contact' seemed an unintuitive and uncomfortable theory to defend. At that time, according to Descartes' theory of *tourbillions*, the normal physical force was force by contact, where each object influences another by 'touch', and if the two objects that are interacting via force are far away then the space must be conceived of as being filled with matter. For this reason, postulating the existence of a force that 'travels' in empty space and 'reaches' bodies at a distance seemed an absurdity. But, as Lange (2002) rightly points out, Newton does not say *why* action at a distance is impossible or why there must be something that carries the action. Just saying that this notion is an absurdity does not sound like a serious and well-motivated reason for discounting it. The same applies to Bohmian mechanics: the claim that the wave-function cannot act on the particle needs to be motivated.

Some help in this regard comes from Clarke: "That one body should attract another without any intermediate means is indeed a contradiction for this is supposing something to act where it is not" (as cited in Lang, 2002, p. 95). This worry looks surprisingly similar to the discussion above concerning the space of the wave-function. If the wave-function is in another space, how can it act in this three-dimensional space? But if we take this to be a worry, we are implicitly assuming that a body should be present in the same space as another in order to have any influence on it. Similarly, Clarke's worry presupposes locality. And this presupposition needs to be motivated further. Why is it the case that two entities cannot communicate unless they live in the same space? Is such communication physically impossible? Or, is this lack of communication only due to metaphysical presuppositions, like the 18th-century locality (which was later abandoned)? Valentini (2009) thinks the latter, arguing that the problem of communication simply arises as a result of our traditional metaphysical conceptions of the world. Just as

Newtonian scholars endorsed non-local action, which was at odds with their metaphysical understanding of the physical world, scholars of Bohmian mechanics should also not be restrained by our own metaphysical criteria that dictate what kind of communication is possible and what is not.

Obviously, before accepting Valentini's criticisms we should ask a few questions. The first is whether the Newtonian example is really a good one: were the 'Newtonians' right when they introduced action at a distance? Indeed, it seems nowadays that the gravitational field is one of the pillars of gravity. However, even if action at distance may not work well in a gravitation context, given that non-local quantum interaction is confirmed by the scientific community, we could certainly claim that they were at least right when they decided to abandon their metaphysical criteria that regarded locality as necessary. Another question we should ask is whether or not the Newtonians were justified in abandoning their metaphysical criteria. Correspondingly, we must ask whether realists of the wave-function are really justified in abandoning theirs. However, comparing and contrasting the two different situations may lead us too far away from the main aim of this book.

The second example that Valentini discusses of where the physics community was forced to introduce new physical ontological categories concerns the electromagnetic field. Many physicists of the 19th century were very skeptical about assigning a physical ontological status to an 'empty' space. More importantly, it seemed highly implausible that a portion of 'empty' space was actually the transmitter of a force by contact. How is it possible that a particle is 'pushed' by a field that is only 'empty' space with some mathematical properties? Also in that circumstance, the scientific community had to revise its criteria for describing physical reality. Therefore, Valentini argues, in the same way that we had to attribute physicality to empty space in the past, we now have to attribute physicality to a higher-dimensional space.

3.4.4.2 Characterization of this Novelty

We have seen that by replying to the challenges of the realist view, Valentini (2009) simply opts for a bite-the-bullet maneuver. However, the issue is that, even if we should embrace new physical entities in our ontology and revise our metaphysical criteria about physicality, we still need to minimally characterize the new physical entity and understand *how* we should revise our conceptions of what physicality applies to. Valentini (1992) attempts some answers to this question, which I will discuss in this section.

According to Valentini, an electromagnetic field is more abstract than material solid bodies because it is a portion of empty space – nevertheless, it is still physical. In the same way, the wave-function is more abstract than normal fields since it lives in configuration space, but we should not regard it as unphysical just because of this ascription. Valentini (1992) argues that the more we progress in our scientific endeavors and the better theories we come up with, the more abstract the entities to which we should rightly attribute physicality become. Indeed, according to Valentini, in the history of physics we have increasingly considered more abstract entities to be physical causal agents. As we just said, Bohmian mechanics presents us with a case of an even more abstract agent than forces and fields – the wave-function. Unfortunately, Valentini does not clarify the meaning of the adjective 'abstract', which sounds vague and confusing. What does it mean for a physical entity to be 'more' abstract than others? It seems to me that this claim may be interpreted in many different ways. An initial gut interpretation could claim that there are different degrees of physical reality depending on the level of the abstractness of an entity; in other words, entities could be classified according to different degrees of physicality. But does the character of physicality admit different degrees? This is at least controversial, and we are inclined to rule out the proposal as unintelligible.[78]

Another way we could interpret Valentini's talk about the abstractness of physical objects is to connect it to the distinction between the interpretation of the field as a particular or just as a collection of properties of the space. We could argue that Valentini perhaps regards the electromagnetic field as a physical particular while he regards the wave-function as a collection of properties of the configuration space (and not as an independent 'concrete' particular undulating in a multi-dimensional space). This is certainly a very charitable interpretation. But would Valentini not claim that the configuration space is also 'more' abstract than the physical space? Indeed he does, and this reveals that Valentini's discussion probably cannot be interpreted in this light. In fact, if the wave-function is just an assignment of properties of the configuration space, then that space must be physical and substantival.

Moreover, the discussion about the abstractness of the wave-function not only has consequences for the intelligibility of physicality, but also for the concept of causality. In fact, Valentini (1992, 1996) stresses that the wave-function is not like the physical causes that we find in classical mechanics. This is because the wave-function is not an efficient cause, but a formal one. It is, however, quite ambiguous what a formal cause amounts to. Any interpretation we could give in light of Aristotle's understanding of formal causes seems to lead us astray, since

---

[78] For a discussion of this see Brown & Wallace, 2005. According to M. Deutsch (private correspondence), this proposal is intelligible, if 'more or less physical' is understood as 'satisfying more or less traditional criteria of physicality'. This is a very interesting and original reading of Valentini's statement which would need to be further elaborated.

in Aristotle's time the 'form' was the 'substance', the 'essence' of an entity. Indeed, here it seems that Valentini's adjective 'formal' refers to the fact that the wave-function acts on the particles neither through an exchange of energy nor via its intensity, but only through its 'phase', which is a structural aspect of the wave-function.[79] The fact that a formal aspect of the wave-function (strictly speaking) is involved in the causal relation between the wave-function and the particle motion pushes Valentini to call the wave-function a 'guiding form'.

It is quite clear that by appealing to the formal character of the causal role of the wave-function, Valentini can respond adequately to the challenges given by the hydrogen atom.[80] As long as the wave-function is not an efficient cause but only a formal one, we can understand why it can still be regarded as the cause of the particle motion even if its presence does not always bring about the expected change in the particle motion. It is not the 'physical' presence of the wave-function that brings about the change, but its structural aspects; namely, how it rotates and what kind of shapes it has. But this way of approaching the realist problems is not satisfactory at all, and that is because it undermines the realist program. Instead of saving it, it sinks it. If the causal role of the wave-function is only formal – if, at the end of the day, the wave-function's physicality does not matter – why should it be regarded as physical? With this sort of line of defense, Valentini seems not only to undermine his realist position with confusing and ambiguous remarks, but he also seems to cause the reasons for endorsing the realist view to fall apart.

3.5 Summary: The Realist View Is Bad for Ontological Results

In the first part of this chapter, we presented and discussed the ontological picture defended by the realist view, and we found it extremely problematic. Identifying the wave-function with a physical causal field brings about a very unintuitive and uncomfortable scenario that does not give due diligence to the familiar categories we normally use when we interpret physical ontologies.

In considering how to face these challenges, the realist is at a crossroad. The first option the realist can take is to adopt a bite-the-bullet maneuver. In this case, the realist's reply is that the realist position requires a drastic change of our outdated metaphysical criteria and that we should embrace the existence of new kinds of physical entities that do not belong to our familiar categories and do not

---

[79] The question that Valentini ought to answer, however, is what 'formal' exactly means and why, as we will see later, 'formal' implies 'not physical'.
[80] For a discussion on the hydrogen atom in Bohmian mechanics, see Dürr & Teufel, 2009, p. 153.

match our old criteria of physicality. This bite-the-bullet maneuver is quite safe since it is impossible to knock it down only in light of metaphysical speculations. What this teaches us is that if we appeal to metaphysical criteria to defeat the position we could end up having nothing at all in the end, because the realist could always be in the position to reply to our criticisms. But this bite-the-bullet maneuver obviously sidesteps the deeper challenges to the realist program. In particular, it fails to develop a specific account of what should count as physical and how we should revise our metaphysical criteria.

The second option the realist can take is to go further and face the challenges of his own view. But in doing so, the realist risks eroding the motivations for endorsing the realist view in the first place. By pursuing this alternative, instead of saving and strengthening the view, Valentini (1992) destroys it.

Therefore, it seems that the only viable option for the realist is to bite the bullet while endorsing a certain primitivist approach according to which it is not possible to specify the wave-function further. In this way, the realist view cannot be knocked down. But this is not a satisfactory position, and if remaining silent about the specification of the wave-function is really the only option available to the realist, then there must be something wrong at the core of their position. But where is the realist wrong? This is the first question we want to ask in the following section. We will see that the answer lies in the reasoning behind the realist's claim that the wave-function is a physical field in configuration space. This claim is the source of all the problems that the realist position incurs. The reasons we have for endorsing the view that the wave-function is a physical field arise due to the kind of methodology adopted by the realist, and this methodology is so misleading that it provides us with sufficient reason to remain deeply skeptical of the realist view.

3.6 The Methodology of the Realist View

3.6.1 The Wave-function as a *physical field* in Configuration Space: A Problem of Reification

In the first part of this chapter (3.1. and 3.2) I presented the realist view, which identifies the wave-function with a physical field. The reasons for identifying the wave-function with a physical *field* (and not something else) rely on the structure of the wave-function. Since the wave-function is a function that assigns, for each point of the space where it is defined, a particular value specified by a complex number it has the structure of a field. One aspect worth noticing is, however, that the wave-function has all the possible particle configurations as its argument,

3.6 The Methodology of the Realist View — 95

hence it is defined over a 3N multi-dimensional space. And from here, from the fact that the ontology contains a physical field that lives in a multi-dimensional space, the realists face a number of difficulties, as presented above. I will now briefly reiterate these difficulties.

The realist interpretation, as discussed in the last section (3.5), is normally criticized for the *ontological results* it presents: that the ontology consists of a physical entity living in a space that is not our space, that this field, from its own space, acts on the particles of our space – and there seems no way to account for how! –, and that this entity does not receive back-action from the particles, contradicting the third Newtonian law, which for centuries has been regarded as a criterion for physicality. Notice that all these criticisms against the realist view concern the resulting ontology and are grounded in metaphysical presuppositions. For this reason, as we have seen, the reply from the realists may simply be a 'bite-the-bullet' maneuver apt to reestablish a new metaphysical criterion for physicality, does include neither spatio-temporality nor back-reaction. Moreover, the realists may find a way to solve the problem of communication between the two spaces by appealing to some kind of metaphysical relation between the two spaces (such as emergence), or by putting the particles in the higher-dimensional space as well. In all this, they might want to claim that our metaphysical principles are outdated and misplaced: in the same way we changed our metaphysical principles when dealing with the electromagnetic theory by attributing physicality to empty space, why shouldn't we change our metaphysical criteria in the case of quantum mechanics? It seems that the dialectic in the literature is going exactly in this direction and there is no way the realist position can be overcome. Certainly, we could engage in a complicated discussion over the differences between various metaphysical criteria for physicality and get lost in the meandering metaphysical nuances that differentiate the electromagnetic field and the wave-function. But do we really need to get into such a discussion?

There is, to my mind, a primary way to argue against the realist interpretation, and that is by focusing not on its ontological results but on its *methodological presuppositions*. In a nutshell, my worry is that the realist conflates mathematics and physics. First of all, the points of the configuration space are mathematical points that represent the possible configurations of the particles. Secondly, the values assigned to these points by the wave-function are complex numbers. Is there anything physical in these considerations? No. The result is clear: the wave-function is indeed a field, since a field is any function that assigns values to space points. However, it is a mathematical field, since there is nothing about this field that makes it physical (at least for now). Mathematical objects are not physical objects. Distinguishing 'merely mathematical features' from 'genuinely physical aspects' of the theory is arguably the main task of philosophers of physics. In light of this worry, we can take note of the following claims by Albert:

> The sort of physical objects that wave-functions are, are (plainly) fields – which is to say that they are sorts of objects whose states one specifies by specifying the values of some set of numbers at every point in the space where they live. (Albert, 1996, p. 278)

Albert's sentence is misleading and unfortunate for two important reasons. The first is that Albert seems to think that the physicality of the wave-function is given by its 'field-structure', which, however, is first of all mathematical.[81] Indeed, he does not even consider the dynamics we discussed above. Secondly, Albert does not differentiate the mathematical object that has the role of 'representing' from the physical object that 'is represented'. Indeed, he asks what *physical* objects the wave-functions *are*, and not the true question of what physical objects the wave-functions *represent* (see Maudlin, 2013). And this confusion applies not only to the wave-function but also to its space. Albert seems to assume that the space where the wave-function is defined is a space that the wave-function lives 'in' physically (hence that it is a physical space).

But a field is physical, or better, a mathematical field represents a physical field, if the mathematical values attributed to the mathematical space, where it is defined, represent physical properties attributed to physical points (which normally are taken to be the space-time points of our three-dimensional space, but which here should be physical points of a high-dimensional space). Therefore, Albert jumps from the mathematical realm to the physical realm, and even worse, he conflates the two, overlooking the important question of whether or not the values assigned by the wave-function – these complex numbers – represent any physical properties. The canonical answer to this question would be that these complex numbers represent the amplitude and the phase of the wave-function. But, again, given that the wave-function is a 'function' (hence a mathematical entity), the 'amplitude' and the 'phase' are two mathematical elements of the wave-function. We should more specifically call the amplitude 'probability amplitude'. Thus the question we asked before still remains, even if at a second level of description: do these mathematical elements of the wave-function represent the amplitude and the phase of a physical field?

To summarize, if it is right to charge the realists with conflating mathematics and physics, or the representative objects with the ontology, then there is a gross methodological mistake at the core of their position. Indeed, if the above criticism is correct, the real question that should be asked is not what the wave-function *is*,

---

[81] This view is also supported in Maudlin, 2013 and Myrvold, 2015.

but what the wave-function *represents*, if anything. We know that the wave-function is a mathematical field. What we still do not know is whether we have any good reasons to regard this mathematical object as representing something physical. Are the reasons that stem from the dynamics enough to regard the wave-function as representing something physical? If so, what does it represent?

3.6.2 A First Reply from the Realist

My criticism, however, might be uncharitable, since the realist position might be subtler than I have presented it here. The realists might indeed respond to my accusation by claiming that they *do* know the difference between representation and being, between mathematical and physical, but that in this case we can avoid any pedantic methodological division between the two realms because there is a one-to-one correspondence between the wave-function (what is representing) and the physical field (what is represented). The former is 'defined' in configuration space while the latter 'lives' in a high-dimensional space, the "wave-space". But the wave-function and the field (the configuration space and the wave-function space) are isomorphic, so why bother with terminological issues?

At this point, however, we have pushed the realists onto more reasonable ground, and we are in a position to push them with further questions. Once they acknowledge the difference between 'mathematical' and 'physical', and once they admit that inferring the physicality of the field from the fact that it is a (mathematical) field is wrong, they find themselves in dangerous waters, as we will see. Does the realist have good grounds for claiming that there is this one-to-one correspondence between the wave-function and a physical field? We still do not know. Do we have good reasons to discard such a correspondence? I think we do.

The first reason to raise doubts about the physicality of a field that is isomorphic to the wave-function is that the wave-function is gauge-dependent. We know that several wave-functions, all related by gauge transformations, lead to the very same particle trajectories.[82] If we take two wave-functions, such that one is a non-zero scalar multiple of the other, then both wave-functions are physically equivalent since they define the same velocity for the particle configuration and the same probability distribution. Given that gauge invariance is a common criterion used to assess the physicality of mathematical entities, the realist should at least claim that the physical field is represented by a class of wave-functions related by gauge transformations. Hence, they should admit that there is not a one-to-one

---

[82] For technical details about this, see Goldstein, 2013.

correspondence between the wave-function (as a mathematical entity) and the putative physical field. Rather, different mathematical objects, in this case 'wave-functions' represent the same physical reality (the field).

The second reason follows similar lines. Once we reject reification and we agree that there is a difference between what represents and what is represented, then there is a criterion we generally adopt to find out what the features of the 'represented' are – that is, the criterion of observation invariance. Normally, we take what is represented to have the sort of structure that remains invariant under different mathematical representations. North (2009) presents a very clear case of this sort of observational invariance applied to the coordinate system that we use in mathematics to represent objects. Suppose you have your Euclidean space and two points on it. The distance between the two points remains invariant, no matter how you change the coordinate system. Whether you shift the origin or rotate the axis, the mathematical distance between the two points still remains the same. There is a geometrical distance between the two points that is coordinate transformation invariant. The criterion of observation invariance says that we should conclude from this that there is a physical distance corresponding to the mathematical distance. The case of coordinate invariance can easily be applied to our case. Is the structure of the wave-function telling us what the structure of physical reality is like? If it is, it should be observationally invariant (or in this specific case, coordinate-invariant). Suppose you have two particles in three-dimensional space (hence six coordinate axes in your configuration space) and you shift the origin of one configuration space axis, x, so that the wave-function is moved ten meters up.[83] In this case, translation invariance is implemented by:

$$\psi(x_1,y_1,z_1,x_2,y_2,z_2) \rightarrow \psi'(x_1+10m,y_1,z_1,x_2,y_2,z_2)$$

Does the wave-function change? It turns out that it does,[84] since the wave-function is coordinate-dependent:

$$\psi(x_1,y_1,z_1,x_2,y_2,z_2) \neq \psi'(x_1+10m,y_1,z_1,x_2,y_2,z_2)$$

Now the question we should ask is whether this change is meaningful. I suggest that it is, since the new wave-function may not even obey the Schrödinger equation. Indeed, the wave-function might satisfy the Schrödinger equation with a potential depending on x but may not obey it with a potential depending on x +10.

---

[83] I would like to thank Dr. Lienert here for having enhanced my argument with mathematical considerations.
[84] Lewis (2004) claims that the wave-function is invariant under coordinate transformations. However, Dr. Lienert, and Prof. Goldstein (private correspondence) agree with my view that the wave-function does change under 3ND coordinate transformation.

Moreover, the change in the equation is not a pure gauge because the probability distribution is not invariant under it. Given the Born rule:

$$|\psi(x_1, y_1, z_1, x_2, y_2, z_2)|^2 \neq |\psi'(x_1 + 10m, y_1, z_1, x_2, y_2, z_2)|^2$$

Notice that now the realist is at an impasse. First we pushed them to give up a one-to-one correspondence between the mathematical entity 'wave-function' (or, if you like, the mathematical entity 'field') and the physical entity (the field). But now we also pushed them to say that if we simply change our representation of the coordinates, the mathematical object does not remain invariant, hence not all of its features should be interpreted as representing physical features. The wave-function is fixed, attached, almost 'glued' to the configuration space in such a way that it becomes itself a representative element with the configuration space coordinate system. Perhaps the wave-function is a mere representational element of the theory.

In this section, I hope I have shown that first of all we should discard the notion that there is a one-to-one correspondence between the wave-function and the physical field. From this, it follows that the realists are simply in the wrong when they do not acknowledge the difference between the level of mathematics and that of physics in their appeal to an alleged and rigid one-to-one correspondence. Moreover, we have seen that the wave-function itself is not a mathematical object that remains invariant under coordinate transformations, hence we should not think that its mathematical structure reveals objective features of the physical world.

3.6.3 High-dimensional Space?

Now that we have ruled out any attempt at reification, as well as any attempt to regard the wave-function as representing an isomorphic objective structure of the physical world, the question is whether we should take the class of equivalent wave-functions related by gauge transformations to represent the physical field that lives in a multi-dimensional space. There are similar cases in the history of physics. For example, it seems that the Aharonov-Bohm effect prima facie presents potentials that seem to be physical entities but, at the same time, are gauge-dependent.[85] Also in this case, a solution would be to take a class of potentials related through gauge transformations and regard that as representing the 'physical entity' called 'potential'. However, it is normally the case that preference is given to

---

[85] See for example Healey, 2001.

interpretations that do not take classes of equivalent potential as real. And this is not the only case. Up to now, in the history of philosophy of physics, this strategy has been proposed many times but rarely supported: in most cases, the final solution has been to regard something else as representing the physical.[86] Therefore, also in the case of Bohmian mechanics, using the class of equivalent wave-functions is just an ad hoc solution, which, if endorsed, needs to be grounded in sound motivations.

Hence, we have good reasons to push the realists to answer the question of why they really need to have a high-dimensional field in their ontology, and I imagine that their line of reasoning might be something like the following. They may be happy with conceding that the wave-function does have extra-structure that is not physically meaningful or that should be taken away in order for the wave-function to be invariant under gauge and coordinate transformation. But they might further claim that we need to keep the structure of a field in configuration space within our physical realm. This may be motivated by appealing to the following two principles:
1) We want to take the mathematical objects that figure in the fundamental laws of the theory as physical.
2) We want to take as physical all the mathematical structure that plays a fundamental role in the theory and that is necessary for the theory to provide complete information about the system.

These two principles are actually the very same principle if we think that fundamental laws can incorporate only elements of the structure that play a fundamental role in the theory. However, for now I want to keep them separate and explain them in slightly different way. I disagree with both principles, and in the following section, I am going to argue against them.

3.6.4 The First Principle

The first principle states:

(1) We want to take the mathematical objects that figure in the fundamental dynamical laws of the theory as physical.

The motivation for endorsing the first principle might be dictated by the nature of dynamical laws, which are 'about what is fundamental'. North presents this view in the following way:

---

[86] For more extensive discussions of this, see: Lyre, 2004; Maudlin, 1998; Healey, 2007.

> This brings me to a very general principle that guides our physical theorizing, from which the other principles I use all extend: the dynamical laws are about what's fundamental to a world. [. . .] The dynamical laws govern the fundamental level of reality; that is why they are guide to the fundamental nature of the world. When I say that the laws 'are guide to the fundamental nature of a world', I mean that we infer the fundamental nature of a world from the dynamical laws. We do not directly observe the fundamental level of reality: we infer it from the dynamics. We posit, at the fundamental level, whatever the dynamical laws presuppose – whatever there must be in the world for these laws to be true of it [. . .]. We posit, at the fundamental level, whatever is required for the laws governing objects. (North, 2013, p. 186)

In sum, the idea is that we assume that the dynamical laws are about what is fundamental, and, for this reason, we take to be fundamental the elements the laws are about. So, if we apply this to the case of Bohmian mechanics, we can construct the following argument:

Premise (1): The dynamical laws are only about what is fundamental.
Premise (2): The dynamical laws of Bohmian mechanics are about the wave-function.
Conclusion: The wave-function is fundamental.

One first reason to be skeptical of this sort of argument is that there are different formulations of the same dynamical laws that make use of different mathematical objects; therefore, more importantly, there are different formulations that are about different sorts of objects. Take again the case of Bohmian mechanics. We do know that it is possible, contrary to what most Bohmians think, to formulate Bohmian mechanics by dropping the universal wave-function. Indeed, we can reformulate the Schrödinger equation and the guiding law of motion with different conditional wave-functions, one for each particle, plus entanglement fields that 'entangle' the conditional wave-functions with each other. In this mathematical formulation, the Schrödinger equation is about the evolution of three-dimensional wave-functions and of the entanglement fields.

This proposal has been developed in Norsen (2010). Norsen starts from the claim that it is impossible to reformulate Bohmian mechanics only in terms of particles and their individual conditional wave-functions. Indeed, we know that the actual evolution of the conditional wave-functions depends on the particles, the structure of the conditional wave-functions themselves *and* the structure of the universal wave-function from which the conditional wave-functions are extracted. Hence, it is often thought that it is impossible to construct Bohmian mechanics without the universal wave-function. But Norsen's proposal is to enclose the information displayed in the configuration space wave-function in a countable infinite number of entanglement fields in three-dimensional space. In this proposal, we construct the Bohmian dynamics with our conditional wave-functions but we supplement them with entanglement fields. Norsen (2010) shows that if we choose appropriate initial conditions for the entanglement fields, then this new formulation of Bohmian mechanics is exactly empirically equivalent to the standard formulation that uses the universal wave-function. In this formulation, the evolution of the conditional wave-functions and of the entanglement fields is dictated by the Schrödinger equation. Moreover, the evolution of the particles is determined by both the entanglement fields and the conditional wave-functions. Therefore, in this version of Bohmian mechanics, the pillar equations are about particles, conditional wave-functions and entanglement fields, but not the universal wave-function in configuration space.

Given this equivalent formulation, the question of how we can decide which formulation provides us with the true fundamental ontology arises. How can we decide which is the 'true' fundamental ontology? If the realist insists on adopting a methodology that infers the fundamental objects of the physical realm from the dynamical laws, then we need to identify how we can select the dynamical laws in the first place, given that many different laws can work equally well when formulating the very same theory.

A second point that I find controversial in the argument is the following. I admit that we would be right to infer the physical reality from the laws of the theory; moreover, I believe that we should take the laws to be our guide to the fundamental nature of the world. But this does not mean that we have to take their mathematical structure as physical. We do not have to assume that what they are fundamentally about is a physical structure that is isomorphic to the mathematical structure. Here again I suspect that there is a sort of process of reification implied. This is an implication that, as we noted above, is problematic. We might agree with the claim that the dynamical laws are about what is fundamental but still acknowledge that the dynamical laws make use of a structure which may or may not be found in the physical world. Take for example Hamiltonian Mechanics, which makes use of the Hamiltonian. No one has ever considered the Hamiltonian to be a physical field in 6N dimensional space. On the contrary, we all know that it is a mathematical function that provides information about the energy of the system. The core issue here is not whether we should take the dynamical laws to disclose the fundamental nature of the world. Rather, the issue arises from the fact that, in order to formulate efficient scientific laws, we adopt some mathematical structure that may or may not correspond to an ontological structure, which may or may not be isomorphic to an ontological structure. We construct our laws with mathematical objects, some of which directly represent some physical objects, and some of which are mainly mathematical artefacts that allow us to have very convenient formulations of scientific laws. And the problem is that we do not know whether the structure of the wave-function reflects a physical field-structure in the world exactly or whether it is in the formulation simply to allow for the most convenient formulation.

The last kind of perplexity in the argument concerns the truth of the laws. North (2013) explicitly claims that we need to posit in the ontology what makes the laws true. In this respect, we can say that the laws need their 'truth-makers' in the world; that is, things that make them true. Her argument may be spelled out along the following lines. Take the sentence: 'An apple is on the table'. Its truth-makers are the apple and the table. Consequently, if the sentence is true, there must be in the world an apple on a table. Take now the laws of Bohmian mechanics, which are the guiding law and the Schrödinger equation. They are about the evolution of the particles and of a wave-function; therefore, the truth-makers for our Bohmian laws are the particles and the wave-function. Hence, we need to consider the particles and the wave-function in our ontology. But the fact that laws need truth-makers (though note that this assumption is highly controversial[87]) does not mean that we have to place in our world the same kind of mathematical structure presented in the laws. My gut reaction is to think that, for mathematical law-statements, things are settled differently than they are for sentences.

First of all, talk about truth-makers is going to become difficult without committing to a particular status of laws: are we taking laws as modal nomological entities or just as descriptions of regularity in this world or as primitive entities? For example, if we endorse a Humean view, then our laws are true in virtue of some stuff in the world.[88] However, if we endorse that nomological entities have a governing role, then laws are above this world, so they are true even though the physical stuff they regulate does not exist! So, it really depends on how we understand laws and on our metaphysical conception of them.

A second very general remark is as follows. Interpreting North's discussion in terms of fundamentality and truth-makers, or using the metaphysical tools of fundamentality and truth-makers to lend support to her view, may lead us astray. For instance, the truth-maker theories and the fundamentality theory might even not be compatible[89] since, according to the truth-maker theories, it is possible to have as truth-maker an object to which the fundamental laws do not refer.

Addressing now the core of the realist view on the need for truth-makers of dynamical laws, I claim that the truth-makers of physical laws – presupposing that

---

[87] A primitivist of nomological entities, for instance, would deny that laws need something to make them true. For the primitivist, laws are brute facts that are not analyzable in terms of deeper truths. I would like to thank here Dr. Asay for his comments on this point.
[88] We will discuss the Humean view on laws in chapter 4.
[89] Thanks to Jack Tak Ho Yip for clarifying this point to me.

our metaphysical view on physical laws admits truth-makers for laws! – may be different kinds of objects and not necessarily a set of physical objects. For example, one could take platonic entities to be the truth-makers of our dynamical laws. Thus, my third point is that even if one grants that physical objects play the role of truth-makers for our dynamical laws, it does not necessarily follow that physical objects need to present a physical structure isomorphic to the one of the mathematical entities figuring in the laws. It is not obvious that the truth-makers of a law need to be structurally isomorphic to its mathematical items. Think again of how Bohmian mechanics and classical mechanics represent physical objects in configuration space. Particles, tables, my computer, you and I – everything is represented mathematically with a point in configuration space. But this does not mean that at the ontological level there is really only one point which makes the laws true. The same reasoning should be applied to the case of the wave-function: the fact that, mathematically, we use a function that maps complex numbers to points in high-dimensional space does not mean that we need the same isomorphic structure at the physical level to make the laws true.

But we can reformulate North's argument so as to make it stronger and more convincing than I made it appear to be. First of all, recall the discussion about fundamentality. North claims that the dynamical laws are about what is fundamental. Now, according to the metaphysical theory called 'best system' (or MRL[90]) account of laws,[91] a statement is a law if and only if it is an axiom of the best system, which refers to the system that best balances strength and simplicity. For example, in this case, Bohmian equations should count as laws if and only if any deductive system lacking them would be inferior in strength and simplicity. Being a law is a special and specific status according to this way of thinking. Here we do not want to go into the more complicated and deeper question of whether or not the Bohmian equations match the metaphysical requirements for equations to be metaphysical law-statements (in other words, whether they are really the axiomatizations of the best system). For now, let us suppose that they are, and so that there are good grounds for claiming that the Schrödinger equation and the guiding law are indeed laws of the Bohmian theory. Then, according to the best system approach, we can infer from the axiomatizations of the best system what the fundamental concepts are, and, consequently, what should be part of our ontology. Indeed, according to Lewis (1986), the axiomatizations constituting the best system make use of only fundamental language. This means that the wave-function is fundamental. According to this connection between lawhood and fundamentality,

---

[90] MRL stands for Mill, Ramsey and Lewis. See Cohen & Callender, 2009.
[91] We will discuss the Best system account of laws in chapter 4.

there is a fact of the matter regarding whether the laws reformulated in terms of entanglement fields are part of the axiomatizations or not. Hence, there is also a fact of the matter regarding whether we should be realists about the wave-function; that is, whether we should think that the wave-function carves reality at its joints.

We can also use some metaphysical tools to support North's claim (North, 2013) concerning the truth of laws. Here I do not want to go into discussion about the truth-makers of laws; rather, I want to approach the problem in a more intuitive yet still rigorous way. North claims that we should posit in our ontology what makes our dynamical laws true. An example that can help us understand this claim, and that offers support to this claim, comes from the electromagnetic field theory. The dynamical laws of classical electromagnetic fields are about points of space. And the question of what kind of fundamental structure of the world could ever make the electromagnetic theory true, according to its laws, has a simple reply: a structure where points of space are concrete particulars. The same line of reasoning should be valid in the case of the wave-function and the configuration space. At the beginning of this chapter, we claimed that the realists make the gross mistake of conflating mathematics and physics by taking the configuration space as physical. Indeed, as we claimed, the configuration space is a mathematical construction. But North's argument seems to reveal that actually this was not a mistake. Rather, it was the result of some other methodological principles according to which we should take what the dynamical laws are about (hence what makes them true) as fundamental. If we take the dynamical laws to be the guides of our investigation into the ontology of the world, then we should differentiate the configuration space in classical mechanics from the configuration space in quantum mechanics. In classical mechanics, the dynamical laws are about the history of the universe represented by a function from times to points in 'configuration space', where 'configuration space' is, ultimately, simply the set of all the functions from particles to points of space (see Dorr, 2009). Hence, if we ask what it is in virtue of that this function accurately represents the history of the universe, the answer hinges on the physicality of the particles and the space points. But in quantum mechanics, the situation is different,[92] since the Schrödinger equation is a constraint on a new kind of function, the wave-function, which describes the history of the universe. This function associates each time to a function from configuration space to a complex number. And it is hard to see in virtue of what these facts are true if we do not take the configuration space points to be physical points or concrete particulars (see Dorr, 2009).

---

92 See Dorr, 2009 for a detailed discussion of this point.

Let me try to reply to this line of defense from the realist. We *could* hold the view that the laws are fundamental facts (in virtue of their simplicity and strength) and that any concepts and any properties that figure into them are fundamental. According to Ted Sider,[93] for example, who is a defender of this view, it is reasonable to take some objects as fundamental if and only if they figure in the maximally simple and strong laws. But we need not be committed to this view. Ted Sider himself acknowledges that at the root of this metaphysical view of lawhood and fundamentality there is a deliberate connection between simplicity-centered epistemology of fundamental reality and concept-fundamentality-centered metaphysics, a connection that is arguable and not compelling.[94] For example, we could follow Cian Dorr's criticism against this view and argue that the best formulation of laws is not accessible to us, or simply that the connection between the two is far more complicated than we thought. Esfeld,[95] for instance, refuses tout court a Siderian approach, claiming that we should never infer any ontology from our dynamical laws and their formalisms but that we should be led by armchair metaphysical criteria.

My second point in my reply to the realist's defense is the following. We should be careful in applying the language of fundamentality in deciding whether the wave-function is a *physical* entity. We may agree that the wave-function is a *fundamental* object in our *ontology*, if we take 'ontology' to be whatever exists in this world. In this case, given that in our fundamental law we quantify over the wave-function, it is definitely true that the wave-function 'exists' in a Quinean sense.[96] However, the question that we should be asking is whether we should think of its 'fundamental' existence as a physical existence. There are different concepts that are fundamental yet not physically real. This does not mean that they are 'less' real than physical entities. They are 'real' but not physical. Without a doubt, the fundamental laws are a guide to what exists and what is fundamental – but the question is whether it is always the case that their fundamental concepts are in a one-to-one correspondence with physical objects.

Concerning the point developed by Cian Dorr (Dorr, 2009), I do not understand why it would be problematic to take the configuration space points as representing the particle configuration. We do not need to reify that space. The facts of the wave-function, which maps points in the configuration space to complex numbers, are in virtue of the different behaviors of the particle configuration.

---

[93] Here I refer to what Ted Sider said during the reading group in metaphysics at Rutgers University (Winter 2016).
[94] Here I refer to what Ted Sider said during the graduate seminar in philosophy of physics at Rutgers University (Winter 2016).
[95] Private correspondence.
[96] Thanks to Dan Marshall for this point.

The things that the facts of the wave-functions are true in virtue of do not need to be at the level of the configuration space, given that the configuration represents more fundamental physical stuff (in this case, particle configuration).

In our discussion of the first principle rooting the realist view, we have shown that the realists' arguments are either quite weak or they rely on controversial assumptions. However, I think that there is still work to do in order to defeat the realist view's methodology. In particular, we need to address the second methodological principle that the realists may want to endorse.

3.6.5 The Second Principle

The discussion of the first principle is made deeper and more complicated through an evaluation of the second principle:

(2) We want to take as physical all the mathematical structure that plays a fundamental role in the theory and that is necessary for the theory to provide complete information about the system.

The second principle explains why we should infer the physical structure from the mathematical one, and provides the realist with stronger motivations to keep a multi-dimensional field and a multi-dimensional space in the physical reality. Let me first reformulate the second principle in more precise philosophical terms. What do the realists mean by 'a fundamental role'? According to the second principle, we should understand the fundamental role of a structure as intrinsically related to the notion of complete information. Is a structure necessary for the laws to express all the information about the system, or can it be replaced by other kinds of structure? A structure is fundamental if and only if I cannot reformulate the laws in terms of other kinds of structure without losing some physical information about the system. If we could replace our mathematical objects with others, then they would not be fundamental, rather they would be reducible. Take for example the Hamiltonian in classical mechanics. Given that the Hamiltonian is a function of the energy of the system, in most circumstances we can replace it with two different energies, kinetic and potential. Furthermore, the kinetic and potential energies are reducible to other particles' properties such as velocity, position and mass. Hence, the Hamiltonian is not a fundamental structure of the theory. What about the wave-function? The realist would claim that the wave-function is necessary to encode in the laws the entanglement relations between the particles and to predict the future evolution of the system.

I will now support this claim with one very general example.[97] Suppose that you have two quantum particles, particle 1 and particle 2. While particle 1 has a 50% chance of being at position A and a 50% chance of being at position B, particle 2 has a 50% chance of being at position C and a 50% chance of being at position D. This can be easily represented in terms of wave-functions. If we want to represent the system in three-dimensional space (Figure 9), then we associate one wave-function with each particle, the wave-function has two equal peaks of intensity, one peak for each region of space that the particle is likely to occupy. Now, in three-dimensional space the system has only one single representation. Once we represent the system in 3ND configuration space, however, we do not have a single representation, but three options (we suppose here a scenario where the Bohmian particles might not be entangled). The three different representations in configuration space correspond to the same single three-dimensional representation, since in configuration space representations differ depending on whether or not the two particles are entangled and, if they are, *how* they are entangled. The three possible scenarios are as follows: either the two particles are anti-correlated, or they are correlated, or they are not correlated at all. While in Figure 10c the two particles are not entangled, in Figure 10a the two particles are entangled in such a way that when particle 1 is at position A, particle 2 is at C, and when particle 1 is at B, particle 2 is at D. In Figure 10b the two particles are entangled in the opposite way, so that while particle 1 is at position A, particle 2 is at D, and while particle 1 is at B, particle 2 is at C.

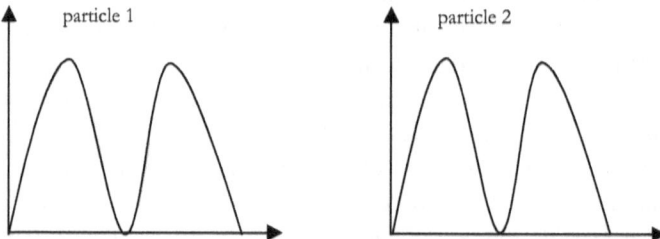

Figure 9: Entanglement in one-dimensional space.

This example shows that we are able to represent the entanglement and the kind of entanglement between particles only with a high-dimensional field living in a high-dimensional space. Indeed, in three-dimensional space, it is not possible to represent complete information about entanglement.

---

97 This example is completely taken from the paper by Lewis (2004).

3.6 The Methodology of the Realist View — 109

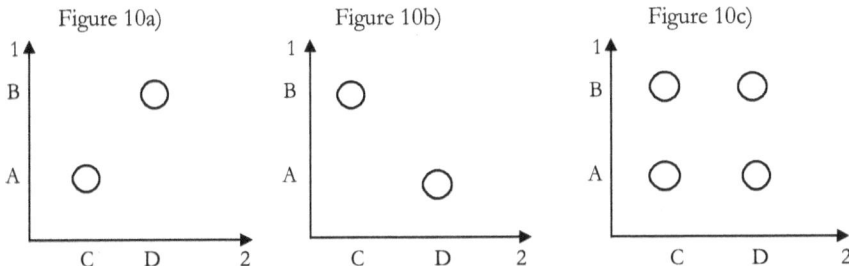

Figure 10a–c: Entanglement in two-dimensional configuration space.

According to the wave-function realist, this implies the following argument:
Premise (1): We want to take as representing physical structure that mathematical structure which is necessary for us to be able to completely represent/describe all the information about the physical system.
Premise (2): Without a high-dimensional wave-function, we would not be able to completely represent/describe all the information about the physical system.
Conclusion: The high-dimensional wave-function represents physical structure.

Obviously, an easy maneuver here would be to remind the realist of the fact that the wave-function can be reduced to set of conditional wave-functions plus entanglements fields. Therefore, we could acquire the complete information about the system not by appealing to a universal wave-function in configuration space but by appealing only to beables in three-dimensional space. However, this response is not foolproof either, and it would trap us in the problem of fundamentality: laws rewritten in that way would be far more complicated and thus could not be part of the best system. Therefore, we cannot take them or their concepts as fundamental. Notice that the same could be said for the Hamiltonian: once we reformulate the Hamiltonian, our laws may not be as simple and as informative as before, and as such they may not be part of the best axiomatization of laws. However, the case of the Hamiltonian is quite controversial, since there is no great difference between the two formulations. In contrast, replacing the universal wave-function with conditional wave-functions would result in an ontology with an infinite (though countable) number of fields.

The differences between the reformulation of the Hamiltonian and the reformulation of the wave-function should definitely be investigated further, but such as investigation would not be appropriate here. In any case, let us take for granted that if we want to keep our best system, we cannot reduce the wave-function further (and we remain agnostic about the Hamiltonian). If we do make this assumption, then it is true that we need the wave-function and its configuration space in order to have information about the entanglement relations obtaining among the particles. We cannot substitute the wave-function with any other term, and we need it necessarily in order to formulate our laws in the best possible way. Should we accept the realists' verdict? Before replying again to the realist, it is time to remind the realist of the distinction we have drawn (a distinction they are likely to have accepted) about the representing and the represented. Keeping that distinction in mind, the second principle should be reformulated as follows:

(2*) We want to take as representing physical structure that mathematical structure which plays a fundamental role in the theory (and) which is necessary for us to be able to completely represent/describe all the information about the physical system.

As we said, the realists might insist on keeping the high-dimensional space structure in the physical reality, because we really need to regard as physical all the mathematical structure that is needed in order to completely represent all the information about the system. In this case, we really need the high-dimensional wave-field in configuration space in order to completely represent all the physical information. Along these lines, Valentini claims that, since the wave-function stores physical information (about entanglement), it must be physical (Valentini, 1992). But this jump is again misleading due to a confusion regarding the distinction between the 'complete representation of all the information' of the system, the 'complete representation of the ontology' of the system and the ontology itself. Valentini jumps from the first level (complete representation of information) to the last (the ontology).

But let me explain what the crux of the problem is, step by step. Firstly, I want to point out the deep difference between 'information completeness' and 'ontological completeness' (Maudlin, 2006). We can introduce this difference by pointing to one example: the electromagnetic field.[98] All the information we need about the system is given by the field. From the information provided by the field, we get not only all the information regarding the field itself, but also regarding the charge. This way, the charge may be eliminated from the representation of the physical information about the system since the information it provides is redundant. But charges do exist, and may generate the field. Therefore, if we

---

[98] This is the example that Maudlin himself uses in order to delineate the difference between informationally complete representation and ontologically complete representation of the system (Maudlin, 2006).

eliminated charges from the ontological representation, the ontological representation would be incomplete. An informationally complete representation of the system is a representation that provides all the information about the system, whereas an ontologically complete representation of the system is a representation whose mathematical elements exhaust, via their representational role, all the ontology of the world. In the case of the electromagnetic field, the ontologically complete representation of the system consists of both the electromagnetic field and the charge. But the charge does not appear in the informationally complete representation of the system.

Now, it is clear that the wave-function is needed in order to have an informationally complete representation of the system. Indeed, without the wave-function, we would not acquire the non-local information we need in order to predict the particles' trajectories (without giving up the best system of laws). But is the wave-function part of the ontologically complete representation of the system? It may be thought that being part of the ontologically complete representation of the system *does not* necessarily imply being part of the informationally complete representation of the system; at the same time, being part of the informationally complete representation of the system *does* necessarily imply being part of the ontologically complete representation of the system. Therefore, it may be argued, the wave-function is necessarily part of the ontological representation. The reasoning behind this argument is that if an element is not needed in order to provide the full information about the system, then it may or may not be ontologically representative; however, if it is needed in order to provide the full information about the system, then it must be part of the ontological representation. This is certainly a line of reasoning that needs to be investigated further, though such an investigation would require a depth of analysis that is out of the scope of this book. In this book, the focus is more specifically on the case study of the Bohmian wave-function. Nevertheless, my general point is that we need to be careful when we transpose one element from the informational representation to the ontological representation and from the ontological representation to the ontology itself. And what I hopefully made clear in this chapter is that even if a mathematical structure is necessary in order to provide the complete informational or ontological representation of the system, it does not follow that there is a physical isomorphic structure in the physical ontology.

Given that we discarded the direct connection between informational representation and ontology, the question that remains to be answered is whether the wave-function is part of the ontological representation and, if it is, what exactly it represents. We will address these two questions in the following two chapters. Before moving to that, however, let me first review an interesting proposal, which is the multi-field view.

3.7 The Multi-field View

The multi-field view is a realist view of the quantum wave-function, without however being in line with what has been dubbed 'wave-function realism'. Indeed, while supporters of the multi-field view believe that the wave-function represents something in our physical reality, and that is a physical field, they also deny that this field is multi-dimensional, rather it is a 3D-multi-field. In their paper *The wave-function as a multi-field,* Hubert and Romano (2018) interpret the wave-function as a multi-field which for a system of N particles specifies a precise value for the entire N-tuple of points in three-dimensional space, thus determining, given the actual positions of N particles, the motion of all particles. In this regard, the resulting ontology is all in our three-dimensional space: the wave-function decorates our 3D physical field and not the 3ND configuration space, as it assigns intrinsic properties (represented by complex values) to particular N-tuples of points of three-dimensional space and not to single points of the configuration space. An alternative, proposed by Romano, is also to take the two fields composing the wave-function, the R-field and S-field as multi-fields. These are real-valued scalar functions expressing the amplitude and the phase of the wave-function, which assign real values to each N-tuple of points representing the actual location of the Bohmian particles, in the three-dimensional space. The multi-field view has also been defended by Chen (2017), who proposes to regard the quantum wave-function as assigning properties to each plurality of point in our three-dimensional space, exactly in the same way we regard the electromagnetic field as assigning properties to each point in our three-dimensional space. Chen further stresses that the multi-field defined over N-pluralities of points in a three-dimensional space is equivalent to the quantum wave-function defined over each point in the configuration space.

This view has the great merit of avoiding the most difficult challenge of wave-function realism, which is that it features a fundamental ontology in a 3ND space. However, several other challenges remain in place. The first one concerns the absence of back-action from the particles to the field. Also in this case, while the multi-field determines the velocity of the Bohmian particles, the latter do not have any influence on the exact configuration of the multi-field. The second problem concerns the fact that the multi-field interpretation violates the view that the space in which a field "lives on" is the smallest space where it assigns a value for each point in that space.[99]

---

[99] For a discussion of these two challenges, see Romano, 2020 and Chen, 2017.

I do not think that these challenges constitute a fatal threat for the multi-field view. In fact, I believe that the multi-field view is a very interesting ontological interpretation for Bohmian mechanics. While supporters of the multi-field view are clearly sympathetic to and officially endorse a realist interpretation of the multi-field as a physical view, one option would be to escape their challenges by adopting a nomological approach to the multi-field, which is exactly the same approach that some philosophers recommend to supporters of wave-function realism. I shall discussion the nomological approach to the quantum wave-function in the next section.

4 A Nomological Interpretation for the Wave-function

This chapter will be dedicated to the nomological interpretation of the wave-function proposed by the Rutgers-Munich-Genova group. First, I will show that at the heart of the nomological interpretation of the wave-function is a particular understanding of the guiding equation (also called the 'law of motion'). Second, I will present the different metaphysical formulations of the nomological view and all of its most important criticisms. Finally, I will investigate its methodology and conclude that, even though the wave-function is a nomological entity, it is still ontologically salient as it represents some ontological features of reality.

4.1 The Guiding Equation

The first interesting questions that we should ask when we are presented with Bohmian mechanics are the following: Why does the law of motion take the particular form it does? What justifies the formulation of the law of motion? Why do we have to believe that particles follow those particular trajectories? Here we will evaluate three justifications proposed by the Rutgers-Munich-Genova group. Each justification will give us the tools to infer what ontological status the wave-function naturally acquires.

4.1.1 Simplicity and Symmetries

Dürr, Goldstein and Zanghì (from now on DGZ[100]) discuss the guiding law with great care (Dürr et al., 1992). We introduced the law of motion in our first chapter, and we saw that it is a first-order equation of motion that describes the motion of particles along continuous trajectories in three-dimensional space. However, when presenting the law, the Rutgers-Munich-Genova group uses a formulation that is different from the one we used by Valentini (1996, 1997). Even though the two formulations are perfectly equivalent and may be used interchangeably, the formulation adopted by the Rutgers-Munich-Genova group is significant in that it allows us to understand their interpretation of the equation and, consequently, of the wave-

---

[100] DGZ is the acronym that stands for the first letters of Dürr, Goldstein, Zanghì, who are the members of the Rutgers-Munich-Genova group.

function. Here, the velocity of one particle is given through the imaginary part of the gradient of the wave-function, whose variables are all the particles' positions, hence the whole particle configuration:

$$v_k^\psi = \frac{dQ_k}{dt} = \left(\frac{\hbar}{m_k}\right) Im\left[\frac{\nabla_k \Psi}{\Psi}(Q,t)\right]$$

The law consists of a first-order differential equation, according to which the velocity of the particles – represented by a velocity vector field v – is given by the gradient of the imaginary part of a function represented by Ψ, where Ψ is the wave-function already presented in chapter 1.

Note that the definition of S (the phase of the wave-function) is:

$$S = \hbar Im log \Psi$$

Given this definition, the DGZ formulation of the law of motion for the particles is exactly equivalent to the one we presented in chapter 1:

$$v = \frac{\nabla S}{m}$$

Let me now explain the equation of motion in detail. The choice to formulate it in this way is motivated and justified by the fact that it is the only law that obeys certain basic requirements (Dürr et al., 1992), which I will list here. First of all, DGZ request the law be the 'simplest' possible law. For this reason, they want it to be based on the velocity of the particles, given by a first-time derivative:

$$v_k^\psi = \frac{dQ_k}{dt}$$

Moreover, they want two wave-functions differing only by trivial transformations (gauge transformations) to be physically equivalent. This means that two wave-functions, where one is a non-zero constant multiple of the other, should be equal:

$$v_k^\psi = v_k^{c\psi}$$

But this is not enough – indeed, they also need to find the form of the velocity field. And this is achieved by symmetry requirements that would render the velocity Galilean covariant. Specifically, they want the velocity field to be rotational invariant. The simplest possibility, given that it has homogeneity of degree zero, is as follows:

$$v_k^\psi = \alpha \left[\frac{\nabla_k \Psi}{\Psi}\right]$$

where α is a constant scalar.

In addition to this, they want it to be time-reversal invariant

$$v^{\psi*} = -v^{\psi}$$

and for this reason, they have to consider only the imaginary part of the gradient of the wave-function:

$$v_k^{\psi} = \alpha Im\left[\frac{\nabla_k \Psi}{\Psi}\right]$$

Finally, their last and most important requirement is that, in order to be fully Galilean-invariant, the velocity field must transform under boosts exactly as any other velocity would. And since the boosts are implemented on the wave-function by

$$\psi \to e^{i\frac{\hbar}{m}v_0 \cdot q}\psi$$

our α must be:

$$\alpha = \frac{\hbar}{m}$$

All these requirements lead to the final DGZ formulation of the guiding equation:

$$v_k^{\psi} = \frac{dQ_k}{dt} = \left(\frac{\hbar}{m_k}\right) Im\left[\frac{\nabla_k \Psi}{\Psi}(Q,t)\right]$$

However, according to Skow (2010), this process of building up the particular *form* of the velocity field according to some requisites is based on the *unjustified belief* that we know how boosts act on the wave-function. Indeed, according to Skow, DGZ assume that the boosts act on the wave-function in exactly the same way they act in the context of standard quantum mechanics, where the wave-function does not represent a physical entity like a physical field but just encodes information about the particle positions. Now, in order to know how the Galilean boosts act on the wave-function, we first need to know the meaning of the wave-function in the theory (i. e. whether it is a physical field or not) – given this, it seems that their construction of the velocity field is based on the fallacy of false presupposition. The fallacy consists in presupposing to know the ontological status of the wave-function, when in actuality the issue is debatable (in the previous chapter, we saw that the wave-function many be regarded as a physical field). However, it seems plausible to think that DGZ are justified in applying the boosts in that way, in the name of coherence since in the Schrödinger equation the wave-function transforms under boosts in this way as well. Hence, I take their presupposition to be well justified and not as fallacious.

Rather, what is worthwhile underlining here is that there is a hidden argument justifying the construction of the guiding equation (Skow, 2010). DGZ start with the claim that the Galilean space-time is the correct space-time upon which we should build the theory. Hence, when formulating the law of motion of the particles, they look for an equation that is Galilean covariant.[101] For this reason, they need to build the equation in a particular way, either by adding factors like α, or by looking only at the imaginary part of the wave-function. In this argument, the connection between space-time and the equation of motion is tight, with the former (the Galilean space-time) determining the latter (that particular equation of motion) (Skow, 2010).[102] The argument runs as follows:

Premise (1): If the ontology lives in our Galilean space-time, then the velocity field must be Galilean covariant.
Premise (2): The ontology lives in a Galiliean space-time.
Conclusion: Our velocity field must be Galilean covariant.

Notice that this argument and Valentini's argument run exactly in opposite directions. Valentini deduced the space-time from the dynamical law, whereas here the inverse obtains.

Given that our space-time is Galilean and not Aristotelian, we *cannot* introduce any force as a cause of velocity. In fact, introducing forces would mean downgrading the Galilean symmetry as fictitious and putting the theory in an Aristotelian space-time. Therefore, the wave-function *cannot* be a causal agent that changes the natural state of the particles from rest to velocity. This way, the guiding law becomes more a *kinematical* law than a dynamical law. Maybe it would be more cautious and respectful to say that there is no room for any classical-dynamical concept in this first-order theory. The guiding law of motion simply describes the natural motion of the Bohmian particles. It is not concerned with the cause of the motion. It does not answer the question of 'why' particles move in the direction they move; rather, it answers the question of 'how' they move. The burning question, then, asks what the wave-function is, given that it can determine motion without being a cause. If the wave-function is not the cause of the particles' motion, if it does not exert any force on the particles, how can it determine the trajectories? And how can

---

[101] See Dürr & Teufel, 2009: "we need to find a Galilean covariant expression for the velocity vector" (p. 153).
[102] See Dürr & Teufel, 2009: "A symmetry can be a priori, i. e. the physical law is built in such a way that it respects that particular symmetry by construction. This is exemplified by space-time symmetries, because space-time is the theater in which the physical law acts [. . .] and must therefore respect the rule of the theater" (pp. 54–55).

we ontologically specify an entity that 'determines' a particular motion without appealing to causality? Given that the wave-function cannot be regarded as *perturbing* the system, but at the same time can be regarded as *determining* the system, Dürr et al. (1997) suggest that we should regard the wave-function as a *nomological* entity – that is, as a law. We should, however, be careful with this comparison. Claiming that the wave-function is like a law does not mean that it should be considered as a law of nature. Instead, this claim simply means that, like laws, the wave-function is a nomological entity that dictates the behavior of the ontology without being part of it. We will dedicate the second part of this chapter to the discussion of the meaning of 'nomological'. Here, for the sake of clarity, I will just say that in the same way any law determines the temporal development of a physical system, the wave-function determines the evolution of the Bohmian particles.

4.1.2 Probability Current

There is another way, according to DGZ, to reformulate the law of motion for the particles. This formulation draws its conceptual tools directly from standard quantum mechanics (more specifically, from how quantum mechanics accounts for the quantum probability current).

In quantum mechanics, the quantum probability current density is defined as:

$$j = \rho v$$

where ϱ is the probability current and v is the velocity field, which describes the flow of the quantum probability current density. In textbooks, j is also commonly defined in this way:

$$j = \frac{\hbar}{m} Im \Psi^* \nabla_i \Psi$$

given

$$\rho = |\Psi|^2 = \Psi^* \Psi$$

where Ψ^* is the complex conjugate of the wave-function.

We could imagine this current density to be similar to the density of a portion of classic fluid enclosed within a specific volume. However, this is only an imaginative analogy, since in quantum mechanics the current density refers to probability flows. We can talk about 'quantum fluids' to render the quantum current more intuitively understandable; however, ontologically we do not have a real fluid flowing through a surface. Quantum fluids refer to the flow of statistical events in our space-time.

Concerning the nature of statistical events, standard quantum mechanics does not commit to a particular ontological interpretation. Bohmian mechanics, on the other hand, interprets these statistical facts as facts about particle positions. As such, the physical meaning of the probability current is that the particles of a Bohmian statistical ensemble move with a velocity given by the probability current. It is not difficult to see that the velocity of the particle motion defined in the guiding law is indeed exactly equal to the velocity generated by the current density.[103]

First take the probability current density:

$$j = \rho v = j = \frac{\hbar}{m_i} Im \Psi^* \nabla_i \Psi$$

and compare it with the guiding law:

$$v_k^\psi = \left(\frac{\hbar}{m_k}\right) Im \left[\frac{\nabla_k \Psi}{\Psi}\right] (Q_1 \ldots Q_n)$$

Indeed,

$$v = \frac{j}{\Psi^* \Psi}$$

If we take this resemblance to be meaningful, then it is the case that the wavefunction (as it appears in the guiding equation of motion) should simply be regarded as mathematically determining the particle motion. From this resemblance one can see that the velocity of the probability flow is exactly equal to the real and ontologically significant motion of the particles.

4.1.3 The De Broglie Equation

Louis de Broglie was the founding father of Bohmian mechanics and developed an equation that is now one of the pillars of quantum mechanics. The de Broglie equation is extremely important because it was the first law that showed the connection between matter and waves. This equation relates the properties of a particle (on the left-hand side) with the properties of a wave (on the right-hand side):

$$p = \hbar k$$

---

[103] For a discussion of the quantum probability current and the law of motion for the particles, see Dürr et al., 1992, 1996; Dürr et al., 1995; Dürr & Teufel, 2009, chapter 7; Oriolis & Mompart, 2012, chapter 1; Sanz & Miret-Artés, 2012, chapter 6.

where p is the momentum of a particle, also expressed as:

$$p = mv$$

while $\hbar$ is the Plank constant and k is the wave number (or wave vector) that gives us information about its wavelength.[104] We can rewrite $p = \hbar k$ as:

$$v = \frac{\hbar k}{m}$$

The equation expresses the velocity of the particles in terms of wave properties; therefore, it tells us that the behavior of the particles is wave-like. This is the first important element: according to de Broglie, particles behave like waves. Bohmian mechanics already demonstrates this 'wavy' particle behavior very explicitly by postulating that the particle distribution displays wave-like behavior given the connection between the probability density current and the guiding law of motion. But the de Broglie equation shows another way to understand the connection between the wave-function and the particles expressed in the law of motion (Goldstein, 1995).

The guiding law of motion may simply be regarded as the de Broglie equation in disguise, or as its reformulation. The formula $p=\hbar k$ leads to Bohmian mechanics and to the guiding equation.

Let me now show why this is the case. Looking at the equation, we may notice that it is formulated only for plane waves.[105] Indeed, not all waves have a wave vector k – only plane waves do. However, we know that the connection between wave properties and particle properties applies to all kinds of waves. The challenge is to find how the de Broglie equation can be expressed for non-plane waves.

First, we can look at how a plane wave is normally defined:

$$\Psi = Ae^{iKx}$$

where A is the amplitude of the plane wave and x is the position vector that defines a point in three-dimensional space.

In chapter 1, we defined any generic wave-function as:

$$\Psi = Re^{\frac{iS(x)}{\hbar}}$$

From this comparison, we see the connection between the plane wave number and the wave-function phase.

---

104 The relation between the wave vector and the wavelength (λ) depends on the context. The easiest relation is in crystallography where k = 1/λ, but in normal quantum mechanics it is k= 2π/λ.
105 Many thanks to Goldstein for pointing out this to me.

$$\nabla S = k\hbar$$

Hence, we can re-write the velocity of a particle not in terms of its wave number, but in terms of its phase:

$$v = \frac{\partial S}{\partial x}\frac{1}{m}$$

which is precisely the law of motion for the particles!

Let me investigate this point a bit further. In light of our discussion, we should understand the guiding equation as a simple reformulation of the de Broglie equation not only on the grounds of invariance under symmetries. The de Broglie equation tells us how particles would *normally* behave, not how they would behave under the influence of some particular forces. Particles, naturally, behave like waves. This reminds us of the birth of Bohmian mechanics and helps us understand how we should solve the puzzles that were already present at its inception.

Bohmian mechanics was developed in order to explain why particles in particular experimental settings were not following straight lines *even though they were not perturbed by (Newtonian) forces*. The observation that their motion was wave-like brought researchers to the idea that the wave-function had a special role in determining the particle trajectories. However, the particle-wave dualism was not easy to understand in terms of the particle dynamics. One of the challenges, for example, was to understand how the particles and the wave interact and how this interaction violates the third Newtonian law (we explained this in chapter 3). But all these problems are solved when we take into serious consideration the idea that, as the de Broglie relation tells us, the particles behave like waves. The parallelism between the de Broglie equation and the law of motion shows that the latter simply is telling us how Bohmian particles *normally* behave (that is, like waves) and how such behavior is their *natural* state.

So, once we establish that the particles behave like waves, and that wave dynamics are defined by the wave-function, then the guiding law of motion also acquires a natural justification and there is no need to introduce further causal elements. Hence, once we consider the claim that particles behave naturally like waves, then we do not need to regard waves as the cause of their behavior.

In light of this, the problem of the violation of the third Newtonian law is no longer an issue, because the guiding law of motion does not tell us that the wave-function interacts with the particles, but simply that the particles display 'wavy' behavior.[106] This consideration may allow us to go one step further. My proposal is

---

106 The problem of the violation of the third Newtonian laws arises only if we think that the wave-function and the particles do interact physically.

that, in order to explain the peculiar trajectories of the Bohmian particles, we really need to regard the Bohmian law of motion as a replacement of the first Newtonian law, which defines the natural state of the particles. This way, the wave-function does not determine the dynamics but instead determines the kinematics (as we have seen above in our discussion of the relation between space-time and the dynamical state of motion). Obviously, claiming that we should replace the first Newtonian law with the guiding equation may be misleading because it seems to suggest that we should keep a classical framework in a quantum context where forces are not fundamental. Moreover, if we take the law of motion as really selecting (in a classical sense) the natural state of the particles, we would certainly incur some problems: for instance, the Galilean space-time may not be compatible with the equation of motion as the law governing free bodies. Indeed, the two may not be compatible at all, since the Galilean space-time naturally selects the law of inertia as defining the natural state of the system, and there seem to be no alternatives. Moreover, it seems rather strange that a law defining the motion of free bodies can have a mass, which is a dynamical parameter. However, this intuitive reading of the law of motion has the benefit of making explicit that the wave-function has a purely nomological status and that the law of motion does not have any room for any physical cause of the motion of particles given that the particles follow their natural state.

4.2 The Resulting Ontology

In this section, we will investigate the different ways in which the nomological view has been interpreted. In particular, we will ask the question of how to understand the claim that the wave-function should be regarded 'as a law'.

4.2.1 The Wave-function as a Law

When the Rutgers-Munich-Genova group introduces the nomological character of the wave-function, they write:

> The main thing we want to discuss here is the status of the wave function: what kind of thing it is. And what we want to suggest one should think about is the possibility that it's nomological, nomic – that it's really more in the nature of a law than a concrete physical reality. (Dürr et al., 2013, p. 266)

> And what it suggests to us is that you should think of the wave function as describing a law and not as some sort of concrete physical reality. (Dürr et al., 2013, p. 267)

In light of these passages, the nomological view has been interpreted as the claim that the wave-function should be regarded as a law. Indeed, in the literature, the Rutgers-Munich-Genova group's view is normally presented with the slogan 'the wave-function as a law' (see Shan Gao, 2014; see also Belot, 2013). For example, Suárez presents the nomological view in these terms:

> Yet another interpretative option is to suppose that the wave-function has the character not of a space or a field, but of a law. This would be a 'nomological' interpretation of the wave-function. (Suárez, 2015, p. 3212)

Notice that here we are talking about the universal wave-function, i. e. the wave-function of the universe. For each possible particle configuration, the wave-function dictates precisely what the trajectories of the particles should be; it determines the behavior of the system in the same way laws do. This interpretation has been severely criticized in the literature for several reasons, which I will now present and discuss.

First of all, we know that the wave-function's temporal development is determined by the Schrödinger equation. This means that the wave-function changes at each instant of time according to what the Schrödinger equation dictates. At each different temporal instant, the Schrödinger equation attributes a different particular value to the wave-function. In light of this, we can regard the wave-function as a time-indexical entity. But if we also regard the wave-function as a law, how can we reconcile its nomological character with its temporal indexicality? Scientific laws do not normally evolve in time; they are not dynamical objects subject to temporal evolution. It is not the case that our laws of nature change as time passes! On the contrary, their role is to determine and dictate the temporal development of the ontology. How is it possible to conceive of a law that is time-dependent?

Notice that this is more than a metaphysical puzzle. We might be inclined to claim that, even if from a metaphysical perspective laws should not be time-dependent, we could revise our metaphysical characterization of scientific laws, after all. However, a time-dependent law is a logical puzzle (Suárez, 2015). Indeed, the first problem with this characterization is that it seems contradictory that a law can determine the future evolution of objects in its domain when the law itself will be different at the next future instant of time (given that the Schrödinger equation 'renews' the wave-function at each instant of time).

Secondly, it seems problematic to accept that a scientific law is subject to a dynamical law. Apart from the temporal indexicality, there is something intuitively unappealing about the view that our law is determined by a dynamical law. Normally, dynamical laws determine the evolution of objects, not of laws! This is further aggravated by the fact that the wave-function not only obeys a law represented by the Schrödinger equation, but it is even its solution! It is doubtful how a law can be the 'solution' of another law (or its 'outcome', to be more precise).

This puzzle is made even more acute if we take the laws to have a modal nomological character. The structure of the Schrödinger equation necessitates the structure of the wave-function, but not vice-versa. Therefore, the nomological character of the wave-function depends on the nomological character of the Schrödinger equation. In a certain way, given that the Schrödinger equation is nomologically stronger than the wave-function, the Bohmian theory presents a hierarchical structure where some laws are more necessary than others, and where the nomological character of some laws is subsidiary to that of more necessary laws. In order to address this issue in full, it would be necessary to enter into a debate on the necessity of laws, which would be impossible to present and address here.[107] However, I think that we are justified in considering this hierarchical nomological structure as a possible threat to the nomological view just presented.

Another reason to be skeptical about the nomological view is the fact that while our laws ought to be simple, the wave-function is extremely complex. Here I do not want to connect this claim with the Lewisian/Humean view about laws (we will deal with that later in this chapter), but I do want to take note of the fact that the wave-function is extremely complex given that it encodes all the possible trajectories that the particles would take according to their initial positions.

Moreover, the wave-function seems to be contingent: the universal wave-function could have been otherwise at the beginning of the universe in the same way that our universe could have been totally flat. This means that the wave-function is 'as it is', like any other physical object. We do not derive its structure from what happens in the world, because the particle trajectories do neither constrain nor necessitate the form wave-function; rather, we derive what happens in the world from its structure.

Finally, the last criticism concerns the fact that wave-functions are normally prepared in laboratories – however, laws cannot be created by human beings! Moreover, what does it mean to say that in a laboratory we 'prepare' different laws associated with a particular physical system? This is certainly another puzzling question that remains to be answered.

---

[107] For a discussion on the necessity of laws, see Wolff, 2013.

4.2.2 The Defense

There are two different ways in which the supporters of the nomological view can reply to the above challenges: they can either 'bite the bullet' or take the criticism and change perspective. Concerning the temporal development of the wave-function, the Rutgers-Munich-Genova group concedes that a law should not be time-dependent and they are happy to think of the wave-function as a time-independent entity obeying a time-independent Schrödinger equation (Dürr et al., 2013). From this perspective, the Schrödinger equation does not determine the temporal evolution of the wave-function but simply acts as its constraint. Ted Sider[108] formulates the nomological view in this way:

$$\exists \Psi(S(\Psi) \& G(\Psi))$$

There exists a law Ψ such that it satisfies the Schrödinger equation and the law of motion in a way that is a-temporal (you can see from the above formulation that the wave-function is not time-dependent). The nomological view is content to regard the wave-function in Bohmian mechanics as the canonical quantum cosmological wave-function of the Wheeler-DeWitt equation, which is static and has solutions that are time-independent:

$$\mathcal{H}\Psi = 0$$

where $\mathcal{H}$ is a sort of Laplacian or a cosmological version of the quantum Hamiltonian that appears in the Schrödinger equation (Dürr et al., 2013). The fact that time does not play a role in the Wheeler-DeWitt equation raises the well-known 'problem of time'. We know that we perceive temporal flow and our physical objects undergo physical change – however, the fundamental object of our ontology, the cosmological the Wheeler-DeWitt wave-function, does not. From this, an important question arises: where do time and change come from?

Given that the universal wave-function loses its temporal dependence, we may wonder how to account for the temporal development of the particles. If the wave-function does not change, why are particles changing their positions? However, notice that the wave-function does not need to be time-dependent in order to determine motion if it is not regarded as a physical entity. If the wave-function were considered a physical field that pushed the particles and caused velocity (see chapter 3), we would need to regard the wave-function as a time-dependent entity as well. But if we accept the nomological character of the wave-function,

---

[108] This formulation is taken from the handouts Sider prepared for the graduate seminar in Philosophy of Physics, Rutgers, Winter 2016.

then it is not necessary to assume time-dependence in order to account for the particles' dynamics. Once it is plugged into the guiding law of motion for the particles, the wave-function still generates the temporal evolution of the particles as its outcome despite the fact that it is time-independent (Esfeld et al., 2014). The Rutgers-Munich-Genova group explicitly compare the wave-function to a doctor and state that time and change are simply 'what the doctor orders' (Dürr et al., 2013). The nomological character of the wave-function is such that it 'orders' or 'dictates' a temporal change in the particle ontology without being affected itself.

Another question that should arise from the time-independent character of the wave-function concerns how we can account for the time-dependent character of the conditional wave-functions. We know that conditional wave-functions are extracted from the universal wave-function, and for this reason, their time-dependence is normally derived from the time-dependence of the universal wave-function. Esfeld et al. (2014) as well as Dürr and Teufel (2009) show that the conditional wave-functions inherit their temporal dependence not from the wave-function but from the particle configuration, in particular from the part of the universe that is not in the domain of the conditional wave-function. This part of the universe (already discussed in chapter 1) was represented by Y(t) and we called it 'the rest of the universe'. If we want to regard the wave-function as being characterized by a strong modal nomological character, then it is its modal nature that 'accounts' for the particle velocity. This way, the motion of the particles is simply dictated by the nomological character of the wave-function, and it is the temporal development of particles that confers time-dependence to the conditional wave-functions.

It is also possible to address the problem of the nomological hierarchy of the Schrödinger equation and the wave-function/guiding law of motion. The line of defense is to admit different degrees of nomological necessity in the structure of a theory. This 'degree view of necessity' deserves much more metaphysical discussion than we can provide here.[109] However, admitting that laws have different degrees of necessity is certainly not a disaster for the nomological view; in fact, this view has recently received some support. Suárez (2015), for example, cites two cases where it is clear that less necessary laws derive their necessity from more necessary laws, where only the latter should be regarded as fundamental laws. What is important to note is that, in these cases, the necessity of the fundamental laws explains and grounds the necessity of the less necessary laws. The cases cited by Suárez (2015) concern the geometrical laws and the laws of optics on the one hand, and the Newtonian and Kepler's laws on the other. The reason why light behaves in a determinate way is due to the fact that, geometrically, it has to behave in that way. The

---

[109] See Wolff, 2013.

reason why the planets orbit in a certain way is due to the fact that necessarily bodies have gravitation, force and acceleration. The only problem is that, as Suárez suggests, in these cases the non-fundamental laws are regarded more as phenomenological laws, while the fundamental ones are regarded as theoretical laws. But can we apply this distinction in Bohmian mechanics? Can we really say that the wave-function is a non-fundamental phenomenological law?[110] After all, it seems that the wave-function is fundamental given that it cannot be derived from any other more fundamental objects.[111]

In this paragraph, let me touch upon the problem of simplicity. If we do not buy into any Humean/Lewisian view on simplicity, what do we mean when we say that laws ought to be simple? Isn't our universal wave-function the simplest tool we have to account for entanglement? The line of response from the nomological view is to point out that there are many different ways to understand simplicity, and the wave-function can be understood as simple in many of these ways.

Concerning the problem of contingency, the answer given by the nomological view may be that the wave-function is not 'contingent' at all – instead, it should be regarded as nomically necessary. The fact that you cannot ask the question of why the wave-function is the way it is does not show that it is contingent; rather, it shows that the wave-function is an object that Bohmian mechanics deems necessary.

Lastly, the claim that wave-functions can be prepared and controlled whereas laws cannot rests on the mistaken assumption that the nomological view applies to the effective or conditional wave-functions, when actually it only applies to the universal wave-function. Indeed, it has never been possible to 'prepare' the universal wave-function in a laboratory! And this is not only because the universal wave-function is *de facto* a function of all the particles of the world, which we cannot manage in a laboratory – it is also because we need to be external to a wave-function in order to control it. This means that any wave-function that can be prepared in a laboratory cannot be universal since it cannot include us.

4.2.3 The Wave-function as a Part of the Law

The kind of discussion the nomologists have been trapped in is, however, off-track. Indeed, I take this discussion to be artificially built upon a misunderstanding of what their view really is. I take it that Goldstein's quotation above on the

---

110 DGZ concede that the Schrödinger equation is not fundamental, but derivative (see Dürr et al., 2013, chapter 12). However, Bacciagaluppi claims otherwise, by appealing to a work by Nelson (see reference below).
111 See Nelson, 1966, and for a discussion on Nelson's work, see Bacciagaluppi, 1999.

nomological status of the wave-function may be easily interpreted as the claim that the wave-function is a law of nature. And surely, claiming that the wave-function is a law is a non-starter: laws have truth-values, but the wave-function can be neither true nor false. However, what the Rutgers-Munich-Genova group wants to defend by appealing to the nomological character of the wave-function is that the wave-function is *more like a law* than a physical field, that wave-functions are *nomological entities*. Now, nomological entities may be laws but they do not only reduce to the subset of laws. For example, the Hamiltonian and the Lagrangian are nomological entities, but they are not laws of nature. A nomological entity is any entity that determines the temporal evolution of the ontology of a system by providing information about it (we will come back to the definition of nomological entity later in the section 4.5 on methodology). For this reason, instead of being a law, it may also be *in* the law (that is, it may be a significant part of the law) given the information of the physical system that it encloses.

The fact that the nomologists understand the wave-function as a part of the law and not as a law itself is also visible in the following passage, where they compare the wave-function to the Hamiltonian:

> We propose that the wave function belongs to an altogether different category of existence than that of substantive physical entities, and that its existence is nomological rather than material. We propose, in other words, that the wavefunction is a component of physical law rather than of the reality described by the law. (Dürr et al., 1997, p. 10)

4.2.3.1 The Wave-function and the Hamiltonian

The Rutgers-Munich-Genova group explains the nomological status of the wave-function by appealing to the classical Hamiltonian, which they regard as a nomological entity as well. The example of the Hamiltonian is not only useful for understanding what a nomological entity is, but also to convince us that the wave-function really is a nomological entity once we observe its striking resemblance to the Hamiltonian.

First, let me introduce some general similarities between the two entities. Both entities live in a high-dimensional space. While the wave-function lives in the so-called configuration space, given by 3N dimensions, the Hamiltonian lives in a phase space, which has 6N dimensions. Indeed, while the configuration space is built only upon spatial degrees of freedom (the particle positions), the Hamiltonian is a function of both position and momentum. Given that both the position and the momentum can be evaluated along the three different axes of our three-dimensional space, the total number of degrees of freedom for the Hamiltonian is six for each particle. Moreover, both functions have the role of encoding information about the physical system such that it is possible to extract the future evolution of the system only from that information.

Having considered these sharper analogies, we can now look at the mathematical structure of how the two functions can be used to predict information about the system.

We have seen that in Bohmian mechanics the guiding law of motion can be formulated through the gradient of S:

$$p = \frac{\partial S}{\partial x}$$

Given that S is

$$S = \hbar Im \log \Psi$$

we can say that the velocity of the particles is given by a sort of derivative (which we do not specify) of the logarithm of the wave-function:

$$p = der(\log \Psi)$$

In classical mechanics, the Hamiltonian generates the velocity of the particles exactly in the same way, through

$$p = \frac{\partial H}{\partial x}$$

which can be reformulated as a generic derivative of the Hamiltonian:

$$p = der(\log H)$$

One more similarity is worth mentioning. Both the functions not only generate particle motion but are also fundamental to generating the correct probabilities of the system. The wave-function, as we know, is the mathematical object that determines the Born rule, while the Hamiltonian determines the Boltzmann-Gibbs probabilities (Dürr et al., 2013, chapter 12; Goldstein & Zanghì, 2013).

4.3 How to Understand Nomological Entities, and Thus the Wave-function: Different Metaphysical Scenarios

Now we know what it means for the wave-function to be *like* a law: it means that the wave-function is not itself a law but is simply a *nomological entity*. However, up until this point we have kept the definition of nomological entities quite loose from a metaphysical point of view, because its specifications really depend on how we should interpret the role of nomological entities in metaphysics. The abundant literature on laws will help us with this matter. Even though the debates found in the literature are related specifically to laws of nature, I take them to be very informative in helping us to understand the more general notion of 'nomological entity'. In particular, these discussions present two main options for understanding the nature of nomological entities: either we endorse a realist attitude and take them as being ontological entities, or we endorse an anti-realist attitude and regard them as non-ontological entities. Normally, this dichotomy exists alongside another dichotomy according to which laws are either external entities or internal entities. If laws are external entities, they are independent of the ontology and indifferent to differences in the ontology; for example, the same law can be compatible with different particle configurations. But if they are internal, then they are dependent on the properties of the ontology. Notice that a commitment to the internality/externality of nomological entities does not imply a commitment to a realist or anti-realist view.[112]

In the next section, I will analyze different proposals concerning the nomological status of the wave-function in terms of different metaphysical conceptions of general nomological entities.

4.3.1 The Realist View on Nomological Entities: Primitivism

We will first analyze how the Rutgers-Munich-Genova group understands the nomological role of the wave-function, and from this we will attempt to derive the kind of conception of laws of nature they would probably endorse. As we have already discussed, the Rutgers-Munich-Genova group believes that both the Hamiltonian and the wave-function should be regarded as 'doctors' that tell their patients what to do. This view is not clear at all; indeed, the image of the doctor is obviously in need of philosophical work. Moreover, the nomological view defended by DGZ seems to regard the wave-function as 'something' that really exists. When asked what the wave-function is, they answer: "It's not nothing, and it's not everything, but it's something".[113]

But what is this 'something'? Even though the Rutgers-Munich-Genova group 'downgrades' the status of the wave-function from being a physical entity to being a law, they still seem to attribute an ontological status to it. They think that the wave-function is 'something' in our ontology, something that is not reducible to the particles' positions and is extremely important in accounting for their motion.

---

[112] For a discussion on the realist/anti-realist view of nomological entities and on the internal/external distinction, see Dorato & Laudisa, 2014; and Cei & French, 2014.
[113] This expression is take from a power-point prepared by Zanghì, for the summer school in Saig, Summer 2016.

4.3 How to Understand Nomological Entities, and Thus the Wave-function

However, they never explained their position more clearly than this. Moreover, one might wonder what they mean by the notion 'ontology'. Most philosophers of physics, for example, are inclined to reduce and limit the ontology to the physical ontology, the physical 'furniture' of this world. But this is clearly not the case in the DGZ nomological view. So what does it mean to put a nomological entity in the ontology of a physical theory?

In order to understand their proposal, which is characterized by regarding the wave-function *qua* nomological entity as substantive (though we do not know exactly in what way) and modally strong, I suggest that we should adopt the primitivist view of laws proposed and defended by Maudlin (2007b). Primitivism about laws comes in two forms, ontological and conceptual. Maudlin presents the primitivist view as follows: "I suggest we accept laws as fundamental entities in our ontology. Or, speaking at the conceptual level, the notion of a law cannot be reduced to other more primitive notions" (Maudlin, 2007b, p. 18).

Let us start to understand what the first form of primitivism – ontological primitivism – amounts to. Consider the following passages from Maudlin:

> My own proposal is simple: laws of nature ought to be accepted as ontologically primitive. We may use metaphors to fire the imagination: among the regularities of temporal evolution, some, such as perhaps that described by Schrödinger's equation, govern or determine or generate the evolution. But these metaphors are not offered as analyses [. . .]. My analysis of laws is no analysis at all. Rather I suggest we accept laws as fundamental entities in our ontology. (Maudlin, 2007b, p. 18)

> Lawhood is a primitive status. (Maudlin, 2007b, p. 17)

These two passages are extremely important because they connect the more general discussion about laws with where we left the discussion on the wave-function: what does it mean for the wave-function to be like a doctor that prescribes what their patients have to do? What does it mean for the wave-function to rule the motion of the particles? Rather than a 'doctor', shouldn't it be regarded as, say, a king? Here Maudlin is clear that images like these are just metaphors that are presented in order to give an intuitive idea of the role of nomological entities, and Maudlin states that these metaphors should not be taken to imply an analysis of what laws are. Instead, he advocates a non-analysis of laws. Laws are ontologically primitive; they have a primitive 'ontological status'. We have already encountered the adjective 'ontological primitiveness' in chapter 2, where we addressed the ontological status of particles. Here I want to apply our discussion of ontological primitiveness to nomological entities rather than to particles:

- Regarding their status, nomological entities are fundamental entities (i. e. they are unreducible *kinds of* entities);

- They exist in a primitive way (their existence is not grounded in anything else, such as properties);
- Their existence (i. e. ontological status) is unique, which means that the 'way' they exist is unique;
- They are non-supervenient entities, which means that two laws may differ without the particle configuration differing;
- They are independent entities as they do not depend on the particle configuration; hence, they are 'external' entities.

The primitivist character of nomological entities can also be interpreted from a conceptual point of view. According to this second reading of primitivism, the notion of something being 'nomological' cannot be analyzed in terms of more fundamental conceptual notions such as causation, counterfactuals, regularity and so on.[114] On the contrary, it is the notion of law that is necessary and sufficient for explaining causation, counterfactuals and what is physically possible. This is how Dorato and Esfeld present this conceptual primitive aspect:

> And if we begin by postulating that at each time and place the temporal evolution of the world is governed by certain principles our convictions about possibilities, counterfactuals, and explanations can be regimented and explained. In this sense, conceptual primitivism about laws implies that the notion of law is necessary (and sufficient) to explain (note, an epistemic notion) the notion of physical possibility. (Dorato & Esfeld, 2015, p. 407)

The governing role of laws is therefore spelled out as a constraint on what happens in our physical world. From this it follows that what is physically possible is determined and dictated by the laws, as the following quotes by Maudlin demonstrate:

> Laws are the patterns that nature respects; to say what is physically possible is to say what the constraint of those patterns allows. (Maudlin, 2007b, p. 20)

> Our world seems to be governed by laws, at least around here. When we say that an event or situation is physically possible we mean that its occurrence is consistent with the constraints that derive from the laws. (Maudlin, 2007b, p. 18)

From this it follows that the modality of the ontology is given by the nomological role of the laws that constrain the physical possibilities of the physical ontology.

---

[114] See for example Hildebrand: "Whenever we say 'it is a law that' that is primitive locution – a primitive operator, corresponding to the relevant ontological primitive laws" (Hildebrand, 2013, p. 5).

4.3.2 Problems

Following the primitivist view on laws, we have seen that laws are characterized as ontological entities: they exist and they have their own independent ontological status. For this reason, they are 'external' entities; they do not supervene on the physical ontology of the world. However, they constrain the physical facts by determining what is physically possible. Our task here is to apply this characterization to the nomological entity we are analyzing, namely the universal wave-function. If we have to interpret the nomological status of the wave-function in terms of primitivism about laws, the wave-function must be primitively substantive and modally strong, besides being external and indifferent to the events of the particles. We can arguably claim that the wave-function does indeed seem to match this first rough characterization. But a natural question arises: if our wave-function is external and not physical (still, ontological), how can it determine particle motion by being the pattern that our particles respect?

In order to answer this question, we can raise it again in the general context of primitivism about nomological entities: How can nomological entities determine the modality of the world? How can they confer modality to the world by being modal in the first place? How can nomological entities determined the modality of the world on account of their own modality? Normally the answer is that the nature of the (causal) properties of the physical entities can be reduced[115] to their nomic roles. This way, a connection between 'laws' and 'physical ontology' is secured. The mass of a rigid body in Newtonian theory, for example, is a property that plays the nomic role of determining a motion proportional to itself and the acceleration of the body:

$$\vec{F} = ma$$

This law determines the motion of a particle subject to a force and constrains its future temporal development by limiting the range of what is physically possible. The final position of the particle is linked to the law in virtue of the fact that the law nomically defines the scientific properties instantiated by the particle.

Let's take a slightly more complicated case where we use the Hamiltonian.

$$v = \frac{\partial H}{\partial p}$$

---

[115] The metaphysical relation between the laws and the properties is still a debatable issue and we do not want to commit to a particular view here.

In this case the Hamiltonian determines the particles' future positions because it nomically defines the total energy of the particles.[116]

But what about the wave-function? What element of the particles is the wave-function connected to? Indeed, the wave-function is not like the Hamiltonian in defining any particle property. Regardless of whether or not we endorse a parsimonious view of properties according to which properties are property-less, the wave-function does not nomically define any particle properties. But if this is the case – if there is nothing that connects the wave-function as a nomological entity with the particles – how can it determine the future evolution of the particles?

The primitivist view about nomological entities presents us with an explanatory gap. On one hand, we have the primitive and substantive wave-function that is modally strong. On the other hand, we have the particles that respect the patterns stipulated by the wave-function. But we do not know how to link the two. In other words, the wave-function is not anchored at all to the particles.

This problem is rendered more acute if we recall that the wave-function is introduced to explain the particles' motion in the first place – in this scenario, the gap between the '*explanans*' and the '*explanandum*' is so wide that the *explanans* seems to have lost its explanatory power.

In summary, we have seen that, according to the primitivist view, the wave-function should be regarded as an ontological primitive entity outside the mosaic of particles' positions, as the entity that restricts the distribution of particles in the mosaic. However, problems arise when we attempt to account for how exactly it constrains the particles. The fact that the wave-function is external and not anchored to the particles creates a gap between the *explanans* and the *explanandum*.

In the next section, I will present two ways to close this gap.

4.3.3 Anti-realism and the Humean View: No Gap, No Explanation

Earlier I claimed that we may regard the nomological view proposed by DGZ as endorsing a sort of primitivism of nomological entities (Maudlin, 2007b). But this creates an explanatory gap because the wave-function is not anchored to any scientific properties of the particles. In order to overcome this gap we can opt to step back from the kind of nomological view that the Rutgers-Munich-Genova group endorses. The fact that the primitivist view creates a gap in Bohmian mechanics is because it claims that nomological laws are external, substantive entities that have a modal role, and the wave-function cannot be anchored to the properties of the

---

116 For a definition of the Hamiltonian in terms of the energy of the system, see chapter 1.

particles. So, one first strategy to avoid the gap is simply to not create it in the first place – that is, by avoiding the presupposition that nomological entities are ontological entities external to the facts about the particles. Hence, the first option may amount to adopting a non-realist view on nomological entities. Very surprisingly, this anti-realist view also sometimes seems to be suggested by the Rutgers-Munich-Genova group. Take, for instance, the following sentence, which seems to go against the primitivist view that we have just discussed: "Everybody knows that the Hamiltonian is just a convenient device in terms of which the equations of motion can be nicely expressed" (Goldstein & Zanghì, 2103, p. 98). By contrast, this quote seems to suggest a sort of anti-realism/instrumentalism about nomological entities.

In this section, I present an anti-realist view about nomological entities that is defended by the doctrine of Humeanism about laws, a view that denies any fundamental existence of nomological entities:[117] if nomological entities exist, they only do so in a derivative sense. However, before dealing with the Humean conception of laws, let me first explain the general idea behind it.

This view goes back to David Lewis' claim that our fundamental ontology consists only of

> [. . .] a vast mosaic of local matters of particular fact, just one little thing and then another [. . .]. We have geometry: a system of external relations of spatio-temporal distances between points [. . .]. And at those points we have local qualities: perfectly natural intrinsic properties which need nothing bigger than a point at which to be instantiated. For short, we have an arrangement of qualities. And that is all. There is no difference in the arrangement of qualities. (Lewis, 1986, p. ix)

According to this doctrine, which has been named 'Humean Supervenience', the fundamental ontology of a theory consists of matter points (or fields) and spatial relations; matter points may (or may not, depending on the kind of Humeanism adopted)[118] instantiate intrinsic properties. It is important to note for the purpose of our discussion that the Humean 'mosaic' comprises the whole universe from the beginning of time until its end; hence, it includes all of space-time, not just the slice of space-time in which we exist now. However, given the reluctance of the Humeans towards any modal entity, when I say 'the whole universe', I mean only all the physical space-time points and all their spatial-temporal relations (and maybe[119] intrinsic properties), and nothing else.

---
117 For a more detailed discussion of the Humeanism, see Lewis, 1994.
118 According to the standard account of Humeanism, space-time points do instantiate intrinsic properties, while according to 'Super-Humeanism' they do not. We will discuss the super-humeanist view by Esfeld in another section (4.3.2.5).
119 Again, it depends on the kind of Humeanism endorsed (see previous footnote).

The fundamental basis of this world is characterized by locality (all that you have is local beables), physicality (only what is physical exists at the fundamental level, assuming that spatio-temporal relations are physical), and non-modality. There are only individual space-time points, their relations and their intrinsic properties. All other physical entities, such as the chair you are sitting on, as well as the laws of this world, and the fragility of a glass are not fundamental but *derivative*. In particular, they are all *supervenient* on the fundamental ontological basis of the world:[120] "Being a commonsensical fellow [. . .] I seldom deny that the features in question exist. I grant their existence, and do my best to show how they can, after all, supervene on the arrangement of qualities" (Lewis, 1986, p. xi).

The relation of supervenience is best spelled out in terms of differences: if A supervenes on B, there cannot be any difference in A without any differences in B. In other words, any change in A must correspond to a change in B. More generally, and more intuitively, we can claim that the relation of supervenience implies that there cannot be a difference in the derivative without there being a change in the fundamental basis. If there is a change in the derivative, then there must also be a change in the basis. This can also be spelled out in relation to possible worlds: if a possible world is different from ours in derivative aspects, then it must also be different in fundamental aspects. If we apply this to the case of nomological entities such as laws, the doctrine of Humean Supervenience claims that there cannot be two different nomological entities that supervene on the very same mosaic (where 'mosaic' refers to the distribution of matter points with spatio-temporal relation and intrinsic properties). The supervenience relation supports the claim that modality does not exist fundamentally, since it can be 'reduced' to physical properties of matter. And Humeans support the view that causality and any other modal relations (such as modal nomological relations) do not fundamentally 'exist' (Lewis, 1994).

We now want to go a step further and apply the discussion of Humean Supervenience to Bohmian mechanics.[121] We said that the wave-function can be regarded as a nomological entity, but if we endorse a realist stance combined with primitivism about nomological entities, then we end up with an ontology with an uncomfortable

---

[120] Notice that even here we classify Humeanism as an anti-realist doctrine of laws. It may be argued, however, that according to the Humean laws exist, even though not fundamentally. Their ontological status is derivative, but still they can be regarded as existing entities. I concede this point, however, with my demarcation between 'realism' and 'anti-realism' about laws, I aim to draw a line between those who take laws to have a nomological-modal role and those who regard them as a descriptive tool. Moreover, most Humeans are instrumentalist about laws as well, which pushes me to regard Humeanism as an anti-realist doctrine of lawhood.

[121] For an application of the doctrine of Humean Supervenience to Bohmian mechanics, see Esfeld et al., 2013; Esfeld, 2014a; and Miller, 2104.

'gap' and an unanswered question regarding how the wave-function dictates a particular motion. We pointed out two strategies: one is to 'eliminate' the wave-function from the fundamental ontology, and the Humean seems to create the perfect metaphysical framework to do just that.

Applying the Humean Supervenience discussion to the Bohmian primitive ontology seems quite easy and straightforward. Indeed, Bohmian mechanics presents a perfect basis for the Humeans: matter points with spatial relations. However, if we apply the Humean discussion to the Bohmian wave-function, it seems that we end up completely off track. Recall that, in the previous chapter, one of the reasons we have for objecting to the realist view is that many different wave-functions all give rise to the same particle configurations. Hence, we have said that different wave-functions are compatible with the same basis. This is clearly at odds with the Humean claim that a change in the derivative must correspond to a change in the basis. And this is the first challenge for the Humean view. The second challenge is quantum entanglement: a peculiar feature of Bohmian mechanics is the modal non-local relations between the particles, but as we have just said above, the Humeans defend a local non-modal ontology. These are two major concerns, and I will try to address them in the following section.

4.3.4 The Supervenience Problem

In our previous chapter, we said that different wave-functions can correspond to the same particle configuration. However, we should be careful in saying this, because there are several ways in which two wave-functions may differ, and consequently there are different ways in which the failure of supervenience can be spelled out. In order to ascertain whether the Humean interpretation can work, we need to be more precise and list these differences.[122]

The first reason why two wave-functions may differ but still be compatible with the same particle configuration is due to gauge dependence: suppose that two wave-functions differ only in terms of a global phase shift by changing all its signs,[123] or in terms of a phase factor so that one is a non-zero scalar multiple of the other. In this case, the differences in the wave-function will never lead to any difference in the particle configuration. Hence, the differences are not physically meaningful. Here, the Humean may defend their view by claiming that the reason why two wave-

---

[122] Here I will list only the two most important differences I considered. For a more detailed discussion, see Miller, 2014.
[123] For a more detailed discussion of the global or overall phase shift, see Bowman, 2008, p. 118. The global phase shift consists of the same change of phase for each component of the wave-function.

functions that share the same particle configuration differ is only due to a mathematical superstructure, which, in turn, is due to the ambiguity of mathematical formalism. The Humean may want to argue that even though the mathematical representation is ambiguous, the two mathematical entities correspond to the very same nomological entity. In a nutshell, they can apply the very same argument used by the realist in regard to the nomological entity. Mathematics makes things ambiguous but the fact that two wave-functions are different in terms of the signs is not meaningful at all – it is just a mathematical aspect of the representation of the same nomological entity.

The second reason why two wave-functions may be different but lead to the same particle configuration is due to an entanglement difference: two different wave-functions can describe two different entanglement relations between particles, but still the resulting configuration may be the same. For example, take two wave-functions that express the same kind of entanglement of particles for measurements along the z-axis but not for the x-axis. If at a certain point we measure both the systems along the z-axis, the result will be the same. However, the Humean may want to argue that it is true that the particle configuration may be the same, but only at one particular time. And since the Humeans do not defend the view that nomological entities supervene on one slice of space-time, but instead support the claim that they supervene on the entirety of space-time, their view is not defeated. Indeed, the two wave-functions turn out to supervene on the entire history of measurements. Given this, the two different wave-functions correspond to two different particle configurations for the entirety of space-time.

At the root of this case is the fact that the wave-function encodes all the possible trajectories that the particles would take, given certain initial positions. Two different wave-functions may have the same particle configuration at one time, but then they can display their differences under other kinds of circumstances. For this reason, if we take the whole of space-time as an ontological basis, then we can be quite sure that those differences between the two wave-functions are spelled out in the particle configurations.

4.3.5 The Non-locality Problem

After evaluating the first problem of the Humean view, the problem of supervenience, we can address the issue of non-locality. According to the standard interpretation of the Bohmian ontology, the dynamics of the particles are non-local, which means that a change of one particle's position in one part of the universe affects the positions of all the other particles of the universe instantaneously. The particles are thus interpreted as being non-locally correlated in a modal way. The realist explains this modal correlation by appealing to the fact that the particles share the same physical wave-function, which is a field that physically directs the particles' motions. The strong nomological version, in contrast, explains this modality by appealing to the nomological power of the wave-function. But the Humeans deny that non-local connections exist in the first place![124] How can Humeans understand the ontology of Bohmian mechanics if they rule out non-locality? Doesn't non-locality prove that the Humeans are wrong about the metaphysics of this world?

In response, the Humeans would just deny that there is any non-local modal relation, in the same way Hume denied seeing any causal connection in the world. The trajectories of two particles 'happen' to be *as if* they were correlated, but they are *not*. There is no modal connection in the world that requires explanation. There are only more or less regular events that can be described in an efficient way with our laws of nature. From this, a consideration arises: it may seem that regarding the wave-function as a derivative nomological entity without any modal power is not explanatory at all. This is certainly true, but it is not a problem for the Humeans. Humeanism does not provide explanations, and the reason for this is, to put it simply, that there is nothing to be explained. Events happen to be a certain way, but there is no 'why', there is no 'cause' – there are no modal connections in the world. The only meaningful action to take is not to explain them but to describe them in the most efficient way. So the question is not whether the wave-function can explain the non-local modality of the particles, but whether it can efficiently describe the particles' motions. And to this question we will dedicate our next section.

4.3.6 Simplicity and Informativeness

Another way in which the Humeans can advocate the Humean nomological character of the wave-function on the particle configuration is by appealing to the Humean best-system account of laws of nature. According to the Humean view, our knowledge of the world should be regarded as a deductive system that is comprised of axioms and those statements that consequently follow from those axioms. Obviously, our knowledge of the world could be systematized with different deductive systems, all containing true statements, but all different with regard to two main criteria: simplicity and informativeness (also called strength). The criterion of informativeness captures how much information is entailed by the system. Reasonably, we want our system to be maximally informative; indeed, we want it to give us

---

[124] To be precise: they do not deny 'non-local relations', but non-supervenient non-local relations. However, we know that, in the case of entanglement, non-local relations are non-supervenient.

information about all the physical phenomena. At the same time, the criterion of simplicity is important because we want our system to contain as few axioms as possible (to avoid an endless list of axioms) and we want its axioms to be as simple as possible. It is not difficult to see that these two criteria require a trade-off. Indeed, the maximum level of informativeness can be achieved either by inserting many axioms or by adopting complex ones, whereas the maximum level of simplicity can be achieved either by reducing the number of axioms or their level of complexity. This does not mean, however, that the Humean view is flawed in this respect. The view claims that we want our system to best balance both simplicity and informativeness. The system that achieves the best balance between these two competing virtues – simplicity and informativeness – is called the 'best system'. Now that we have presented the 'best system', we can also understand what laws are according to the Humeans. Laws are true generalizations that play the role of axioms in the best system. Another requirement that Humean laws must satisfy, and that we have already discussed, is supervenience: the laws must supervene on the mosaic of matter points and their spatial relations.

If we apply this to our Bohmian case, then the Humeans may claim that as far as the wave-function is part of this best system of laws, then it can be understood in a Humean framework as a nomological entity emptied of any modal power. In this way, the wave-function is a nomological entity not because it dictates the particles' trajectories, but because it is part of the best system. It is an essential part of formulating the laws of Bohmian mechanics (i. e. the Schrödinger equation and the guiding equation).

The last question that we must address if we want to endorse the Humean scenario is whether it is reasonable to think that a complex entity such as the wave-function can actually constitute a system that must have the virtue of simplicity.

Answering this question in a detailed way would certainly be an important endeavor – however, such an exploration is beyond the purpose of this book. Here I will only mention some general considerations. The wave-function encodes all the single possible changes of the particle configuration and in this way can represent all the configurations of space-time in its entirety. Obviously, it must be 'complex' to some certain degree: it has to deal with 10^{80} particles! However, it allows for a very concise formulation of laws; hence, it allows for the best system to consist only of one Schrödinger equation (and not many). We have seen that a formulation of the Bohmian laws that does not use the universal wave-function should enclose a countable infinite number of entanglement fields and many conditional wave-functions, all determined by the Schrödinger equation. Hence, in order to construct such a theory, we would need a countable infinite number of Schrödinger equations, one for each entanglement field and one for each conditional wave-function. This would render the system as informative as the one with the universal wave-function, but definitely not simpler, given the number of axioms in the theory. As such, I do believe that the wave-function, despite its complexity, does provide the best balance between simplicity and informativeness. Indeed, one complex element gets rid of a long list of axioms that would invalidate the simplicity of the theory even further.

4.3.7 The Unsatisfactory Humean View

So far, we have seen that the Humean view can provide a coherent account of the wave-function by regarding it as a nomological entity that is part of the best system of laws. The question now is whether we should endorse it. Many reject the view because it does not provide any explanation for the peculiar dynamics of the Bohmian particles – however, as I have shown above, faulting the Humean view for not providing this explanation is not going to work. This is because the Humean view rejects the idea that natural phenomena should have an explanation in the first place. Therefore, if one is inclined to think that this Humean scenario is quite unsatisfactory on account of it being explanatorily wanting when applied to Bohmian mechanics, the Humean may tell them that they only have their own biased anti-Humean metaphysical intuitions to blame. The Humean view is perfectly coherent with Bohmian mechanics, and Bohmian mechanics even provides a natural Humean *mosaic* given that it postulates a distribution of point-like matter.

I do agree that there is nothing conceptually inconsistent with applying the Humean stance to Bohmian mechanics. However, I argue that there is a certain unnaturalness in doing so. The reason why we need the universal wave-function (and why reformulating the dynamics with conditional wave-functions would imply adding a countable infinite number of entanglement fields) is because the dynamics is itself holistic. The Humean can go on claiming that it is only a matter of appearance, and that there is no modality, and that there are no non-local correlations in the Humean framework. It is certainly true that we could claim that the wave-function is just the best mathematical instrument we have in order to describe the dynamics and acknowledge that it does not reflect any ontological feature of the mosaic. But there is a sort of unnaturalness in regarding the Bohmian mosaic as local. And the reason for this relies exactly on the fact that a universal wave-function can achieve a very informative and simple system of laws. Why is it the case that if we really pretend that our Bohmian system is local, and we reconstruct the theory with conditional wave-functions, the empirical predictability of the theory disappears? Why, in order to keep the theory empirically adequate, do we need to insert many entanglement fields? This, I take it, tells us that the mosaic is non-local. Notice that this is perfectly in accord with the fundamentalist version of MRL, which claims that what is in the laws is a 'natural kind', hence 'carves the nature at its joints'. The wave-function is part of the best system of laws, hence it is a natural kind and, consequently, carves the nature at its joints.[125]

4.4 The Dispositional Interpretation

After this discussion of the nomological view, we have not quite yet reached a stable consensus. We criticized the primitive nomological view for creating an explanatory gap between the governing role of the wave-function and the particles, and we criticized the Humean view for not being a natural interpretation of Bohmian mechanics. Recall now that at the end of the section on primitivism about laws, we claimed that we had two options for avoiding the gap. The first was not to create it in the first place by adopting an anti-realist stance about the wave-function as nomological entity. We tried that route and we found it unsatisfactory. The second option, we said, would be to add properties in the ontology in order to anchor the wave-function to the particles. In this section, we are going to pursue this proposal.

In order to fill in the gap between the strong nomological status of the wave-function and the particles' behavior by introducing a property in the physical ontology, we may look to Esfeld's proposal of combining the nomological view with a dispositional one (Esfeld et al., 2104). According to him, we can regard the nomological role of the wave-function as grounded in some dispositions of the system. In light of this, we could say that the wave-function has a certain nomological modality because it is grounded in some dispositional properties. This view seems to offer a much better ontological picture than the one presented by the Humeans and the primitivists. Indeed, it recognizes the modal status of the wave-function and at the same time 'fills' in the gap between the wave-function and the particles.

This dispositional interpretation takes inspiration from those who, much earlier, proposed a dispositional interpretation of the wave-function (Thompson-Jones, 2005; Belot, 2013). For this reason, the literature on the dispositionalist interpretation of the wave-function helps us better understand this dispositional-nomological program. Our main question is what kind of dispositions the nomological role of the wave-function should be grounded in, and we will answer this question by

---

[125] According to Deutsch (private correspondence), this criticism against the Humean view is based only on armchair metaphysics, and not on any physics; for this reason, according to him, I am contravening my own methodology, which aims to navigate between metaphysical presuppositions and considerations on the mathematical formalism. But I guess that in this case it hard to separate 'metaphysical' considerations from 'physical ones'.

looking at the different dispositional interpretations of the wave-function offered in the literature.

The first proponent of the dispositional interpretation was Martin Thompson-Jones.[126] Unfortunately, his manuscript on this issue was never published and is still unfinished; as such, it is difficult to exactly reproduce his thoughts here in a comprehensive way. But I will try to reconstruct his view with rigor. If we regard the wave-function as the mathematical entity known as a 'function', we can easily see that it generates a long list of truths. Take for example the addition function. The addition function maps 2 and 5 to 7, 3 and 5 to 8 and so on. For this reason, we can say that any mathematical function generates a list of truths.[127] Suppose now that your universe consists only of one particle with its own wave-function. If we now turn our attention to the wave-function, we can see that it maps each possible particle position to its respective possible velocity vector in configuration space. The correspondence is unique given that no more than one velocity vector can be attributed to the same possible particle position. Given that we are talking about a 'possible' particle position, the wave-function corresponds to a long list of subjunctive conditionals of the following kind:

(1) If the particle position were x, its velocity would be v.

(2) If the particle position were x', its velocity would be v'.

(3) If the particle position were x", its velocity would be v".

This is the case for all the possible particle positions. The question we could ask now is concerned with truth-making: what is it in virtue of that these counterfactual statements are true? To answer this question, we just need to be aware that physical dispositional properties are normally explained under the form of counterfactuals. Take the fragility of a glass vase, for example. We can reformulate the property of fragility in terms of a counterfactual. What does it mean that the glass vase is fragile? It means the following: 'If the vase were struck under such-and-such circumstances, it would break'. As such, we can list all the possible circumstances which would cause the vase to break. In this regard, in the same way the subjunctive conditional on the glass vase describes the dispositional property

---

[126] Thanks go to Martin Thompson-Jones for sending me his thoughtful manuscript, which, despite being unpublished, acted as a precursor to the dispositional view that is now advanced by Esfeld and Suárez.

[127] Thanks to Dr. Asay for this point.

of fragility, the subjunctive conditional on the particles describe their dispositional property of moving in some circumstances.

Previously, we presented an artificial case where the Bohmian system includes only one particle. But what about the many-particle case? In this case, the Bohmian system is deeply non-local, because it presents a dynamics where each particle's motion depends on the positions of all the particles of the universe. In this regard, a dispositionalist would claim that the disposition of motion of each particle depends on all the positions of all the particles of the universe. In particular, each particle has a particular disposition of motion depending on where all the other particles are. If the configuration of all the particles is Q, a particle will have the disposition of moving along a certain path; if the particle configuration is Q", the particle will have the disposition of moving along another path.

Thompson-Jones presents his view in the following way:

> We can simply have Ψ assign dispositions to each particle of such a sort that the relevant circumstances for the manifestation of the dispositions involve positions for the other particles. That is, what Ψ says about particle 1 at $r_1{'}$ (amongst other things) is that it has a disposition to move in such-and-such a way when the external circumstances external to system are so-and-so *and the positions of the other particles are $r_2{'}$, $r_3{'}$, . . ., and $r_N{'}$, respectively*, a different disposition for the same external circumstances but with the other particles at $r_2{''}$, $r_3{''}$, . . ., and $r_N{''}$, and so on. (Thompson-Jones, 2005, p. 4)

Notice that introducing dispositions keeps the action non-local:

> Unsurprisingly, nonlocality looms large. To put it briefly: if particle 1 has a lot of dispositions the manifestation of which depends not only upon (say) the local electromagnetic potential it experiences, but also on the positions of all the other particles in the system (particles 2 through N), then in order to decide what to do next at any given moment, so to speak, particle 1 has to know the location of the other particles at that moment. (Thompson-Jones, 2005, p. 7)

Notice also that the positions of all the other particles play the role of triggering a particular disposition. As with any other dispositional property like the fragility of a glass vase, the disposition of motion manifests itself only under certain circumstances. Indeed, a dispositional property is not always manifest, and only if it is triggered by certain circumstances will it become apparent. For example, the glass vase would never show its fragility if I kept it safely in my cupboard. I see that it is fragile only when I wash it and it breaks in my hands. According to this view, then, what triggers each disposition is a particular condition of all the other particles. But what Thompson has in mind here is that a particle has a single different disposition for each particular velocity it would take. As such, it has a myriad of dispositions. This way, our ontology will present a very long list of dispositions.

We can understand this last point on the myriad of dispositions in light of Suárez' paper (2015): Suárez also claims that each Bohmian particle instantiates many dispositions, one for each different particle configuration. Suárez's paper has the merit of having developed the view in a more rigorous way, which helps us understand what Thompson-Jones had in mind.

We know that the wave-function generates a velocity vector field, which lives in configuration space. This velocity vector field attributes one vector to each point of the configuration space (for each time). But each vector in configuration space corresponds to a set of vectors for each point in space-time. Suppose now that a system consists only of two particles living in a one-dimensional space, hence representable in a two-dimensional configuration space. Now suppose that you want to see what kind of velocity one of the particles will have when you keep the particle fixed (this velocity is going to depend on where the other particle will be). In particular, we want to know for all possible circumstances what the particle velocity would be if the particle were at that particular fixed point in space. This simply amounts to asking what the velocity of that particle would be for all the possible positions that the other particle would take. This can be easily represented in configuration space by fixing the first particle's position and moving it along the axis of the other particle's possible positions (Figure 11).

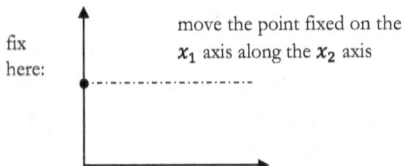

Figure 11: The dispositional interpretation of the wave-function.

This generates all the possible velocities that that particle would take. The actual position of the other particle would trigger the manifestation of a certain velocity. Now the dispositional interpretation claims that each particle position in three-dimensional space has the disposition to move in all the possible velocities that are represented in configuration space by one vector, and in three-dimensional space by a set of vectors. Only one disposition is manifested and this manifestation, as we have said, depends non-locally on the position of the other particle. Which velocity vector will be true depends on where the other particle is. According to the position of all the other particles, the particle will choose a particular velocity vector to follow. So, the manifestation of the disposition depends on a kind of trigger and this dependence is described by the laws of nature.

This would be quite simple in a scenario where we had only two particles. But think of 10^{80} particles – each particle would have an almost infinite number of dispositions!

Going back to where we started, if we use this dispositional interpretation to advocate a weak nomological view of the wave-function, we can say that the nomological character of the wave-function derives from the myriad of dispositions that each particle has.

Esfeld (Esfeld et al., 2014), in contrast, provides a more parsimonious dispositional interpretation. Instead of postulating a myriad of dispositions for each particle, he claims that there is only one relational dispositional and holistic property for all the particles. His view may be spelled out as follows. Take the velocity vector passing through one point in configuration space and regard it as representing one dispositional property for all the particles' positions that that point in configuration space corresponds to. This may erroneously lead us into saying that we should actually take the point in configuration space as representing Albert's marvelous particle (Albert, 1996)[128] and to regard the dispositional property as being instantiated by that single particle. However, this is not what Esfeld has in mind. Esfeld still regards the fundamental ontology to be in our three-dimensional space. Hence, we should think that the dispositional property is instantiated by all the particles taken together as a whole. In this sense, we should understand his characterization of the dispositional property to be relational and holistic.

However, there is one point that deserves some consideration. Indeed, we normally take dispositions to be triggered by an external circumstance. But the problem is that, as we all well know, the Bohmian system comprises all the particles' positions of the universe. Now, if we regard the dispositional property as being instantiated by all the particles of the universe, then what triggers it? The answer we have now is that we should really understand the dispositional property as we understand the fragility of the glass vase, hence as a property that is manifested if and only if something external happens to it. However, perhaps instead we should understand it like the decay of an atom, hence as a spontaneous disposition, which occurs without any external triggering. In this scenario, the nomological character of the wave-function derives from this holistic relational dispositional property.

---

[128] For those who are not familiar with Albert's marvelous particle, here is an explanation. According to Albert what the particle ontology in Bohmian mechanics does not consist of several particles' positions in three-dimensional space, but it consists of only one particle in configuration space. The ontology is constituted of the wave-function and this 'marvelous' particle in a 3ND space. See Albert, 2013.

4.4.1 The Dispositional Property of Motion

It is important here to get a better grasp of the ontology of the dispositional property that we have just introduced. This dispositional property may seem quite strange. How can it be understood in terms of more familiar dispositional properties?

The answer is that it should not be understood as a normal dispositional property like the fragility of a glass vase; instead, it should be thought of as a dynamical property (Esfeld et al., 2014). Whenever Esfeld talks about dispositional properties he refers to dynamical properties, which were incorporated into the theory only in order to account for the dynamics. Why do particles behave in the way they do? It is not because there is a physical entity that is pushing them or performing any kind of action on them; it is not because there is a law (which really exists) that dictates the motion. Rather, it is because the particles have the disposition to move in a certain way.

In this way, the particles are not completely property-less, as they have this disposition. The 'observable job of the wave-function' is not determined by categorical properties such as mass or charge but by their dispositions.

This view is perfectly in accord with the nomological view that regards the particle motions generated by the wave-function as the natural state of the particles (where 'natural' should not be understood as being in contradiction to the dynamical state, since as we have seen the distinction between dynamics and kinematics does not make sense here).

4.4.2 The Mumford Dilemma

It seems that the nomological-dispositional interpretation is a suitable way to frame the nomological interpretation of the wave-function. However, in order to fully understand the proposal, we need to step back and introduce the dispositional account of laws of nature, just as before we presented the Humean view of laws.

In order to understand the proposal of regarding the wave-function as a nomological entity, we are applying the debate on the ontological status of laws (or on general nomological entities) to Bohmian mechanics. In the literature, the debate on the status of laws normally concerns whether we should be realists about laws and their governing role. While the Humean view presents us with a clear anti-realist position, according to which laws merely express regularities of the world, the primitivist view is a clear case of law-realism, according to which law-like entities have a proper modal-nomological role. The law-like entities are 'above' our physical stuff in the world and they choreograph, guide and determine it.

But what about the nomological-dispositionalist view? Here, we presented the view as it is normally presented in the literature; that is, as a proposal that adheres to realism about laws. Indeed, the version we presented does not consist in replacing the nomological role of nomological entities with dispositional properties. On the contrary, dispositions only play the role of grounding the nomological role in the ontology and bridging the two realms. Applied to Bohmian mechanics, this means that the wave-function does exist, it has a nomological role, and this role is grounded in the dispositional properties of the particles (or one holistic dispositional property of all the particles taken together as a whole). The problem is that this scenario faces a dilemma: what is it that really does the job of determining the particle configuration? The wave-function, or the particle disposition? This dilemma has already been brought up in more general metaphysical terms as the 'Mumford's dilemma' (Mumford, 2004; Cei & French, 2010), which I will now apply to Bohmian mechanics.

If the wave-function has the role of governing the motion of the particles, then it cannot be properly grounded in a relevant dispositional property. If, on the other hand, the dispositional property does exist and grounds the wave-function, then the wave-function has only a descriptive role, and it loses any nomological role it had. This dilemma amounts to asking whether the wave-function is independent of or dependent on the dispositional property. Only if we consider the wave-function to be an external and independent entity can we regard it as governing and determining the dynamics. Otherwise, if we say that the wave-function is internal and thus dependent on the dispositional property of the particles, what really does the job of constraining and determining the particles' dynamics is the dispositional property. In a nutshell, this is the dilemma: either we drop the wave-function as a fundamental, substantive and nomological entity from our scenario and just give it a descriptive role, or we drop the dispositional property. Now, there is one thing we should be careful about. Mumford (2004) may be regarded as committing to a false dilemma. Denying that laws have a governing role does not necessarily mean denying their existence. As I said at the beginning of this discussion, being externalist (or internalist) about laws does not necessarily commit to a realist (or anti-realist) stance about laws (see Bird, 2006, for a defense of this view). However, I agree with Mumford that if laws do not have any governing role and dispositional properties do all the work of determining the future evolution of the system, then the laws become so weak and impoverished that they should rationally be dismissed. Applying this to the Bohmian wave-function, we can say that if the dispositional property of the particles fully determines their temporal evolution, then the wave-function as a nomological entity is devoid of any ontological significance. Certainly, it could be still regarded as a kind of Humean nomological entity, whose role is not modal but descriptive: it describes the regularities of the world. However, we do not have any reason to attribute an ontological status to it. Hence, the wave-function should be best regarded as a conventional instrument for describing the Bohmian system, and nothing more.

In conclusion, I agree with Mumford that, at the end of the day, we have two options: either we claim that dispositions determine the evolution of the system or we claim that dispositions do not exist (while the laws play a modal role). Applying this to Bohmian mechanics, either the wave-function does not exist or its existence creates a gap between itself and the particles. Hence, the nomological-dispositional view only superficially progresses the debate within the nomological camp.

4.5 Esfeld's Super-Humeanism

Given that in this section we are discussing the status of the Bohmian wave-function, I will briefly re-discuss the recent radicalization of the Humean view by Esfeld (Esfeld, 2020). As we saw in chapter 2, when discussing the ontological status of the particles, according to his view, which is called 'Super-Humeanism', the primitive ontology is devoid of any intrinsic properties; properties become 'nomological' parameters, hence parameters that are essential in order to build the best system of laws. Mass, charge and spin are all 'parameters' that figure in the law in order for the law to describe the events of the world while achieving the best balance between simplicity and informativeness. This way, they supervene on the mosaic of particle trajectories. The same treatment is employed towards the wave-function. The wave-function supervenes on the motion of all particles' trajectories from the beginning until the end of the universe in virtue of being a dynamical parameter that appears in the dynamical structure of Bohmian mechanics (the set of laws of nature) that constitute the lawhood best system. In recent works (Esfeld, 2019, 2020; Esfeld et al., 2017), Esfeld explains that the wave-function does not exist over and above particles' trajectories, but it is located in them:

> The wave-function can therefore be taken to be located in the motion of matter as defined by the change in the distance relations among featureless point objects only. (Esfeld, 2020, p. 7)

In this sense, the wave-function is nothing more or reduces to particle trajectories by ontological reduction. Its only benchmark is that it enables the formulation of laws that simplify the representation of the temporal evolution of the configuration of matter.

While Humeans commit to a world devoid of modality and dispositionalists re-pristinate it, Esfeld's Super-Humeanism remains neutral concerning modality. The mosaic may or may not be modal. What is important is rather the fact that there are neither modal intrinsic properties such as mass, charge, spin, nor modal entities like a causal field, that induce a modality in the mosaic.

4.6 General Problems of the Nomological View

4.6.1 The Problem of Underdetermination

In this chapter, we have seen that many different metaphysical interpretations can be compatible with the claim that the wave-function is a nomological entity. We could have an ontology devoid of properties, or one full of dispositional properties, but nothing would change. It seems there is no way to reject one metaphysical view with any surety. As in the case of the realist interpretation of the wave-function, we have to face a problem of underdetermination. Moreover, this underdetermination is particularly problematic, because it seems that all the alternative metaphysical interpretations are equally *bad* (as opposed to faring equally *well*) given the difficulties we presented above.

4.6.2 The Physicality of the Wave-function: The Wave-function Can Kill!

The second kind of problem the nomological view has to face is that it must account for all the experiments that seem to be explainable only if we take the wave-function to be a physical entity. I have already presented one such experiment regarding the Bohmian properties of the wave-function in chapter 2. Here I will provide a more vivid example of the physical significance of the wave-function.

Detecting the physicality of the wave-function is extremely difficult because it would require us to learn how to differentiate the effects of waves from the effects of particles. Normally, our measurement devices are constructed in such a way that they detect physical properties such as mass, charge or angular momentum. But, given that these properties may be attributes of both the wave-function and the particle, it is not always possible to understand which property belongs to which entity. The ideal measurement device should be able to deal with an 'empty' wave-function, but it is impossible to create an empty wave-function without the particle. The wave-function is introduced in the theory only as long as the particle is in it. However, even if we cannot prepare empty wave-functions in our laboratories, we can manipulate the wave-function in such a way that it splits into different branches. Moreover, given that the particle of a wave-function does not split but only follows one predetermined path, we can create and measure empty branches of the same wave-function. Let me reinforce this point, since it is a distinctive characteristic of the Bohmian system. Whenever the wave-function associated with a particle splits into two waves through a beam-splitter, only one of the two waves is 'full' or 'occupied', which means that only one contains the particle while the other does not (i. e. it is empty). If Bohmian mechanics is right, and if we can hold this distinction true, the question is whether we can measure empty waves and if so how (here, the term 'measurement' is to be understood in a very weak way; that is, as a sort of detectability via some observable effects).

After provocatively asking "Can empty waves kill?" Vaidman (2005) presents some important experiments that seem to prove the physical ontological status of empty waves. Here I will describe one *gedanken* experiment. Imagine that the wave of a bullet, after meeting a beam-splitter, splits into two equally uniformly dense spherical wave-packets that differ only in the sense that one of them contains the bullet and the other does not. Now, Bohmian mechanics tells us that the velocity of the bullet can be calculated in this way:

$$\vec{v} = \frac{\vec{j}}{\rho}$$

from which we can see that the velocity depends on the current density and the wave-density at the location of the particle, since ρ is:

$$\rho(\vec{x}) = |\Psi|^2$$

and j is:

$$\vec{j} = \frac{\hbar}{2im} \{\Psi^* \vec{\nabla} \Psi - \Psi \vec{\nabla} \Psi^*\}$$

Imagine further that the two wave-packets of the bullet are forced to overlap again, as in a Mach-Zehnder interferometer with only one beam-splitter. In the region of the overlap, the velocity of the bullet is then given by:

$$\vec{v} = \frac{\vec{j_1} + \vec{j_2}}{\rho_1 + \rho_2} = \frac{\vec{v_1} + \vec{v_2}}{2}$$

and its horizontal component is zero. What is surprising is that after this region of overlap, the bullet changes waves and starts occupying the wave that was empty previously. It is as if in this region there was a sort of competition between the two waves regarding which of the two would take the particle. At this point, some doubts on the physicality of the empty wave arise. How could the particle "feel" and follow the empty wave if it were not physical?

A second interesting experiment concerns an experiment in a bubble chamber (Aharonov & Vaidman, 1995; Vaidman, 2005), which is a kind of measurement device that records the particle trajectory. As charged particles travel in the chamber through a particular liquid, tiny bubbles start forming along the particle trajectory. Imagine now that a very fast particle is sent towards an interferometer in a special bubble chamber where the bubbles, on the contrary, develop, very very slowly. This way, the bubble record is time delayed, since the record of the passage of the particles is very slow. What is surprising is that what we see at the end of the experiment is the formation of bubbles not along the trajectory in which the particle really moved, but along the path of our empty wave. In other words, the bubbles show the trajectory of the empty wave! What is even more surprising is that in this experiment, after the region of overlap, the bubbles do not change wave – on the contrary, they keep following the track of the wave that was empty (the same track that grabs the particle after the region of overlap). These two experiments show that if Bohmian mechanics is right, and if the distinction between full and empty waves is meaningful, then we should definitely have some grounds to claim that the wave-function possesses physicality even when it does not contain any particle. However, if we have a closer look at both experiments, then we can see that the wave causes an observational effect only if at the time of the observation the Bohmian particle is inside it (Vaidman, 2005). Indeed, in both experiments, the wave shows its physicality only once it is no longer empty. In the first example, the empty wave manifests its physical reality only when it grabs the particle, while in the second experiment we can see the bubbles forming the empty wave trajectory only once the particle has occupied the wave after the region of overlap.

So, this experiment leaves us with some doubts: we can detect the physicality of the wave-function only when the particle is there. Fortunately, it is possible to modify the experiment so that we can really measure the empty wave-packet. We can do this with weak measurements. We can modify Vaidman's experiment with a Dewdey experiment (Dewdey et al., 1993) – that is, we can put a measurement device along the empty path of the wave-function before the two paths meet and interfere with one another. The surprising thing is that, in this case, the measurement device 'ticks', which means that it does really measure something. But what is that something? It is not the particle, given the measurement device is put along the empty branch of the wave-function; therefore, it must be the wave-function.

To summarize this experimental approach, we begin by constructing a measurement device such that it 'ticks' or simply changes its physical state whenever it interacts with a physical entity. Indeed, any time it interacts with the particle it ticks. However, in this case, it ticks even though the particle is not there. Therefore, it means that the empty branch of the wave-function is physical.

This is certainly a great challenge for the nomological view. Indeed, the most straightforward explanation for the tick of the measurement device is that the wave-function itself has some physical dynamical properties and that it physically interacts with the measurement device. This reminds us of the experiment performed by Brown (1994) that we described in chapter 2, which seems to confirm that the wave-function (even the empty wave) does have properties such as mass and charge.

4.7 The Methodology

In the previous section, we saw that there is a lot of confusion over what the core of the nomological view is. This confusion encompasses a number of issues. The first is that it is not clear whether we should interpret the nomological stance as making the claim that the wave-function is a law of nature or the claim that it is a part of our laws that gives us information about the system. Moreover, it is not clear how we should interpret its 'nomological' character: is it a governing entity with modal power or simply a descriptive mathematical tool?

Here I want to address the nomological view in light of the distinction we drew in the previous chapter between informationally complete representation, ontologically complete representation of the system, and the ontology itself. The nomologists would certainly claim that the wave-function is part of the informationally complete representation of the system but not of the ontology. The interesting and challenging question I want to ask now is whether the wave-function is part of the ontologically complete representation of the system.

Let us approach this in steps. First of all, I would like to recall the division within the nomological view that causes the nomologists to split into two different camps.

The first camp, defended by Esfeld, uses the Humean framework in order to argue that the wave-function does not exist (over and above particles' trajectories). This camp, which I call 'the nomological-instrumentalist' camp, takes the alleged supervenience of the wave-function on the particle configuration to support the view that the wave-function is not ontologically relevant.[129] The second camp, sometimes defended by the Rutgers-Genova-Munich group, seems to put the wave-function in the ontology not for its physical salience but in virtue of its strong nomological status.

---

[129] To be noticed is that Esfeld has recently offered a more cautious description of his view, by acknowledging the ontological significance of the wavefunction. However, he still endorses the view that the wavefunction is 'located' in the particle trajectories, and so is nothing over and above the particle trajectories. In this sense, to me, the wavefunction is still not ontologically significant.

The proponents of this second view, as suggested above, may draw their metaphysical conception of the wave-function from the primitivist views about nomological entities.

I think that both camps adopt a problematic methodology. We will first start by analyzing the nomological-instrumentalist view. One way would be to motivate the nomological status of the wave-function by apriori metaphysical considerations, claiming that our ontology reduces to our primitive ontology that consists only of the minimal set of entities necessary to make up all the rest of the ontology. This armchair approach is for instance what Esfeld seems to adopt in his most recent works (Esfeld, 2020). While an armchair metaphysics is perfectly coherent, it raises several doubts on its epistemic justification. Another way would be to justify the nomological-instrumentalist view of the wave-function by appealing to supervenience. The claim is that the supervenience of the wave-function on the particle configuration has some ontological implications, namely that the wave-function is not an ontological entity but, at best, can be regarded as a nice summary of the history of our space-time. But the claim of supervenience needs to be investigated further before it is able to imply anything about the wave-function's ontological status. What kind of supervenience is involved? Indeed, there are different kinds of supervenience. For example, let us first analyze the kind of supervenience between the chair you are sitting on and the particles that constitute that chair. If we take the particles to be the only physical constituents of your chair, then, obviously, any difference in the chair must correspond to a difference in the particle ontology. The chair, in this sense, can be said to be reducible to the ensemble of particles – or, more strongly, to be nothing over and above the particles. This kind of supervenience implies a particular view on the ontological status of the chair that is at least 'derivative'. More strongly, if we apply the Ockham's razor principle to our case, given that the chair is nothing over and above the particles, the chair may also be eliminated from the ontological representation of the system. Certainly, once we have to define which entities need to appear in the complete ontological representation of the system, the chair will not be among them while the particles will be. In this case, implying a sort of ontological reduction from a supervenience claim is legitimate: given that the chair supervenes on the particle distribution, we only need the particles in our ontologically complete representation of the system.

Now, Maudlin (2009) presents a case where this implication cannot work. Take for example the state of the deterministic system at a certain time, and also take the state of the same deterministic system at a later time. We can say that the state of the earlier time supervenes on the state of the later time. But this does not mean that there is ontological reduction between one state and the other; it does not mean that the first state is ontologically 'spooky'. In particular, we could say that this supervenience does not have any direct effects on our ontological commitments because it is nomic, which means that the future state of the system can be derived from the previous one through the physical laws of the theory. The supervenience does not tell us that the later state is 'made up of' the earlier state. Maudlin also presents us with another case that is not entirely clear-cut but nevertheless has merit in that it effectively demonstrates the complexity of the issue. The case is drawn from electromagnetic theory (we have already touched upon this in our previous chapter) and draws the status of the charge into focus. The charge distribution supervenes on the electromagnetic field: any change in the electromagnetic field must correspond to a change in the particle distribution. But this supervenience does not have any direct ontological implications. Indeed, this supervenience is not ontological (as it was in the case of the chair) but nomic: "The charge distribution nomically supervenes on the field values since one uses a physical law – Maxwell equations – to derive the former from the latter" (Maudlin, 2009, p. 3152). We could claim that this nomic supervenience implies an ontic supervenience, but this is not straightforward and needs to be substantially motivated.

With these clear examples in mind, we can analyze the Bohmian case of the wave-function that supervenes on the particle configuration. What kind of supervenience is involved here? We can quickly rule out any ontological supervenience, as the wave-function is not physically constituted by the particles. Hence, we have to investigate whether the wave-function nomically supervenes on the particles, namely whether we can derive the former from the latter through the laws that govern the particles. Although to date there is no published work supporting this, I am happy to concede that this is actually possible. Even so, just as in the case of the electromagnetic field, this nomic supervenience does not have any direct implication in the ontological status of the wave-function.

Hopefully this discussion has shown that the nomological instrumentalists adopt a problematic methodology when they claim that the supervenience of the wave-function implies that it is not ontologically relevant but that it is merely a convenient and excellent device to write our laws of nature.

Now we may focus our attention on the camp that takes the ontological status of the nomological role seriously. This camp acknowledges that the wave-function is ontologically important, but then they reify the wave-function as a nomological entity and include it in the ontology. However, this creates confusion and is not satisfactory. Indeed, the questions that we were asking were as follows: How can a nomic entity be part of the ontology? How can it physically influence the particles if it is not physical? The primitivist view is right to attribute a strong ontological character to the wave-function; still, it fails to acknowledge that what we really need is not to reify the nomological entity by upgrading it to an ontological entity. Rather, what we really need, as we saw when we dealt with the problem of the gap between the wave-function and the particle configuration, is a physical way to ground the nomological entity in the particles.

The Hamiltonian gives us an idea of what we are looking for and points to a route by which we may guide our discussion. The Hamiltonian is a nomological entity, but this does not mean that it is detached from the physical world. Indeed, even if it is a mathematical function, it is a function that expresses the energy of the physical system. The Hamiltonian is a field in a 6N dimensional space, and it is a mathematical field; hence, it does not represent an isomorphic physical field in a concrete 6N dimensional space. It is a nomological entity in the sense that it gives us information about the particles' evolution without pushing or pulling the particles around. Still, even if it is a nomological entity and does not represent a physical field in a 6N dimensional space, it has physical significance since it is grounded in the physical energy of the system. We could say, loosely, that it mathematically represents or expresses the energy of the system. This way, even if we endow the Hamiltonian with a strong modality, this does not create a gap between the Hamiltonian and the physical ontology. So, in the same way the Hamiltonian expresses some physical features of the world, which grounds and explains its nomological role, we need to find what it is in virtue of that the wave-function acquires its own nomological role. In other words, we need to answer the following question: what does the wave-function 'express' in the physical ontology? The fact that we categorize it as a nomological entity does not mean that we have to rule out the fact that it can express physical features of the world. If we allow this, then we do not need to reify the wave-function as a nomological entity in order to explain its ontological significance and how it can govern the particles' motions.

This last proposal can also accommodate the problem that the nomological view has to face when it comes to explaining the experiments involving the empty branches of the wave-function. What those experiments show is that the wave-function does have a physical salience in our world. Regarding it as a mere instrument for calculating the velocity of the particles, or as a primitive entity with nomological status but also ontological relevance, does not address the puzzle that empty branches of the wave-function causally interact with our measurement devices.

Given this discussion, it is now time to ask the question that we wanted to ask at the beginning of this section, which is whether the wave-function is part of the ontologically complete representation of the system. In order to answer this question, we first need to have a specific definition of the ontologically complete representation of the system in mind. Consider the one given in Maudlin (2009): "An ontologically complete description of a physical situation should provide – in a relatively transparent way – an exact representation of all the physical entities and states that exist" (Maudlin, 2009, p. 3154).

I take this sentence to be vague enough to create discontent. What does "in a relatively transparent way" mean? What is an "exact representation"? If the above definition of 'ontologically complete representation' implies that the structure of the representative entity is conserved in the physical ontology, then the wave-function should not be regarded as part of the ontologically complete representation. Indeed, the discussion of the realist view in chapter 1 showed us that putting an entity isomorphic to the wave-function in our physical ontology is conceptually and practically unreasonable. However, if the above definition just means that components of the ontologically complete representation are supposed to describe physical elements of the ontology, then I think that the wave-function should be considered as part of the ontologically complete representation of the system. This is because, as we saw while discussing the nomological view, the wave-function does mathematically describe some physical element that exists in our world, and that causes the experimental outcomes we just presented above.

The aim of the next part of this book will be to investigate what the wave-function represents. While one could endorse the multi-field view and claim that the wave-function represents a 3D multi-field in the next chapter, I shall investigate this by adopting a perspective borrowed from ontic structural realism.

IV The Structuralist View

5 Ontic Structural Realism: The State of the Art

5.1 Introduction

In the introduction to this book, I argued that Bohmian mechanics offers an obvious, simple, and clear formulation of quantum mechanics. Indeed, following Goldstein (1996), we targeted the physics program of Bohmian mechanics as 'OOEOW': 'obvious ontology evolving in an obvious way'. However, the whole discussion on the Bohmian ontology has revealed many problems that are difficult to tackle. Let me order them briefly.

First of all, there are problems concerning the resulting ontological picture. The realist view offers quite a mysterious ontology where a high-dimensional field in a high-dimensional space performs a causal action on particles, bringing about their velocity. The challenging questions are: how can a multi-dimensional entity/space be physical? How can it be physically connected to our space and our familiar ontology? In addition to this, there are problems coming from the principle of reciprocity or back-reaction: how is it possible that a physical entity physically interacting with another does not receive any reaction? Should we abandon the principle of reciprocity as a criterion for physicality?[130]

If we endorse a nomological view, however, we get quite a mysterious ontology too. First of all, it is dubious that a temporal entity can count as a law; secondly, it is not clear how this law-like entity is connected to a property-less ontology, or how it can externally dictate its motion. Thirdly, even if we add dispositions to this ontology, we are faced with Mumford's dilemma of whether we should attribute the power to the wave-function as a law-like entity, or to the particle disposition.[131]

Moreover, we saw that there are problems concerning not only the ontological status of the wave-function, but also the other two elements of the theory: the particles and the physical properties. Concerning the status of properties, in Bohmian mechanics, physical properties are completely different from how they are conceived in classical mechanics, and it is not clear how to define their contextual status; moreover, it is dubious how and by what entities they are instantiated (only by the wave-function or by the wave-function *and* the particles?). Regarding the status of the particles, it is still an open question how we should conceive of 'property-less' particles if we decide that physical properties only belong to the wave-function. If, by contrast, we grant properties to the particles, their roles seem to be spooky.[132]

---

[130] See chapter 3.
[131] See chapter 4.
[132] See chapter 2.

Concerning the methodological presuppositions, I also presented some objections against the methodologies adopted by the realists and by the nomologists. The realists' methodology relies on a process of reification and mistakes the elements necessary for an informationally complete representation of the system as parts of the ontology. The nomologists, on the other hand, take elements that are not needed in the informationally complete representation of the system as non-representative of ontological objects and as non-physically salient. Once we discard any process of reification and we inquire into the complex linkage between the 'informationally complete representation' of the system, the 'ontologically complete representation' of the system, and the ontology itself, both views seem unsatisfactory. We argued that the wave-function is a representative element of the system, but, at the same time, is not a physical field; this statement left us with two nagging problems. The first is to spell out the relation between the mathematical entity – the wave-function – and the physical entity it represents. The wave-function is indeed a nomological entity, which represents 'indirectly' and in a 'non-transparent way' something of the ontology that cannot be reduced to the particles' properties. The second problem is to detect what that entity is supposed to be. Indeed, we know from chapter 3 that the mathematical structure of the wave-function and the physical structure of the entity represented by it do not differ only in terms of abstractness (as the realist view seemed to believe), as they are also really different in *kind*.

In this part of the book, I will present and discuss a third view that can account for the ontology of Bohmian mechanics – that is, ontic structural realism. I will argue that a structuralist view provides the best interpretation of the wave-function and also the best conceptual tools for understanding the ontological status of property-less particles. Moreover, I will show that its methodology takes on aspects of both the realist and the nomological views, and, for this reason, can be regarded as a reconciliatory view between the two rivals.

Given that this part is going to be quite dense, let me preannounce here the main important steps. I will dedicate chapter 5 to the presentation of the structural realist view as it is normally understood in the field of philosophy of science. In particular, I will focus on its ontological version, which is called ontic structural realism (from now on OSR) and its different specifications. My aim will be to present not only its ontological commitments, but also its methodological program. Once we get a clear understanding of its methodology, I will be able to develop a structuralist interpretation of the Bohmian ontology, to which I will dedicate chapter 6. In particular, I will first apply a structuralist methodology to Bohmian mechanics and elaborate the resulting structuralist ontology. Later, I will check which kind of ontic structuralist specification the Bohmian ontology matches best. It will turn out that the Bohmian ontology matches the moderate ontic structural realist program. In chapter 7, I will present and discuss some potential challenges that the structural realist view may have to face. Finally, I will claim that the ontic structuralist view reconciles the two views, since it takes on aspects from both sides. I will conclude with the hope that my defense of OSR not only is convincing in its application to the Bohmian case, but that it also shows that OSR provides an appealing methodological and metaphysical framework to interpret physical theories in general.

5.2 The State of the Art

5.2.1 Structural Realism

Structural realism was born with the paradoxical aim to save and discard the scientific realism program at the same time. We could regard it as a 'moderate' form of scientific realism. The scientific realism program claims that we should be realist about the observable and unobservable entities presented in our best scientific theories. Moreover, realists are committed to a literal interpretation of scientific claims and they take theoretical and observational statements at face value. According to realists, our scientific theories do represent the world faithfully; hence, we should infer our ontology from a literal interpretation of the scientific claims (Psillos, 1999).

More specifically, this view is committed to three different claims concerning three different areas of philosophy. The first commitment is ontological: there is a fundamental reality out there in the world. This reality is mind-independent, and as such does not depend on our mental representation or subjective experiences. Science aims to investigate this kind of reality through objective and trustworthy methods. For this reason, its results can be reasonably regarded as revealing the truth (or approximate truth) of what the physical reality is, independently of our mental categories and ways of representing the world. The second claim is semantical: as we said, the realists take all the scientific statements – theoretical and observational – at a face value. Not only do they interpret them literally, but they also believe that it is possible to attribute them truth-values. Finally, they are committed to the view that all the theoretical and observational claims constituting a scientific theory are epistemologically relevant; hence, these claims constitute a reliable system of knowledge of our world.[133]

---

[133] For a discussion of the three different commitments of scientific realism, refer to Chakravartty, 2016.

An important aspect that I should stress is that whenever I say 'scientific theories', I mean 'successful' and 'mature' scientific theories, hence theories that have been corroborated and that are empirically adequate. This obviously lets an aspect of arbitrariness and vagueness sneak into the scientific realist view, since it is difficult to really specify the level of corroboration and empirical adequacy that a scientific theory should have in order to be regarded as 'mature' and 'successful'.[134] However, here we just want to give a 'taste' of the scientific realist view, and it is not our aim to dig into this matter.

The scientific realist view is mainly supported by the so-called 'no miracle' argument (Putnam, 1975), which is based on the claim that science is successful. According to this argument, given this premise, the only reason we could grant for the success of science is that science does track the true nature of the world, or in more metaphysical words 'carves reality at its joints', otherwise its success would just become an unexplainable 'miracle'.

This view, however, finds serious challenges from the pessimistic meta-induction argument, which claims that shifts from one scientific theory to another reveal that we cannot and should not be realist about the content of our scientific theories. This argument focuses on a set of cases where mature and successful scientific theories were proved to be false after years of corroborations (Laudan, 1981).

Given this challenge, structural realism comes to the rescue of the realist attitude of scientific realism, but only by discarding one of its most important pillars. Indeed, on the one hand, the structural realist asserts, in agreement with scientific realism, that we should be realist about our scientific theories. On the other hand, the structural realist argues that we should not be realist about the content, but of the structure. This way, we can defeat the pessimistic meta-induction by claiming that there is a continuity across different shifts of scientific theories, and this continuity is a 'structural' continuity. The fact that successful and mature scientific theories were proved to be false is due to the fact that their terms failed to refer to the right objects, about which we should not be realist. The birth of structural realism is normally associated with the year 1989, when Worrall published his seminal paper titled "Structural Realism: The Best of Both Worlds?", where he writes: "There was continuity or accumulation in the shift, but the continuity is one of form or structure, not of content" (Worrall, 1989, p. 117).

The most pressing question for our work is to understand what is meant by 'structure' here. Many advocates of structural realism (Shapiro, 1997; Cao, 2003b) take the formal mathematical expression of the laws to be 'the structure' that ontic structuralists refer to. In light of this interpretation of 'structure', structural realism

---

[134] For a definition of a 'mature' and 'successful' scientific theory, see Laudan, 1981.

is sometimes regarded as the Pythagorean/Platonist metaphysical position, according to which we should be realist about the mathematical structure.[135] For this reason, it has been accused of not being able to account for our physical reality and for how the mathematical structure of the theory can provide the empirical content about which we should be realist. Others, in contrast, claim that 'structure' refers to the concrete physical relations among the objects of the theory (Esfeld, 2004, 2009; French, 2006; French & Ladyman, 2003). But then, a common argument against this view is that if the structure is so specific, it is not the kind of structure that can be retained through theory change. Another major view is to approach scientific theories from a semantic perspective and claim that the structure is the set-theoretic 'model' of the theory (Brading, 2010). Here I do not want to deal with the discussion of what meaning should be preferable, nor what Worrall really meant in his paper. Rather, I just want to explain the meaning that will be used in this book and that we are going to develop and clarify step by step.

First of all, I want to refer to a citation by Worrall himself:

> From the vintage point of Maxwell's theory, Fresnel was as wrong as he could be about what waves are [. . .], but the retention of his equations [. . .] shows that, from that vintage point, Fresnel's theory was none the less structurally correct: it is correct that optical effects depend on something or other that oscillates at right angles to the direction of transmission of the light, where the form of that dependence is given by the above and other equations within the theory. (Worrall, 2007, p. 134)

I believe that the above citation helps us clarify the meaning of the structural realist claim that the continuity is not at the level of the content but of the structure. Notice that Worrall claims that 'the retention of the equation' shows that a theory is correct 'structurally'. This does not mean that we should identify 'the structure' with the 'equations' themselves. On the contrary, the equations are only hints about what the structure is. Later, Worrall argues that the theory is 'structurally' correct insofar as some effects depend on 'something' that has a particular behavior, and he stresses that 'the form of the dependence' is given by the equation. The content, in this case, is the nature of waves, while the structure is the kind of dependent relation that optical effects entertain with a certain kind of oscillation. And it is exactly this form of dependence that is spelled out by the Fresnel laws.

Given this passage, we can reasonably regard 'structure' to be the physical kind of relations that connect different aspects of the world, which bear a sort of

---

[135] Normally Pythagoreanism is associated with the view that identifies mathematical and physical structures (Ladyman & Ross, 2007, p. 159). The platonic view is normally regarded as the view asserting that the boundaries of what is real and what is mathematically possible coincide (Ladyman & Ross, 2007, p. 234).

dependency on one another. More precisely, we can define it as the concrete network of first-order relations between specific kinds of relata, which may be objects or quantities (French, 2006; Esfeld, 2004). We will spell out this characterization in detail later on.

5.2.2 Ontic Structural Realism

There is a question that divides the structural realists into two opposing groups. The question that structural realism asks is: why should we be realist only about the structure and not about the content of our theories? And more deeply: why is it the case that we are often not right about what the content of our theories is, or better what objects the theory refers to? Two different lines of reasoning normally answer this question.

The first, which is the core claim of epistemic ontic structural realism, finds the reason in the limits to our knowledge: we cannot be realist about the objects, because what we can know is only the structure of physical reality. According to epistemic structural realism (ESR), there is a hidden content of our physical theories – hence, the unobservable/theoretical terms of our theories do refer to objects really existing in our world, but to what objects exactly we do not and cannot know. Metaphysically, the epistemic structural realist may be happy to concede the existence of 'unobservables',[136] hence of individuals such as electrons and quarks. However, she argues that they are inaccessible. Normally, there are two ways to support this claim: one is called the 'upward path' to ESR, and the second is called the 'downward path' to ESR.[137] The former, which draws back to Russell (1912), Maxwell (1968) and Poincaré (1968), claims that our sensory data

---

[136] What counts as 'unobservable' is open to debate. According to direct epistemic structural realism (DESR), for example, we can have structural and non-structural knowledge of chairs, tables and every macroscopic individual, since they are regarded as 'observables'. According to the indirect epistemic structural realism (IESR), by contrast, what counts as observable is only what is the immediate object of our sensory data, hence only of our perception. Therefore, even macroscopic objects such as chairs, tables and books count as unobservable. (For a clarification about this distinction, see Frigg, 2011). The distinction between DESR and IESR is sometimes reformulated in terms of 'weak' and 'strong' ESR (see for example Ainsworth, 2009). This distinction is also behind the two kinds of epistemic structural realism delineated in Psillos, 2001: the upward path to ESR, and the downward path to ESR (see the next footnote).

[137] The distinction between IESR and DESR is behind the two kinds of epistemic structural realism delineated by Psillos (2001): the upward path to ESR, and the downward path to ESR. Normally, the structural realists that defend the upward path to ESR support IESR, while structural realists that defend the downward path to ESR support DESR. For a better explanation about this, see Frigg, 2011.

of the world are such that we can be realist only about the structural aspects of our perceptions.[138] According to the latter, scientific theories do not provide knowledge about the non-structural nature of individuals, hence about what individuals are above and beyond the relations they entertain. Therefore, it is not possible to be realist about the intrinsic nature of individuals, but only about their structural aspects.[139] No matter which path is taken, the general and common conclusion drawn is the same: at the fundamental level of our reality there are unobservable individuals interrelated with other unobservable individuals through relations; however, since they are unobservable, they cannot constitute our objective knowledge of the world. Even though ESR is normally happy to concede the existence of unobservable and unknowable individuals at the fundamental ontological level, some of its proponents prefer remaining 'silent' concerning their existence, and they rather endorse a sort of skepticism or at least agnosticism. This is, for example, the view to which Worrall (2012) has recently turned to and the view that Morganti (2004) defends.

The second way to answer the question would be to go radical and claim that we cannot know about the objects described by our physical theories simply because there are no objects.[140] This is how Ladyman and Ross present this view:

> A first approximation to our metaphysics is: "there are no things, structure is all there is."
> (Ladyman & Ross, 2007, p. 130)

This claim turns structural realism into an ontological and metaphysical position, and for this reason it is called 'ontic structural realism'.

Historically, the main motivation for supporting OSR comes from a problem that is widespread in the philosophy of physics – the problem of underdetermination of physical theories.[141] The particular kind of underdetermination that the

---

[138] Since in this work I will not deal with ESR, I will not specify the different kinds of arguments supporting this view here. Mainly, there are three arguments supporting the upward path to ESR: the argument for perception (Russell, 1912, 1927; Maxwell, 1968), the transmission argument (Poincaré, 1968), and the argument from predictive power (Votsis, 2005, chapter 4).

[139] The arguments supporting the downward path normally come in two forms: the pessimistic meta-induction (Laudan, 1981), and the argument from mathematical representation (van Fraassen, 1997).

[140] Normally, the defenders of OSR identify objects with individuals, so their view amounts to the claim that there are no objects. In this respect, the OSR defenders support IESR. But there are exceptions. For example, Brading (2010) distinguishes objects from individuals. I will discuss the different views on this matter later in this section.

[141] For a discussion of the problem of underdetermination, see Papineau, 1996 and van Fraassen, 1991.

ontic structuralist deals with[142] is metaphysical underdetermination, which obtains whenever there is one single theory with one single formulation but different ontological interpretations. In other words, within the same theory, there are different alternative ontological interpretations that presuppose radically different ontologies. An example is the classical debate between individuality and non-individuality of quantum particles. Here is how Ladyman presents this case:

> Even if we were to decide on a canonical formulation of our theory, there is a further problem of metaphysical underdetermination. In the case of individuality, it has been shown [. . .] that electrons may be interpreted either as individuals or as non-individuals. (Ladyman, 1998, pp. 419–420)

Here Ladyman is referring to a famous case presented in quantum statistics. In quantum statistics, the distribution of statistical weight to different microstates – all compatible with the same macrosystem – is such that two microstates that differ with respect to which particle occupies which position share the same statistical weight, as if they were not two different microstates.[143] This leaves us with a two alternatives: either the quantum particles are not individuals, or they are individuals but are restricted by some symmetry conditions. In a nutshell, we have two competing ways of explaining why permutation does not generate a statistically different physical state, and both are equally compatible! How should we choose between them? The ontic structural realist responds to this problem by cutting it at its roots and claiming that there are no such things as individual objects.

In this specific case, by claiming that structure is all that exists, the ontic structural realist is safe not only from embarrassing metaphysical questions that cannot be answered due to underdetermination, but also from any metaphysical

---

142 There is another form of underdetermination that the ontic structural realist can solve. This kind, called 'Jones Underdetermination', refers to the case where there is the same theory with different formulations that imply different sets of world-furniture, hence different 'ontological' commitments. The most important debate in this field is the Lagrangian and Hamiltonian formulations of classical mechanics (see North, 2009; French, 2014, section 2.2).

143 Suppose that our macrostate informs us that two particles A and B are distributed across two boxes 1 and 2. Then we have four possible microstates compatible with our original macrostate: (1) both particles are in box 1; (2) both particles are in box 2; (3) A is in box 1 and B is in box 2; (4) A is in box 2 and B is in box 1. While in classical mechanics each of the microstates has its own distinct statistical weight and all the microstates have equal statistical weight, in the case of quantum statistics, the two last microstates (3) and (4) do not have their own individual statistical weight – rather, they share the same statistical weight. Permutation of particles in one microstate does not create another possible microstate. The two possible microstates are the very same microstate, just labeled in different ways.

commitment detached from the sound realm of empirical experience that confines and limits our epistemological contents.

In conclusion, by being 'structural realist' and at the same time 'ontic structural realist', it is possible to overcome not only the problem of scientific theory shifts, but also the problem of underdetermination. This is, again, what Ladyman writes:

> So we should seek to elaborate structural realism in such a way that it can diffuse the problems of traditional realism, with respect to both theory change and underdetermination. (Ladyman, 1998, p. 420)

Most ontic structural realists are regarded as 'realists' insofar as they conceive of the structure – which consists of the physical relations among objects – as being at the most fundamental levelof our mind-independent reality. But there are other approaches within ontic structural realism that blur the division between the epistemic and the ontic versions of structural realism.

Differences within the OSR view not only concern the kind of realism they endorse, but also its core statement that structure is all that exists. Indeed, OSR should be best regarded as a cluster of different metaphysical positions concerning objects. Here I will explain three different families of positions, without the presumption of exhausting all the different alternatives. All the positions are against the traditional object-oriented metaphysics according to which the building blocks of our world are individuals which instantiate intrinsic and extrinsic properties. However, while some positions reject the existence of objects, and consequently of individuals, others differentiate between objects and individuals and reject the existence of individual objects. Lastly, other positions defend the existence of individuals (which, however, are purged of any intrinsic identity).

Ontic Structural Realism against Objects
1) Radical Ontic Structural Realism (ROSR): This view (Bain, 2013) focuses on uninterpreted relations (relations that are characterized by their extensional meaning) and takes at face value the OSR claim that relations are all that exists. This position is normally criticized for being 'unintelligible' and for lacking physical content, since the relations it refers to are uninterpreted.
2) Eliminative Ontic Structural Realism (EOSR): This view (French, 1998, 1999, 2003; Ladyman, 1998, 2001; French & Ladyman, 2003a; 2003b) focuses on interpreted relations (relations are characterized by their intensional meaning) and claims that relations are more fundamental (or prior to) objects. Given this, relations do not need objects in order to exist. This claim can lead to two different positions: according to the first position, objects exist but they are superfluous, redundant entities, and for this reason they may be eliminated. The second position claims that objects are fictitious; hence, they do not exist. In this sense,

we have 'free-standing' relations that constitute a network. This position is better than ROSR because it accounts for physical content, however it is normally accused of being as unintelligible as ROSR.

Ontic Structural Realism against Individuals
3) Intermediate Ontic Structural Realism (IOSR): This view (Lyre, 2011) differentiates 'objects' from 'individuals' and claims that objects do exist, while individuals do not. Objects are identified by those intrinsic properties that are invariant quantities.
4) Bundle Theory (BT): Even though the BT has its own story that is independent of the structuralist position, it is sometimes invoked by the structuralist because of the anti-individualistic metaphysics it defends (Morganti, 2004). The BT takes objects to be secondary, while properties and relations are taken as more fundamental. Objects are nothing over and above properties and relations.

Ontic Structural Realism against Intrinsic Properties
5) Moderate Ontic Structural Realism (MOSR): This view (Esfeld & Lam, 2006) takes individuals and relations to be on the same footing, both ontologically and conceptually.

5.3 Ontic Structural Realism: The Methodological Program

In the previous section, we presented the different kinds of ontological commitments endorsed by the proponents of OSR. In this section, I will look at the methodological program of the ontic structural realist view. I believe that the choice of methodology should always be the first grounding step for any ontological interpretation of a theory. First, we choose what methodology seems more promising, and later we apply it to the theory under investigation in order to infer its ontology. In doing so, we avoid any armchair metaphysics, while the methodology takes a major role in our work of understanding the ontology of the theory. For this reason, any sound metaphysical program (if it aims to escape the route of armchair metaphysics) needs, first of all, to be founded in a coherent and sound methodological program.

Concerning ontic structural realism, as far as I can tell from the literature, there is no stable consensus of what the right methodology should amount to. In many cases, it really seems that the supporters of OSR endorse even opposite methodologies.[144] However, OSR seems to be committed to certain general methodological principles that inform us about how it approaches both physics and metaphysics. Here I shall make explicit the principles I find most relevant for my project.

5.3.1 Ontic Structural Realism: An Anti-armchair-metaphysics Program

Ontic structural realism characterizes itself, first of all, as an anti-armchair-metaphysics program, meaning that it refuses any ontological commitments that derive from our metaphysical criteria rather than from the results of our best scientific theories. Instead, it takes our best scientific theories to be the starting point for our ontological inquiry about the world. The link between the two realms – the epistemological domain, which is confined within the scientific theory's statements, and the ontological domain – is very tight, with the former determining the latter. This, however, does not mean that we should read off the ontology from the formalism of our theory. It simply means that we should not jump out of the epistemic domain that our scientific theories draw. Therefore, we should infer our ontology from the scientific theories, so that the resulting ontology lies within what is epistemically supported by the theory itself. This methodology does not simply imply that we should not include in our ontology entities that the theory does not postulate. Rather, it implies something stronger: we should ontologically commit only to what may not be the cause of a case of metaphysical underdetermination. We should not commit ourselves to more than what the theory is strictly committed to already. This general direction of the ontic structuralist program may be more specifically summed up in the following terms.

1) Physics should inform Metaphysics[145]
Physics should always be the starting point of our metaphysical inquiry (Ladyman & Ross, 2007). According to OSR, philosophy is only a meta-reflection of the world presented by physics. The role of philosophical inquiry is not to add knowledge, but to clarify it. The primacy of physics over metaphysics has another implication, which is that the results of our research in physics should have an impact on our metaphysical inquiry. An example is the principle of identity of indiscernibles by

---

144 Another problem is that OSR seems to defend the view that mathematical and physical structures are blurred; there is no clear and neat distinction between the realm of mathematics and that of physical world. I shall discuss this later in the same section 5.3.1.
145 I am using an expression used by Ladyman & Ross, 2007.

Leibniz.[146] Leibniz defined the notion of individuality as reducible to the sum of all its qualitative monadic properties. According to his principle, it is impossible to have two individuals with the same monadic properties. In case two 'things' have the same qualitative monadic properties, then they must be the very same 'individual'. Obviously atomic physics reveals the presence of identical particles, which are particles that are 'identical' concerning all their qualitative monadic properties. Hence, it would be inappropriate to still endorse the Leibnizian principle. For this reason, in light of the scientific findings, we have to loosen the criteria for individuality by adding spatio-temporal properties as the properties to which individuality is reducible.

2) From Laws to Ontology

According to OSR, laws play an enormous role in determining the ontology since they express the physical relations (hence the physical structure) that constitute our physical reality. According to the structural realist, whenever we have to infer the ontology, the first step consists in taking the laws of the theories and regarding them as revealing the features of the world. Laws are constructed in such a way that they qualify the kind of structure that the theory describes. Moreover, according to OSR, laws give the identity conditions for both properties and objects,[147] and they delimit our epistemic and ontological domain. Concerning the properties, given that we cannot know about a property more than what the laws tell us about it (see 6.6 for a discussion on properties and laws), their identity is given by their nomic role, hence the role they play in the laws of the theory. Regarding the objects, the very fact 'of being an object' is given by the way it is constituted in the laws of the theory (Brading & Skiles, 2012): the relations expressed in the laws shape the nature of objects by determining their particular behaviors. According to this line of thought, it is not the case that objects instantiate some relations in virtue of possessing some intrinsic properties (either categorical or dispositional). On the contrary, it is the case that objects manifest some properties because they enter into certain specific physical relations dictated by the laws.

3) Modesty

The program of the ontic structural realist is dictated by the virtue of 'modesty', which captures two important aspects: humility while inferring the structure of the world and parsimony of ontological commitments. Humility consists in recognizing and rejecting what is beyond our epistemic domain, while parsimony is a

---

[146] For a discussion of the principle of indiscernibles, see Dorato & Morganti, 2013.
[147] This depends on the OSR version that is under consideration.

criterion that should guide us in the application of Occam's razor. Both are crucial ingredients in helping us to avoid any problem of underdetermination. First of all, we need to recognize which claims we are entitled to commit to and which claims we are not entitled to commit to. Moreover, we need to keep our ontology parsimonious and as unambitious as possible. These two strategies help us to avoid any commitments to underdetermined ontological claims. This means that the ontic structuralist wants to minimize all the ontological commitments and to endorse only those that are needed for the theory to work in the physical world. I am sure that this may sound vague and arbitrary and needs to be spelled out in more detail. I think that Chakravartty (1998) helps us better reformulate the ontic structuralist application of the principle of 'modesty'. He writes:

> We must turn to the equations with which we attempt to capture phenomenal regularities, and ask: what do these mathematical relations minimally demand? We must consider not what possible metaphysical pictures are consistent with these equations, but rather what kinds of property attributions are essential to their satisfaction – consider not what is possible, but what is required. (Chakravartty, 1998, as cited in French, 2014, p. 61)

Whenever we infer the ontology from the laws, we should not ask what is 'compatible' or 'consistent' with the formalism, but what ontological features are necessary (essential) for the laws to be satisfied. In Faraday's words: "Why then assume the existence of that of which we are ignorant [. . .] and for which there is no philosophical necessity?" (Faraday, 1844, p. 291).

Therefore, OSR accepts only the metaphysical stances that are minimally required for the interpretation of our theory. In a nutshell, according to the OSR,

> #All things being equal, we should prefer the most parsimonious ontology.

This is not only a very useful principle to get rid of all redundant entities – it is also crucial because it is connected to the main point of the ontic structural realist program delineated above, namely that the epistemology should draw the boundaries of our metaphysics. Given this, the main aim of OSR is not to create gaps between the epistemology and the metaphysics: "Humility is handled by eliminating the inaccessible posits whose existence opens this gap between metaphysics and epistemology" (French, 2014, p. 60). It is exactly through this gap, indeed, that the problem of underdetermination sneaks in.

Up to now, we have dealt with the family of principles that help us close the gap between epistemology and metaphysics. But we are still left with the question of how exactly we should infer this ontology, and this is addressed by further methodological principles.

4) The Mathematics and the Physical World

In the section on the methodology adopted by the realists, we argued against their failure at distinguishing between what 'represents' and 'what is represented'. While the former is normally in the realm of mathematical formalism, the latter is in the physical realm of our world. Sometimes the mathematical object and the physical one are in a one-to-one correspondence, but sometimes they are not. Structural realism has been charged with the same accusation, i. e. it does not differentiate the mathematical structure from the physical structure, since it blurs the distinction between the mathematical structure of the equations figuring in the laws and the physical picture of the world.

Actually, French and Ladyman seem to have been guilty of this sort of blurring: "The structural dissolution of physical objects leads to a blurring of the line between the mathematical and the physical" (French & Ladyman, 2003, p. 41).

Indeed, if the ontology does not contain objects that instantiate relations, it seems that we cannot really differentiate between the relations instantiated in the world physically and the relations that our mathematics formulate. As I claimed before, OSR may sound like a Pythagorean view (the world is a mathematical structure) and a Platonist view at the same time (we are realist about mathematical structures). However, despite those controversial claims, the OSR methodological program is quite coherent and in line with what we defended previously when arguing against the realists. This can be demonstrated with the following quotation from French:

> It is through the mathematical presentation of the relevant features of scientific theories that the structures we are interested in can be identified and thus, at that level, the mathematics is only playing a representational role, rather than a metaphysically constitutive one. The metaphysical nature of the structure of the world should not be identified with its mode of presentation. (French, 2014, p. 11)

Hence, OSR aims to retain the distinction between what represents and what is represented. The objection sometimes put forward is that it does not succeed, and the charge is that it cannot succeed because it does not have the means. This is because, as we have seen above, it cannot differentiate the mathematical features from the physical features of the world once it denies the existence of objects. But in this work we will try our best to keep the distinction, and we will show that at least some moderate versions of OSR have the tools to do so. This clear distinction between the way mathematics presents the physical world and the ontology itself avoids the danger of reifying mathematical objects.

5) Objectivity and Invariance

We already mentioned invariance as the criterion we should use in order to decide whether a mathematical object/structure is objective and whether it should be taken as revealing the structure of reality. Objectivity is not built on the presupposition that there is a mind-independent reality 'out there'; on the contrary, it is constituted by inter-subjectivity, given by invariance under different 'observations'. The connection between invariance and objectivity is given, very simply, by the fact that what is 'invariant under different observations' is really accessible through different ways of observation, and, for this reason, it is possible to formulate a universal agreement on its nature, which is irrespective of the different perspectives and ways that set up our observation. Think, for example, of physical systems where the invariant quantities indicate the real structure of the space where the theory is formulated. Those invariant quantities do not depend on our coordinate transformations, nor do they depend on any other arbitrary descriptive tools. Whenever we transform one allowable coordinate-dependent description of the system into another, those quantities remain invariant under those transformations. For instance, that there is a distance between two points is a fact that is independent of whether we are using Euclidean or angular coordinates.

In this regard, OSR matches Cassirer's view of objectivity as 'de-anthropomorphized' conception of reality:

> It is no longer the existence of particular entities, definite permanencies propagating in space and time, that forms "the ultimate stratum of objectivity" but rather "the invariance of relations between magnitudes". (Cassirer, 1957, p. 476, as cited in French, 2104, p. 91)

In this process of 'de-anthropomorphization', the role of a relational conception of nature, which refuses a substantive understanding of those entities that are far away from our epistemic domain, is crucial.

6) Modality

There is another fundamental aspect that OSR upholds as pillar of its methodology. It may seem that all this insistence on parsimony and modesty may lead directly to a Super-Humean ontology where there are only matter points without any properties, and where laws (and what we might categorize as modal entities) supervene on the particles' motions. But OSR is committed to another principle that can be stated as follows:

> **All things being equal, it is preferable to have an ontology with modality, rather than an ontology without modality.[148]

According to OSR, modality is in the world, since the relations that describe the laws of nature are modal relations. We will spell out in detail the character of modality later in our applications to the Bohmian case. Now it would be methodologically misleading to dictate the nature of modality without having a scientific theory as our reference point. Even though Esfeld (2009, p. 179) criticizes French for not specifying the features of modality, this, I think, can only be done case by case.

5.3.2 Summing up: The 'Danglers'

Now I want to sum up all the discussions on the ontic structuralist methodology in a simple principle:

> ***All things being equal, it is rational to prefer a theory without danglers rather than a theory with danglers.

The term 'danglers' is used by Dasgupta (2009) to refer to those entities of a theory that are both unobservable and redundant. This definition of dangler, however, is certainly too broad, and many philosophers, not only ontic structural realists, would subscribe to the above principle. This section aims to illustrate the characterization of 'danglers' in light of ontic structural realism. According to the structuralist view, 'danglers' are all those entities that, given their epistemic inaccessibility, create a gap between the epistemic domain and the ontological domain and, for this reason, are good candidates for a case of metaphysical underdetermination. They are all those ontological entities that do not constitute our objective reality because they are not purged of any anthropomorphized character. Finally, they do not constitute the minimal ontology that is essential for the understanding of the theory: their redundant character makes them unnecessary elements of the ontology. Danglers are those theoretical and unobservable entities that are normally put in the theory in order to explain some observable or predictable phenomena; moreover, most of the time, their mathematical structure is coordinate-dependent.

---

148 See, for example, Ladyman & Ross, 2007: "We will argue that the marriage of scientific realism and Humeanism about modality is an unhappy one" (p. 79).

5.3.3 An Example: The Aether

I think it would be a good idea to provide a very quick example of 'danglers' that have populated our theories. This example will turn out to be useful in our evaluation of the status of the wave-function in Bohmian mechanics. One of the most blatant danglers in the history of physics was for sure the luminiferous aether,[149] which was first proposed by Descartes for purely philosophical difficulties, which involved the definition of void and then discarded by Einstein with his general relativity. The aether was postulated in order to understand all the transmission of gravitational effects such as Newtonian action at a distance and electromagnetic effects such as the traveling of light, Faraday's lines of force, and Maxwell's electromagnetic waves. The idea supporting the notion of aether was that it is impossible to think of transmissions of physical forces in an empty, void space. If the space between two masses is void, i. e. there is nothing between them, how is it possible for those two masses to interact? If we think of the Newtonian gravitational force, we might think that the 'force' is a transmission of small particles that hit a body. But in this case, we have to postulate the existence of 'particles' in the space, particles that 'move'. In case we think of 'waves' traveling through space, then we need to understand 'waves' as vibrations, but a process of vibration can happen if and only if there is a medium that can be 'distorted'. The aether, in a nutshell, was introduced to be the material 'transmitter' of physical interactions. It served many scientific theories, and it acquired a long list of different physical properties in order to satisfy all the cases where its presence was needed. But the firm belief in the aether started to lose strength when Maxwell, with his electromagnetic theory, and Einstein, with his general relativity, proved that it was possible to understand the space itself as the place of physical transmissions and perturbations. Given that the space could play the same role that the aether was playing, why bother introducing the aether? The aether suddenly became a superfluous, redundant entity, just an invented name to support the verb 'undulate'. Ontic structural realists suggest that we should not believe in these kinds of entities in the first place. Their strategy is to focus the attention not on the substantial character that those entities might have (whether they are molecules or fields) but to the relations that they bring into the scene, and to be realist about those relations. Our discussion of Bohmian mechanics in the next chapter will provide an example of what I have been proposing.

---

149 See Worrall, 1994 for a discussion of the aether and ontic structural realism.

6 Bohmian Mechanics and Ontic Structural Realism

In this chapter, I will turn to Bohmian mechanics and investigate what its resulting ontology would be if we applied the ontic structural realist methodological program. Our main guiding questions will be the following: does Bohmian mechanics turn out to present a structuralist ontology in line with OSR? If so, what kind of OSR? In order to answer those questions, several steps are needed.

6.1 The Problem of Underdetermination Given by the Wave-function

My first step consists in analyzing the status of the wave-function. In particular, I would like to inquire whether the wave-function could be considered by the structural realist as a 'dangler' in Bohmian mechanics.

First of all, it is worthwhile stressing that whatever we know about the wave-function is gained via indirect access, mediated through the particles' behavior (Maudlin, 2013). Moreover, we have seen that there are no empirical grounds that may constrain a specific ontological interpretation of the wave-function instead of another. The only thing we know about it is that it determines a particular particle velocity, and as we saw while discussing the nomological view, the wave-function is the simplest mathematical object we have in order to specify a vector field. But this, *pace* the realists, does not tell us anything about the ontological interpretation.[150]

Given this, there is a gap between the epistemic domain of our information about the wave-function and the metaphysical interpretation of its ontological status. Any metaphysical interpretation would always imply more than what we could ever know. Through this huge gap, the problem of underdetermination sneaks inside the theory in a very significant way. Indeed, the different metaphysical status that we could attribute not only shows that the wave-function could be a physical entity or a nomological entity, but also that we are completely unaware of fundamental features, for instance whether the wave-function is time-dependent or time-independent.

Maudlin addresses this very same point regarding the quantum state in general:

---

[150] See chapter 3 for a discussion on this topic.

> We agree that we do not know enough about the quantum state to determine even the most generic features of its behavior. But then we are in no position to make reliable pronouncements about what it is. We do not even know the right general ontological category in which to put it. (Maudlin, 2013, p. 151)

Given our scarce knowledge of the wave-function, it is not even possible to categorize it without any arbitrariness, since different categories would be equally good.

6.2 Is the Wave-function a Dangler?

I take it that this metaphysical underdetermination gives us prima facie grounds for thinking that the wave-function is a dangler and should be handled with particular care.[151] However, unobservability and underdetermination are necessary but not sufficient criteria for establishing whether an entity is a dangler. We also need to check whether the wave-function is dependent on any arbitrary mathematical representation, and whether it is redundant. Concerning the first feature, I think that our discussion in chapter 3 was already very clear: the wave-function does depend on an arbitrary mathematical representation, since it is almost 'glued' in configuration space. Concerning redundancy, in order to assess whether the wave-function is redundant if considered as part of the ontology, we have also seen that it is possible to have an ontology without the 3ND physical field. In particular, we have seen that the nomological view develops an ontology without appealing to any physical field. For this reason, I argue that it is redundant. However, it is also true that the ontology proposed by the nomological view turned out to be quite unsatisfactory for several reasons.

In the following sections, we will inquire into another parsimonious ontology that does not postulate a 3ND field, one that is developed according to ontic structural realism. Our main focus will be to investigate how the structural realists interpret the wave-function, while only few sections will be dedicated to the particles. Our structuralist ontological interpretation will be the result of a methodological work that follows the principles presented in the previous part of this chapter (coordinate transformation invariance, parsimony/modesty, and laws and physics should inform metaphysics). First of all, we are going to explain why, according to the ontic structural realist, the wave-function does not represent an entity living in 3ND. The

---

[151] According to Max Deutsch (private correspondence), the question of whether the wave-function is a dangler should be better formulated as the question of whether the wave-function as physical wave-field in 3ND 'dangles'. However, I believe that in the literature, this way of presenting the issue is widely accepted.

argument we will use still concerns the invariance under coordinate transformation, but it will be slightly different from the one presented in chapter 3 and, we hope, richer and more convincing. After this, we will ask whether the wave-function represents anything at all, and if so what.

6.3 The Problem of Invariance and Objectivity: What the Wave-function Represents Cannot Be in 3ND

In this section, I will suggest that if we applied the principle of invariance endorsed by OSR, we would have to reject any commitment to the 3ND space, hence we would have to reject the idea that the wave-function represents a physical field in 3ND (as the realists claim).

In our discussion of the OSR methodology, we presented the view according to which invariant quantities should be taken to reveal the real structure of the world. In particular, we looked at the view according to which invariant quantities should be taken to indicate what the real space is, and what objects and symmetries are there in the world. We can divide the mathematical structures into three different categories: the coordinate structure, which helps us localize a mathematical object, the coordinate-dependent mathematical structures, and the coordinate-independent mathematical structures. Only the latter reveals the objective nature of our physical world.[152] In the case of Bohmian mechanics, we have seen in chapter 3 that the wave-function is not a coordinate-invariant mathematical structure. Indeed, we saw that if we shift one coordinate axis of the configuration space (such as translating the axis five meters up), the resulting wave-function may differ so significantly that it may not obey the Schrödinger equation anymore.

But there is a further point that creates a serious problem that is worth spelling out with an example. Suppose that we have a fixed correspondence between our 3D axes on the one hand (which identify the mathematical space of our particles) and the 3ND configuration space axes on the other, such that we may label the 3ND axes in this way:

$$\{x_1, y_1, z_1, x_2, y_2, z_2\}$$

where the numbers label the three-dimensional particle position, while 'x', 'y' and 'z' label the axis-coordinates of our Euclidean space (so that x_1 corresponds to the 3D x-axis coordinate of a particle position identified by '1', y_1 corresponds to the 3D y-axis coordinate of the same particle position identified by 1, and so on). All

---

[152] Our example was the distance between two points in a Euclidean space.

the different 'x's, 'y's and 'z's – one for each particle – constitute the axes of the 3ND space, and all the coordinates $x_1, y_1, z_1, x_2, y_2, z_2 \ldots$ pick out several particles' positions in 3D, hence a particle configuration that consists of different particles located in different 3D positions. We know from chapter 1 that all these coordinates pick out one 3ND point that corresponds to all the 3D particle positions. Given this, we could say that the configuration space is only a convenient descriptive or representative space of our physical space. It allows us to conveniently represent all the particles' positions with one point in 3ND. However, if we change one and only one of these coordinates (e. g. x_1), the particles' dynamics in 3D will differ: the particles will take other trajectories and they will be related by different entanglement relations. But this seems strange. The 3ND coordinates are representative coordinates for the 3D system. How is it possible that the particles' dynamics change only because we change one axis of the 3ND coordinates? According to the principle of coordinate invariance, any arbitrary change of the coordinate system should not change the physical system.

The obvious, intuitive answer would be to notice that the change of one 3ND axis, let's say 'x', corresponds to a change of only one particle's 'x' axis and not all the particles' 'x' axes.[153] Since the Hamiltonian is not invariant to that kind of 3ND coordinate change (Lewis, 2004; Albert, 1996), it dictates a completely different dynamics of the wave-function, depending on any 3ND transformation. And since the wave-function, in turn, determines a particular entanglement between the particles, different Hamiltonians dictate different evolutions of the wave-function and different particle entanglement. But the structural realist wants laws to be the guide to our ontological interpretations, and given that invariance needs to be a requirement for objectivity, our laws must be invariant if they are supposed to reveal the objective features of our world. Changing the laws of Bohmian mechanics, however, turns out to be inconvenient, since they are the simplest we could ever achieve (see chapter 4 for a discussion of this point). In the following, we will investigate another strategy.

Suppose that we change not only the first 3ND coordinate x_1 but all the 3ND coordinates x (x_1, x_2, x_3), such that this amounts to a transformation of one axis in 3D for all the particles. In this case, the Hamiltonian turns out to be translationally invariant. Hence, the dynamics of the wave-function will not change

---

153 A first reaction would be to think that the change in the particles' dynamics is due the fact that the translation of one axis is such that the 3ND coordinates pick up another particle configuration in the 3D space. This is certainly right. But the issue here is that, even if we do not suppose a rigid correspondence between the 3ND and the 3D spaces, we are still forced to admit it, if we want to keep our laws invariant under arbitrary transformations. More specifically, we are forced to admit that the 3ND space is not an autonomous physical space.

and, at the same time, the particle entanglement will not undergo any change. What we did was to change the coordinates in such a way that our dynamical laws are translationally invariant. In particular, our coordinate transformations of the 3ND space leaves the potential that figures in the Hamiltonian invariant, and the reason for this is that the 3ND transformations respect the 3D symmetries, and the potential in the Hamiltonian is invariant under 3D symmetries.

Strictly speaking, in order to keep our laws invariant for 3ND coordinate transformations, we need to treat the 3ND space as if it was not really a 3ND space with all the coordinates independent of one another.[154] In conclusion, in order to keep our laws 'invariant', we do not change the laws, but we have to reduce all the possible different translations we can have in 3ND to the set of possible translations we have in 3D. But this, obviously, amounts to reducing the 3ND space to the 3D space. In order to have invariant laws, the degrees of freedom of the system are reduced from 3ND to 3D. Lewis (2013) suggests that while the wave-function and the configuration space may be said to be specified by 3ND parameters, only three of them are strictly speaking spatial.

To sum up, if we keep invariance as revealing the physical structure of the world, then we have to give up the configuration space as the real space of our objective reality. The only way to keep our laws invariant is to treat our 3ND space as 3D.

Our argument can be summed up in the following two arguments. Both arguments show, in slightly different ways (one focusing on the invariance of laws, the other of quantities), the incompatibility between the OSR commitment to the role that invariance should play in our ontological interpretations and the 3ND space-realism. Hence, both arguments show that, if we endorse OSR, we cannot claim that the wave-function lives in 3ND space.

1° Argument:
    Premise (1): Either we give up our invariant laws, or our space is 3D.
    Premise (2): According to ontic structural realists, our laws of nature need to
            be invariant.
    Conclusion: According to ontic structural realists, our space is 3D.

2° Argument:
    Premise (1): If we are realist about the 3ND space, we should give up the invariance criterion.
    Premise (2): Structural realists do not want to give up our invariance criterion.
    Conclusion: Structural realists cannot be realist about the 3ND space.

---

[154] For a similar discussion, see Albert, 1996; Lewis, 2004.

The question at stake now is the following. If 3ND is not a physical space, as postulated by the theory (because if it were, then the laws would not be invariant under arbitrary translations), then either the wave-function does not represent anything, or the entity represented by the wave-function must be in 3D space. What is the wave-function? Is it just a mathematical tool? If not, what does it represent in 3ND according to the structural realists?

6.4 What the Laws Reveal

The second question we should ask is whether the ontic structural realist would be happy to regard the wave-function as insignificant, as a mere mathematical tool useful for the theory to achieve empirical adequacy. I claim that the ontic structural realists would reject the idea that the (universal) wave-function does not represent anything and that it is just a merely mathematical object, devoid of any physical significance. The reason is that the wave-function is a fundamental ingredient of the dynamical laws[155] and, according to structural realism, laws are the features of reality. Take the guiding law of motion and the Schrödinger equation. In both equations, the wave-function plays a crucial role: if we took away the wave-function, the laws would not be informative at all.

In order to get a clear idea about the specific role of the (universal) wave-function, we can check what happens if we try to reformulate the laws of Bohmian mechanics without using it.

As we saw in chapter 3, the wave-function can be replaced; hence, the pillar equations can be rewritten by substituting the universal wave-function with other mathematical objects. Specifically, according to Norsen (2010), the wave-function can be replaced with a (countable) infinite number of entanglement fields associated with the effective wave-functions of the particles.[156] As we have seen, it would be impossible to retain the empirical predictability of the theory only with the effective wave-functions, without those entanglement fields. This means that the entanglement relations described by those fields are exactly the features of reality that the universal wave-function, *qua* part of the laws, represents.[157] Regardless of the particular formulation of the laws adopted, the Bohmian laws depict entanglement relations as features of reality, either via the mathematical object called the wave-function or via the mathematical objects called entanglement fields. The

---

155 For discussion about this point, refer to chapter 3.
156 The wavefunction can also be regarded as a multi-field (Hubert & Romano, 2018).
157 Even within the multi-field view, the behaviour of a given configuration of particles is intrinsically non-local.

guiding law of motion shows that the velocity of the particles' configuration is given by the kinds of interdependent relations obtaining between the particles, which are given by the wave-function. Hence, the relations that capture the interest of the structural realists are fundamentally spelled out by the wave-function. Given this crucial role of the wave-function in the law, given its unique role in shaping the relations between the particles, it is right to say that it carves the world at its joints by revealing the kinds of relations obtaining in our physical space. The role of the wave-function, indeed, is to map each particle position to all the other particles' positions for each time to a complex number.[158] Therefore, its physical significance is to build dynamical relations of interdependence between particles' positions in 3D.

One consideration that is worth examining is the following. The fact that the wave-function can be replaced – and so that we could have a different formulation of the laws of motion and of the Schrödinger equation – is not important to the structural realist, since both reformulations depict the very same feature of reality. This shows an interesting insight into the advantages of structural realism, which is worth spelling out with a comparison between the structural realist attitude and the realist one.

If we compare both attitudes, it is clear that the structural realist one is better. The realist needs to know the exact formulation of the laws in order to infer the reality of the world (hence whether the laws should be reformulated with the universal wave-function or entanglements fields), because her methodology in interpreting the ontology rests upon a process of reification (the realist reads off the ontology from the mathematics). By contrast, the structural realist only focuses on the relation that the laws spell out. Regardless of whether the guiding law is formulated in terms of the universal wave-function or in terms of the effective wave-functions plus the entanglement fields, the structure on which the structural realist focuses is the same. The difference between the realists and the structural realists may be more clearly elucidated as follows.

Realists focus on what is needed in order to write down the laws of motion for a theory – in other words, they look at the mathematical objects that are necessary for the laws to be predictive, and then they take those objects at face value and they reify them (i. e. they interpret those mathematical objects as physical objects). Realists adopt a literal approach. For instance, in the case of the wave-function, they start from the guiding law, they look at the wave-function as a collection of values of a multi-dimensional space, and they argue that the wave-function is essential and

---

[158] Within the multi-field view, The multi-field is a non-local beable that assigns properties to all N-tuples of points of space (Hubert & Romano, 2018).

fundamental in order to write down the guiding law of motion. Given its fundamental and essential character, according to their methodology, we should be realist about that mathematical field as a collection of values in the configuration space and regard it as a physical field. Now, the resulting ontology would be completely different if we took Norsen's formulation of the guiding law as the 'true' formulation. In this case, indeed, we would take the different conditional wave-functions, along with the entanglement fields, as constituting the physical ontology, and the ontology would turn out to consist of exclusively local beables. For this reason, it is of crucial importance for the realist to establish which formulation is the true one.[159] In order to do this, we suggested that the realist could endorse a sort of Humean fundamentalism, according to which we should take the simplest and most informative laws to be spelling out the fundamental ontological entities. However, we argued that this is certainly debatable and it depends on the kind of metaphysical stance of laws one endorses.

The ontological interpretation of the structural realist, in contrast, does not rely on a particular formalism; hence, the structural realist does not need to choose between competing formulations of the same laws. Differences in the formalism are not ontologically significant. Indeed, the structural realist focuses not on the mathematical objects that are needed to formulate the theory, but on the resulting structure. As a result, the structuralist has an advantage over the realist. This is what Brading claims:[160]

> Now consider the proposal offered by the ontic structural realist. She says: pay attention not to the mathematical devices that seem unavoidable in making it possible to write down the theory; pay attention instead to the resulting structures. (Brading & Skiles, 2012, p. 15)

The structuralist ontology is not derived from a reification of a particular formulation of the Bohmian laws (whether expressed in terms of the wave-function or in terms of entanglement fields) – rather, it must be compatible with more different mathematical formulations because it underpins what all the different formulations agree on. In this way, the structuralist ontology must be obviously more modest and parsimonious since it cannot include all the features that correspond to the differences in the mathematical formulations, i. e. those aspects that may be an issue for different ways of formulating the theory. It includes only the minimum ontological commitment it can take. In the case of Bohmian mechanics, we take it that the entanglement relations constitute the minimum ontological commitment. Moreover,

---

[159] For the same considerations, see chapter 3.
[160] The following quotation is taken from a first version of Brading & Skiles, 2012 (last accessed 13.03.2017, URL: https://www.kbrading.org/papers).

by committing to a minimalistic ontology, the structural realist successfully closes the gap between the epistemic domain and the ontological one. It only commits to what the laws of the theory reveal and nothing else. The ontology is restricted to what we know through the laws of nature.

To recapitulate, we have seen that the ontic structural realist rejects the fact that the wave-function is a 3ND field because 3ND space cannot be taken as a physical space, otherwise our laws would be not invariant under coordinate transformations. However, the ontic structural realist still wants to attribute ontological salience to the wave-function, given its primary role in the laws of nature. And we claimed that the role of the wave-function is to represent entanglement relations.[161] Indeed, if we substituted the universal wave-function with effective wave-functions, we would have to add entanglement fields.

One may think that the structural realist could also be happy with an ontology of only local beables, of only local fields, plus entanglement fields, as in the picture described by Norsen (2010). While it is true that we could, in theory, regard the wave-function as representing wave-fields and entanglement fields in 3D, this would create a gap between the epistemology and the ontology. Consequently, this would certainly constitute a case of underdetermination. In the same way we do not know enough about the wave-function in order to give a particular ontological interpretation, we do not know enough about those fields. Moreover, it would lead to a less parsimonious ontology, given that we would need an infinite number of entanglement fields plus one field for each particle, adding fields in the ontology. Lastly, a collection of entangled and non-entangled fields is certainly redundant. The nomological view has shown, indeed, that it is possible to understand the dynamics of the particles without bringing any external physical entity in the ontology. In the following section, I will spell out the characterizations of the entanglement relations.

6.5 Modality

In the previous section, we claimed that our wave-function represents entanglement relations. Now it will be our endeavor to characterize this structure (constituted by entanglement relations). The first characterization we should give is that it is a *concrete and physical* structure, for the following reasons:

---

[161] Notice that regarding the wave-function as representing entanglement relations was briefly suggested in Esfeld et al., 2015 and in Esfeld, 2015. Moreover, this structuralist reading has been defended by Lam (2015). However, given that we reach the same conclusion by very taking different paths, I will discuss their views only later, when addressing the status of the particles.

1) *It is instantiated by physical objects*: The entanglement relations are instantiated by the Bohmian particles, which play the role of their 'bearers'.
2) *It lives in our space-time*: The entanglement relations are instantiated in our space-time, since they connect particles that live in our space-time.
3) *It is empirically detectable* (although indirectly): Experiments performed on the particles reveal the presence of their entanglement relations.

Moreover, we should characterize this structure as *holistic*, for the following reasons:
1) *It does not supervene on any intrinsic property of the particles*: The structure cannot be reduced to any intrinsic properties of the particles. A change in the structure does not imply a change in the particles' intrinsic properties.
2) This structure is *non-separable*: It is impossible to break this structure into different one-to-one particle relations. The whole network of entanglement relations is not conceivable as the sum of different one-to-one relations between any two particles. On the contrary, the structure takes all the particles together as a whole.

This is clearly manifest in the fact that no matter how we reformulate the laws, the same entangled structure is always depicted.

Moreover, we know that we can characterize structures as modal or non-modal. For example, non-modal structure are space-time structures.
3) The structure is *modal*: It constrains and determines the dynamics of the particles.

Any entity that constrains or determines another entity is modal. But how should we spell out its modality?

The first step would obviously be to regard it as *nomological*. After all, its identity is given precisely by its nomological role, i. e. how it nomologically determines the particle motions. Here, however, we have to clarify the following. We said in our discussion on the reality of the wave-function that different wave-functions, related through gauge transformations, give rise to the same empirical scenario (that is, to the same particle dynamics). Hence, we were doubting the physicality of the wave-function. For this reason, it is better to underline that, from an ontic structural perspective, we take the structure not as entertaining a one-to-one correspondence with the wave-function. On the contrary, a group of equivalent wave-functions, all related through trivial transformations (gauge and coordinate transformations), represents the same structure. This way, the ontic structuralist assumes that the structure is unique in determining the particle dynamics, which means that:

> \# There cannot be two different structures that, given the same initial particle positions, determine the same entire evolution of the universe in all circumstances.

This way, the uniqueness of the structure is safeguarded, and it is possible to define its identity through the resulting particle dynamics it generates. Moreover, we safeguarded the invariant principle and we are safe from any arbitrariness or underdetermination objection: there is no gap between the epistemic domain and the metaphysical one.

Now the question is whether this structure of entanglement relations is sufficiently explanatorily powerful. We have seen in chapter 4 that a nomological character is not completely satisfactory. Moreover, given that the relations are concrete, it is not the case that they are merely nomological. Should we say that they are causal?

The relations are nomological given that they are spelled out by the laws, but they are also concrete, physical, and causal. They do not bring about the motion in an abstract way, but are concretely and dynamically involved in the physical system.

In this scenario, the entanglement relations have the causal seat that we would normally attribute to the particles. This ontological interpretation should cast new light on the problem of the absence of back-reaction in Bohmian mechanics that we discussed in chapter 3. Let me restate what the problem was. According to the realists, the wave-function is causally connected to the particles, as a physical entity. However, it violates the principle of back-reaction, which all physical entities are expected to respect. Indeed, the particles do not back-react on the wave-function. How is this possible? In an ontic structural realist scenario, this problem no longer arises because it does not present two physical objects as acting on one another through causal relations. By contrast, in the structuralist scenario, the relations among the particles have a primitive modality, while the particles have a derivative modality. There is no causal mechanistic force involved. It is the modality of the wave-function that confers modality to the particles. This way of conferring modality from the structure to the particles is very similar to the nomological one. However, here the relations are concrete and physical, they are dynamical, and this way there is no gap between the entity that confers modality and the receivers. In sum, in this scenario, there is no external entity with which the particles interact (whether physical or nomological). By contrast, the relations are themselves, with their laws, the primitive active principles. In Bohmian mechanics, contrary to the Newtonian case, laws do not support the back-reaction principle for the simple fact that the evolution of the relations among the particles is fundamental and not derivative; in other words, it is primary and not determined by them. Once again, particles appear to be causally inert as in the realist case, but this is not a problem because there is no entity on which they are supposed to react back; by contrast, the particles are dependent on the web of relations spelled out by the laws of the theory.

However, there is still a problem. The problem is that even if we may be happy to concede that the entanglement relations do constitute the active principles for the motions of the particles, it is still not clear why those relations change in time, given that they are not back-reacted by the particles. The Bohmian particles are not seats of causation.

This worry is not strictly related to the Bohmian scenario, but it is a general threat for OSR, given that normally OSR rules out any ontology of particles. One of the proponents of this worry is Chakravartty. While arguing against OSR, Chakravartty (2003) claims that "given a concrete instance of some set of relations, we have no explanation for what constitutes the active principle that transforms this set of relations into another" (p. 872). Later he goes on: "Unable to supply these missing links, OSR thus runs afoul of the explanatory-role principle. Hence there is a gap of explanation" (p. 872). This particular worry[162] concerns the active principle that transforms the set of relations from one to another. Applying this worry to Bohmian mechanics, our theory seems to be explanatorily wanting because it does not account for what changes the network of entanglement relations between the particles so that at time t_1 is S_1 and at time t_2 is S_2. There is no explanation for what constitutes the active principle that transforms the relations among the particles S_1 at time t_1 to the structure S_2 at time t_2. In a classical scenario, objects constitute the 'active principle' that transforms the relations between entities. Take the case of two charges: the relations between the two charges, expressed in Coulomb's law as a force change depend on the properties of the charges (their magnitude, their sign, their position). But what about the relations expressed by the wave-function? What can change them? Since in Bohmian mechanics it is clear that particles are not – and cannot! – be these active principles, given that the evolution of the wave-function is free and not determined by them (see chapter 2 and 3, where we said that the wave-function is a free function that is not determined by the evolution of the particles), it is not clear what entity can provide this active principle.

This worry, however, does not apply to Bohmian mechanics if we endorse the commitments of ontic structural realism. According to ontic structural realism, we should regard objects as causally powerless and inefficient – that is, no longer as the seats of causal power – and instead take the laws and nomological relations as causal. In this regard, the Schrödinger equation plays the role of active principle in

---

[162] The criticism by Chakravartty is much more extensive than this little worry. However, here we will consider only this one.

Bohmian mechanics, causing a particular evolution of the entanglement relations between the particles. This obviously does not mean that the Schrödinger equation *causes* the wave-function to change through time and to evolve the way it does. We cannot take the law to be the seat of causation in the same way objects would be.[163] But in a certain and limited way, we can and we should. French presents the view in the following way:

> Does the Hamiltonian in Schrödinger's equation cause the wave-function to evolve in the way it does? Even in Newtonian physics [. . .] can Newton's third law be regarded as causal? [. . .] It would seem that, at first glance at least, one cannot say that it is not the case that Schrödinger's equation causes the wave-function to evolve in the way it does, or at least, not in anything like a thick sense. Still, this is causation in a thin sense. (French, 2014, p. 227)

Ontic structural realism replaces the classical mechanistic conception of causation with a 'thin' one, which is applicable to nomological entities and nomological relations, and empowers them as 'active principles'.

6.6 Particles, Properties and Structure

We will turn now to the question of the ontological status of properties. The discussion on the ontological status of scientific properties in Bohmian mechanics addressed two main problems.

The first concerned the underdetermination involving the ontological interpretations of properties. We presented the dilemma of whether we should endorse a 'generous' view, and attribute the properties both to the wave-function and to the particles, or the 'parsimonious' view, which regards the particles as property-less and the wave-function as instantiating all the properties. Both ontological interpretations face equally strong challenges that are difficult to solve. Therefore, it is impossible to endorse one instead of the other without an element of arbitrariness.

The latter was at the core of the status of properties. We saw that Bohmian properties do not match the classical Newtonian conception of scientific properties. Indeed, Bohmian properties are either contextual, or non-localized, since they can never be regarded as properties that 'follow' the particles along their trajectories in a continuous way and persistently in time. Indeed, we have seen from the spin-experiments that some properties suddenly change, leading the particles first to take one path and then to take another path, while the Brown

---

[163] For a discussion of this point, see French, 2014, p. 227.

experiments showed that properties such as mass, charge and angular momentum violate the localizability condition of properties (see chapter 2).

The first question we should ask is whether properties are true 'danglers' for the theory, and this amounts to asking two different questions: whether they are directly accessible by an epistemic agent and whether they are redundant.

Given that Bohmian mechanics presents two different kinds of properties, one that is contextual (like spin) and one that may be regarded as non-contextual and intrinsic (like mass), here I will separate the discussion accordingly.

Starting with contextual properties such as spin, let me recall how we measure them. Whenever we measure the observable of a contextual property like spin, we prepare an experiment where a system of interest and our measuring device are going to interact physically. However, the meaning of this interaction is not straightforward, yet it needs to be interpreted through the Bohmian theory. Given the theoretical system of Bohmian mechanics, we know that the result of any experiment depends on the initial conditions of the wave-function and of the particle configuration. Putting what I said more simply, and supposing that the system we are measuring consists of only one particle, we can say that the result of any experiment depends on 1) the position of the particle; 2) how the measuring device is set up; and 3) the form of the wave-function. These elements determine the trajectory of the particles and consequently what the result of the experiment is. Postulating the presence of properties in the system beyond position would commit us to redundancy. We have discussed all this in chapter 2, where we saw that how the apparatus is set up will involve property ascriptions to the properties. And this is already a first hint that tells us to be suspicious about scientific properties such as spin. This presentation of the spin property tells us that 1) spin-properties are not directly accessible (we access them through the particle position) and 2) spin-properties are redundant.

Concerning putative intrinsic properties such as mass, we may suppose that they are needed in our ontology because they explain why a particle takes one trajectory instead of another. Let us insist in particular that the reason why an electron goes to the right-hand side of our experimental device is in virtue of the fact that it has a particular cluster of intrinsic properties (mass, charge) that make us label it 'electron'. As I said before in chapter 2, the reason why we may want to label it 'electron' is that it behaves in some sort of way under some circumstances. And our properties like mass have been introduced in the theory through their causal role, which is supposed to be the role of triggering a particular motion. Again, what we do know are the causal relations that correlate the particular cluster of properties with the motion. These causal relations are given by the guiding law of motion. This, obviously, does not mean that intrinsic properties do not exist! Nor does it mean that we should consider intrinsic properties as 'danglers'. However, it is important to stress this, since inaccessibility is one necessary criterion for an entity to be considered a dangler.

The second problem of properties is redundancy. In order to see why intrinsic properties are redundant, however, we first need to spell out another problem, generated by indirect access: the problem of underdetermination. The gap between what we know (the entanglement relations) and what is there in the world (the intrinsic nature of particles) can bring up two scenarios (Jackson, 1998; Esfeld, 2015). In the first scenario, given the gap between the intrinsic properties and the relational properties, there might be different intrinsic properties with the same causal profile, meaning that they instantiate the same kind of relation (a causal-nomological relation). In this respect, two different objects, which instantiate two different intrinsic properties, may have the same kind of relations. The problem in this scenario is that we would never get to know whether this is the case, because we would just know the relations that objects have with one another. As such, we would fall into the problem of underdetermination. In addition to this, if we actually had two systems with different intrinsic properties but the same dynamical relations, we would have to count two different scenarios despite their indistinctness. In a nutshell, even if we had two different systems, the difference between them would be undetectable because the difference in their intrinsic properties does not make any difference in the end! This scenario would provide an uncomfortable situation for the ontic structural realist, who does not want to commit themselves to any case of underdetermination! So, let us keep the intrinsic properties but let us also endorse the view that it is impossible to have a scenario where different intrinsic properties instantiate the same relations. In this second scenario, the causal profile of the properties and the intrinsic properties are tied together. But then, why should we keep them both in our ontology?

It is clear that intrinsic properties are redundant. We have seen that OSR is committed to the parsimonious view and the modesty principle. In virtue of the modesty principle, which rejects the commitment to claims vulnerable to underdetermination and non-parsimonious ontology, it seems clear that the ontic structural realist has to step back and refute any commitment to intrinsic properties.

Particles seem to manifest some properties in virtue of the relations they entertain, but those properties are redundant and ungraspable and they create an issue of underdetermination; hence, according to OSR, we should not commit to their existence.[164]

---

[164] Remember that, according to OSR, we should commit only to those ontological entities and features whose difference make a difference for our epistemic knowledge.

6.7 The Individuality of Particles

Up to now, we have inquired into the ontological status of the wave-function and of the properties. What we found is that both the wave-function and the properties are danglers according to the realist, and for this reason they both need to be reconceptualized through a structuralist perspective. The question we should now turn to is whether a structuralist methodology would push us to eliminate not only the 3ND physical field and the properties, but also the Bohmian particles as point-like individuals. This way, only one entity would remain: the structure. Recall that the structural realist methodology targets danglers, i. e. entities that are redundant, not directly accessible and that create issues of underdetermination. Given this, I do not think that the individuality of particles should be considered an issue here, as long as we adopt a reductivist anti-Leibnizian notion of individuality – that is, as long as we can reduce individuality to the spatio-temporal properties of the particles. If we reject any form of primitivism about individuality, and we define individuality as nothing over and above the collection of all the properties (including spatio-temporal ones), then Bohmian particles are individuals. Indeed, we can rightly individuate and label different particles thanks to their trajectories. Just imagine that I have two property-less particulars in my pocket, and I present one of them first, then return it to my pocket. After that, I show the other one later: how do you know which one is which? The only way to know would be that you must be able to track their motion. Suppose that I put the first in my right pocket and I take the second out of my left pocket, then you know that I am showing you a different particle. Therefore, the fact that in Bohmian mechanics each particle has its own continuous trajectory cuts at the root of any doubt about their individuality.

Let me spell out in detail the discussion we are addressing. Whenever we have to establish the individuality of the particles, there are several notions of individuality to which we can appeal (Dorato & Morganti, 2013).

First of all, individuality may be regarded as a primitive concept. In this case, individuality is a fundamental concept, non-derivative and transcendental. This means that a particular is itself in virtue of an intrinsic and primitive property that makes it itself.

Alternatively, individuality may be regarded as a derivative concept. And in this case, there are several ways to spell it out:
- **Strong Individuality:** Individuality is a derivative concept, reducible to uniqueness of qualitative properties;
- **Moderate Individuality:** Individuality is a derivative concept, reducible to uniqueness of properties (where properties also include spatio-temporal properties);

- **Weak Individuality**: Individuality is a derivative concept, reducible to irreflexive relations.

In Bohmian mechanics, it is clear that if we rule out any primitive and strong account of individuality, and, by contrast, we admit that individuality is a derivative concept reducible to spatio-temporal properties, then Bohmian particles are individuals. This is possible given that Bohmian particles are always identified with their positions, for each instant of time (Esfeld, 2015; Lam, 2015).

Moreover, not only is each particle identified with its trajectory, but we can also classify particles and group them into different (non-fundamental and emergent) 'natural kinds' by examining the particular trajectory they would take in some experiments.

6.8 The Bohmian Ontology and Moderate Ontic Structural Realism

The important status of the Bohmian particles, which are considered proper individuals, reveals an ontology that is definitely incompatible with any strong version of ontic structural realism. Hence, the resulting picture we get, after applying a structuralist methodology to Bohmian mechanics, is in accordance with moderate ontic structural realism. Moderate ontic structural realism (MOSR) was introduced as a valid alternative to strong versions of OSR by Esfeld and Lam (2009). Their account of MOSR is based on two pillar points:

(1) Relations require relata (individuals);

(2) Relata do not necessarily have intrinsic properties over and above the relations that they entertain with one another.

This second claim, which was endorsed at first, has actually been replaced by a stronger one:

(3) All the properties of individual objects are relations to other objects.

Elaborating these two claims further, MOSR accepts the existence of objects in our fundamental ontology, but those objects are not characterized by intrinsic properties, in virtue of which they enter into relations. On the contrary, relations themselves are part of the fundamental ontology and intrinsic properties simply do not exist. Objects seem to instantiate intrinsic properties in virtue of the relations they instantiate. But, since intrinsic properties are, as we argued before, 'unknowable' and redundant, they do not constitute, according to the OSR methodological principles, our ontology.

Moreover, according to MOSR, objects and relations are on the same ontological and conceptual footing. Ontologically, this means that neither of them has an ontological priority over the other, and while relations cannot exist without objects, objects are nothing but what is in a relational structure. Moreover, this means that objects and relations are conceptually mutually dependent because, in the same way relata cannot be conceived without relations, relations cannot be conceived without their relata.

The dependence between relata and relations is normally spelled out in terms of identity conditions:

(4) The identity conditions for objects are provided by the relations they instantiate; the identity conditions for relations is provided by their relata.

Concerns may arise, however, regarding the identity of objects. Indeed, in the traditional object-oriented metaphysics, only intrinsic properties can constitute the identity conditions for individuals. This concern has been expressed by Chakravartty, among others:

> The non-eliminativist takes entities and their properties to be dependent on their relations (whether asymmetrically or symmetrically); their identities are relational: they are constituted by an extrinsic system of relations. But then a worry arises immediately. Can the identity of a particle depend solely on the relations on which it stands? Typically, on the standard metaphysical picture, intrinsic properties of entities play an important role in constituting identities, and one might wonder whether purely extrinsic characterizations can suffice in making such identities intelligible. (Chakravartty, 2015, p. 12)

In contrast, according to Esfeld and Lam (2008), it is legitimate to assume that the identity conditions are provided by the relations, given that those relations are regarded as physical and concrete. Concrete relations can fulfill the role of identifying an object and distinguishing it from others in the same way intrinsic properties do. For instance, if we consider three different objects A, B and C, we may want to identify B with the following sorts of claims: B is heavier than A but lighter than C; B is longer than C but shorter than A, and so on and so forth. In agreement with Esfeld and Lam, I do not see any reason why relations cannot provide identity conditions for objects (Esfeld & Lam, 2008).

Now let me recap. First, we argued that according to structural realism the wave-function is a dangler of the theory and, for this reason, cannot be reified. By contrast, according to a structural perspective, the wave-function mathematically represents entanglement relations in our three-dimensional space. Moreover, we have seen that, according to the structuralist methodology, while intrinsic[165] properties do not exist, particles do. We argued that the application of a stucturalist methodology to Bohmian mechanics leads to an ontological picture that is advocated by moderate structural realism. After this, we presented moderate structural realism in detail, and we want to check now whether the Bohmian ontology perfectly matches all the pillars grounding moderate ontic structural realism. In particular, our inquiry will focus now on pillar (4), which concerns the identity conditions.

With regard to the identity conditions for the entanglement relations represented by the wave-function, given the requirement of uniqueness that we established in section 6.5, it is natural to regard the entire history of particle trajectories as providing the identity conditions for the structure. 'Two' entanglement structures are the very same structure if and only if they determine the very same history of particles' trajectories for the entire space-time. What would actually provide a better identity condition for the entanglement relations would be all the possible particle trajectories, not only the actual ones. However, it is practically impossible to empirically detect whether the possible trajectories are the same, given the limited number of experiments we can perform. However, we are quite confident that the entire history of the universe does provide enough time and opportunity to 'test' and manifest the identity of the entanglement structure.

With regard to the identity conditions for the particles, an initial question immediately arises: is it also the case in Bohmian mechanics that relations identify particles?[166] We have just discussed in chapter 2 of this book that positions do play the role of *principium individuationis*. But now we are claiming that according to moderate ontic structural realism the identity conditions for particles should be the relations that they instantiate. In this respect, is the Bohmian ontology perfectly in accordance with moderate ontic structural realism?

In order to answer this question, we would need a long excursus on the metaphysical nature of the property 'position'. If position turns out to be intrinsic, then we would have only a very weak account of moderate structural realism.

---

[165] Here the domain of intrinsic properties is restricted to what philosophers of science call 'scientific' or 'theoretical' intrinsic properties, such as mass, charge, angular momentum and so on.

[166] The problem of the individuation of Bohmian particles has been addressed by Esfeld (2015) and Lam (2015) as well. They both support a structural individuation. While Esfeld claims that the *principium individuationis* is provided by spatial relations, Lam defends the position that the *principium individuationis* is given by the entanglements relation. In this chapter, we will combine the two views, by appealing to a different approach.

6.9 Particle Positions: Extrinsic or Intrinsic Properties?

In this section, I want to briefly inquire into the metaphysics of the particle position in Bohmian mechanics. This is of extreme importance given that, depending on whether position turns out to be an intrinsic or an extrinsic property, moderate ontic structural realism may be regarded as fitting the Bohmian ontology or not. If position turns out to be intrinsic, then Bohmian mechanics presents a very weak structuralist ontology that may not even seem structuralist at all. Indeed, in this weak-moderate ontic structuralist scenario, objects are conceptually and ontologically independent, since their identity conditions are provided by their intrinsic nature. So why should we call it a structuralist ontology in the first place? Structural realism would seem to be reducible to the mild and weak claim that we should not be realist about danglers and should regard them in structural terms; it would thus no longer be the metaphysical position that claims that objects do depend on structure.

We have explained in chapter 2 why particle positions play a major role in Bohmian mechanics: they alone (given a wave-function) determine the future development of the system, and they are the non-contextual properties to which all the other properties can be reduced (with the exception of mass and charge). Moreover, they are the only properties that belong only to particles (they do not violate the localizability condition). The question now is whether we should consider positions to be intrinsic or extrinsic properties. If position is an intrinsic property, this would mean that relations do not play the role of providing identity conditions for the particles, but intrinsic properties do. And this would amount to discarding MOSR. First of all, let us define what is intrinsic and what is extrinsic. The definition of intrinsic and extrinsic property can be spelled out as the following:

(1) p is intrinsic iff, necessarily, for any x, x has p in virtue of how x is, as opposed to how x is related to things that are wholly distinct from itself.

(2) p is extrinsic if it is not intrinsic.

In the case of Bohmian mechanics, imagine that p is our property and x is our particle. *Prima facie*, it may be argued that an object has a position not in virtue of how other physical objects are, but in virtue of the fact that it is physical and, consequently, it occupies a certain spatial region (or points). The fact that the object has a position does not depend on whether other physical objects exist, since it would have a position even if other objects did not exist. For this reason, position should be regarded as an intrinsic property. But this line of reasoning certainly needs more spelling out. First of all, it would be interesting to understand what a particle position amounts to. In our reasoning above, we defined a particle position as amounting to an occupied point of space. But what is an occupied point? We will turn to this question in the rest of this chapter.

6.10 Position as Extrinsic and a Relational Space

To the question 'what is the difference between an 'occupied' point and an empty one?', Esfeld (2015) responds as follows: points are matter points because there is a non-vanishing spatial relation between any two such points. The essence of a material point is that it stands in spatial relation to other material points. In this framework, we completely abandon a dualistic perspective in terms of matter on one hand and space on the other. On the contrary, the spatial relations among points individuate them as 'matter points' by establishing a spatial distinction between any two such points. There are no physical points in the world that are not individuated by metrical relations; if a point is not individuated by spatial relation is not an occupied point.

In this metaphysical framework, we define a particle position in terms of the spatial relation that it bears to other matter (occupied) points; hence, it turns out to be an extrinsic property. Not only can we satisfactorily reply to the question of what the nature of the matter points is, but we can also recover an 'orthodox' moderate version of ontic structural realism.

6.10.1 A Speculative Relational Bohmian Mechanics

However, this view does encounter significant problems because it implies a relationalist view about space/space-time. Indeed, when Esfeld refuses the ontological dualism between 'occupied points' and 'empty points', he commits himself to a relationalist view, according to which the most primitive spatial relations are the ones between matter points, and not between 'empty' spatial points (Greaves, 2011; Pooley, 2005). The relationalist view, indeed, rejects the notion that there is a dualism between points of space and particles, claiming instead that whenever we talk about spatial distance, we talk about relations between objects; those relation are not reducible to any other more fundamental relations (such as the relations between spatial points). Therefore, the question we should ask before endorsing Esfeld's solution is whether Bohmian mechanics is compatible with such a relational view of space-time.

The endeavor of constructing a relational Bohmian mechanics seems particularly challenging. Since the danger here is to get lost in a very detailed discussion

6.10 Position as Extrinsic and a Relational Space

on space-time that will cause us to lose track of our inquiry into the particle positions, I will just engage in some relevant and conceptual considerations.

First of all, let me briefly outline key debate here. On one hand, the defenders of absolute space claim that space is 'absolute' (or substantival), which means that space "in its own nature, without relation to anything external, always remains similar and immovable" (Newton, 1999, p. 285). On the other hand, according to the relativists, space is "merely relative, an order of coexistences, as time is an order of successions" (Leibniz, 2000, p. 297b).

The debate between absolutists and relationalists about space was recently linked to the notion of background dependent and background independent theories (Rickles, 2008). In light of this, the concept of relational space has been revised, enriched and clarified, and it has been related to how properties are conceived in physical theories. In background dependent theories, properties of physical objects are defined with respect to some fixed entity that plays the role of reference for the system; for example, in Newtonian mechanics, each particle has a position and a motion that are defined by referring to the absolute space and the absolute time, taken as referents. These referent-entities are called the 'background' and have the peculiar feature that they do not change in time, and they are necessary to define the kinematics and the dynamics of the theory (Smolin, 2006). In contrast, background independent theories suggest there are no background entities, hence no fixed entities that play the role of referents for the properties described in the system. According to this view, the 'properties' of the entities postulated in the theory consist fundamentally of the relations among them. The dynamics of the theory is hence defined by the system of these relations, and how these relations evolve in time according to the law of motion postulated in the theory. Indeed, according to this view, the entities are just nodes connected through relations, which determine the dynamics of the system according to a specific law, and which change as time varies. Smolin advances the suggestion that we should understand this scenario with the model of the graph:

> An example of a purely relational kinematics is a graph. The entities are the nodes. The properties are the connections between the nodes. The state of the system is just which nodes are connected and which are not. The dynamics is given by a rule, which changes the connectivity of the graph. The entities are nodes. (Smolin, 2006, p. 200)

Background independent approaches are regarded as in alignment with the relationalist tradition about space and ontic structural realism. For this reason, in the recent debate, philosophers have defined the approach of these kind of theories as 'eliminative relationalism' so that 'background independent' theory and 'relational' theory have become synonymous. Often, it is not the case that one theory is either completely background dependent or background independent, since the same theory may present some background structure as defining some properties and some relations defining other properties. However, given the recent preference for relationalism, it is auspicable that theories should be reconstructed as completely background independent. In this case, relationalism becomes the strategy (Smolin, 2006) of taking the background structure and replacing it with a system of relations evolving according to a law.

Now, far from being a relational theory, Bohmian mechanics is clearly framed in an absolute space-time and is a background dependent theory (see Vassallo, 2015). Here we can list some of the reasons for this:[167]

1) Bohmian mechanics needs a clear definition of absolute simultaneity to account for non-locality.
2) In Bohmian mechanics, positions are taken to be in a Euclidean 3 space, and are the privileged variables.
3) The dynamics is framed in an absolute Newtonian background.
4) The equations and laws are written in a specific coordinate-dependent language.
5) While the space-time affects the motion of the particles, the space-time is not affected by them.

This reasonably should lead us to be cautious of endorsing Esfeld's proposal (2017) concerning the relational individuation of the Bohmian particles. The only way to endorse his proposal would be to completely reformulate Bohmian mechanics as a background independent theory, an enterprise that has just been attempted in Vassallo (2015). Since Bohmian mechanics is background dependent in the very same way classical mechanics is, Vassallo suggests that we should adopt the same kind of strategy that Barbour adopted to transform classical mechanics into a background independent theory. Here we do not have the space to develop the whole mathematical argument;[168] however, the core of Barbour's strategy is to prove that the background structure represented by the space is not fundamental but emergent.

But a lot of work still needs to be done, and this would certainly lead to a reformulation of Bohmian mechanics with huge implications on the kind of formalism used and on the conceptual notions of configuration space and the wave-function. Hence, we do not think that it is fair to redefine the identity of particles on the

---

[167] One may also worry that the wave-function seems to be a background structure given that it determines the motion of the particles, but its development is not influenced by them (I owe this point to J. Wolff; see Vassallo, 2015, for similar considerations).

[168] Refer to the paper by Vassallo (2015) to see that it is possible to have a background dependent Bohmian mechanics.

basis of a hypothetical version of Bohmian mechanics that has not been discussed, and that has not still been recognized by the scientific community. Following the OSR principles against armchair metaphysics, we do not want to speculate on hypothetical theories; rather, we just want to take the laws of an actual and confirmed theory as the starting points for our philosophical considerations. It is physics with its laws that has the role of informing metaphysics, and not vice-versa.

Given this, the worry that position is intrinsic and that the Bohmian ontology is only very weakly in line with the OSR metaphysics is still present.

6.11 Position as Intrinsic and a Substantival Space

Another definition we could give to an occupied point is that what distinguishes an occupied point from an empty point is not the spatial relations it bears but some intrinsic properties. We can say that a particle position *is* a spatial point with some particular features. But what features? In our previous discussion, we have ruled out an ontology of intrinsic scientific properties such as mass, charge and so on. This means that we cannot answer the question by appealing to any property. We cannot say that 'mass' occupies a point, for example. The absence of an ontology of properties puts us in quite an embarrassing situation.

It seems that the only way to distinguish an occupied point from an empty one is to reintroduce the properties. If we had an ontology of properties, for example, answering the question of what distinguishes an occupied point from an empty point would be extremely easy: while the former instantiates mass, the latter does not.

If this is correct, then we should conclude that the identity conditions of particles are not given by relations but by intrinsic properties. This way, the property of position instantiated by a particle is not reducible to a two-place relation between that particle and the space. And in light of this, position seems to be an intrinsic property. Given that the identity of the entanglement structure is given by the entire history of the particle trajectories, while the identity of the particles is given by their intrinsic properties (namely their positions), we witness an antisymmetric dependence between the particles and the structure which is not in line with the orthodox MOSR.

Let me just pause and express my concerns here. I am extremely reluctant to endorse this view according to which particle positions are spatial points of some sort. The first reason is that this view implicitly assumes a particular conception of substantival space, which we can define as follows:

Super-substantivalism: Space is the basic material object; other material objects consist of this space taking on various properties. Objects are adjectival, while space is the only material-physical entity.

But this scenario – where all spatial points are physical, and material objects are only a bunch of physical pointswith some additional properties – is more suited to an ontology of fields rather than of particles. Space becomes more like a field than an arena where physical concrete entities live. In particular, this would be particularly insufficient for explaining the particles' motions. We could no longer endorse the view that particles travel in space, following some trajectories. Rather, we should understand movement as an event where one spatial point is occupied at time t_1, while at t_2 that point is empty, and the next point is occupied. And this is certainly *not* in line with Bohmian mechanics, where particles are taken as moving concrete physical entities.

For this reason, I refuse a metaphysics of occupied points in terms of properties, and there is no need to invoke an ontology of properties, which we had ruled out before.

The question of what an occupied point is receives another answer by the supporters of the bare particulars. According to Ted Sider (private conversation), there is a very obvious answer to that question. Particle positions are defined in terms of points occupied by bare particulars, and that is end of the story. We characterized the Bohmian particles as 'property-less' stuff (meaning that they do not instantiate monadic properties, except for spatio-temporal ones), which in metaphysical language would be called 'bare particulars'. Bare particulars, according to Ted Sider, do not have a metaphysical status spookier than that of electrons or my own. Their nature is simply given by their failing to instantiate any monadic properties. In particular, the Bohmian bare particulars fail to instantiate mass, charge, spin and so on.

This particular view on occupied points reveals a conception of space as a 'container' that surrounds particles and englobes them. It is as if the space had little holes occupied by bare particulars. This view seems to adopt a particular stance of substantivalism:

Container Substantivalism: Space and material objects are equally basic types of entity; material things are enclosed by or embedded within substantival space. Space is outside and between material things. (Dainton, 2010, p. 152)

In this case as well, particle position seems to be an intrinsic property, since each particle's position is independent on other particles' positions and since any position is reducible to a point occupied by property-less stuff.

Certainly, this defense of bare particulars creates some troubles in our intuitive understanding of the world, So, let me present here only some rough considerations.

We may be happy to concede the existence of bare particulars – this is exactly what we do in Bohmian mechanics, and we are also happy to state that what differentiates an occupied spatial point from an unoccupied spatial point is simply that the former is occupied by a bare particular, while the latter is not. But there are two worries. The first is that this ontology of bare particulars does not fare better than any ontology where property-less stuff has its own primitive 'thisness', since, *pace* Sider, it remains entirely mysterious what these bare particulars are. Moreover, what philosophers of physics are concerned with is not really whether it is metaphysically possible to have bare particulars occupying spatial points, but is what makes that object a scientific object, a scientific 'individual'. There may be some property-less objects in this world, with an intrinsic spatio-temporal position, but as long as this characterization of the object does not make it a scientific individual, then we cannot be realist about it. What makes a physical object a scientific object is the relations it has with other physical objects. Then, we may wonder whether these relations obtain in virtue of their intrinsic properties, or whether those relations are fundamental. For this reason, we rule out the bare particular solution on account of it being unsatisfactory.

6.12 Position as Extrinsic and a Substantival Space

Now we are at an impasse. It seems that the only way to defend an extrinsic nature of position, and so recover moderate ontic structural realism, is to presuppose that Bohmian mechanics is in relative space, which is not. But there is a last fourth alternative. According to this option, we define the particle positions in terms of spatial relations and dynamical relations. Here I will present how.

First of all, we can define a particle position by appealing to the spatial relation it bears with the space. For example, on a standard version of substantivalism, having a position is a fundamental two-place relation, which stands between a physical object and spatial points or regions. This kind of substantivalism can be defined as follows:

Relational Substantivalism: Space and material objects are equally basic types of entity; there is a primitive relation of "spatial locatenedess" that holds between objects and places within space. (Dainton, 2010, p. 152)

Position properties are then defined in terms of this relation so that, for any spatial point or region r, there is a position property p of being located at r. To see that such properties are extrinsic, let r be a spatial point or spatial region, let p be the property of being located at r, and let x be a material object that has p. Since, according to substantivalism, x is wholly distinct from r, x has p in virtue of how it is related to something wholly distinct from it, namely r. Given this, p should count as extrinsic.[169]

However, the reason why the particle has that position and thus instantiates that particular relation with space is in virtue of the dynamical relations it is in (in particular, the entanglement relation represented by the wave-function). That the particles have certain spatio-temporal properties does not ultimately depend on their scientific intrinsic properties such as mass or charge, but on the kind of entanglement relations they bear (Lam, 2015). The fact that one particle has a trajectory depends on the kinds of entanglement relations that link it to all the other particles. The reason why it is in certain kinds of relations is in virtue of its positon. Indeed, if it were five meters up, it would bear other kinds of relations. There is, indeed, a sort of dependence of the particles' spatio-temporal properties and the structure represented by the wave-function, which should not be omitted. This makes the position of the particles dependent on where the other particles are (recall the holistic nature of the entanglement structure). We can build a hierarchical structure here: the individuality of a particle is given by its position, but its position is an extrinsic property that the particle bears with the space, and the particle bears a particular relation with the space in virtue of the entanglement relations it bears with other particles. So there is a certain way in which the individuality of a particular is contextual, given that its position is grounded in dynamical holistic relations. The same conclusion is also supported by Lam:

> In this perspective, it seems to make sense to claim that for each Bohmian particle, the fact of being this very particle, which includes its own trajectory and dynamical features, depends on the structure it is part of. (Lam, 2015, p. 89)

This picture recovers completely moderate ontic structural realism: while the identity of the entanglement structure represented by the wave-function is given by the particles, the particles' identity is given by the entanglement relations through their positions (Lam, 2015).

---

[169] I owe this formulation of the property of position to Dr. Marshall.

6.13 Example: Singlet and Triplet States

Before drawing a conclusion with some general considerations on the structural realist view, let me sum up the structuralist view applied to Bohmian mechanics with a clear example, where three wave-functions describe the entanglements between two particles' spin. Before dealing with a particular example, remember that in Bohmian mechanics, spin is not a property with ontological significance, as we discussed in chapter 2. Even though the Bohmians still concede 'spin-talks', facts about spin are reducible to facts about particle positions. Whenever we say that a particle is 'z-spin up', we just mean that, in a particular measurement of the 'z' spin, the particle chooses the exit 'up' instead of the exit 'down'. Moreover, it is worthwhile recalling that Bohmian mechanics is a non-local deterministic theory, so it is a matter of fact that the particle will deterministically choose the up or the down exit, depending on its own initial position and on the positions of all the other particles. The guiding equation secures exactly this non-local and deterministic behavior.

Suppose that I have two particles A and B, and three wave-functions Ψ, Φ, Θ:

$$\Psi_{AB} = \frac{1}{\sqrt{2}} |z\uparrow>_A |z\downarrow>_B - \frac{1}{\sqrt{2}} |z\downarrow>_A |z\uparrow>_B$$

$$\Phi_{AB} = -\frac{1}{\sqrt{2}} |z\uparrow>_A |z\downarrow>_B + \frac{1}{\sqrt{2}} |z\downarrow>_A |z\uparrow>_B$$

$$\Theta_{AB} = \frac{1}{\sqrt{2}} |z\uparrow>_A |z\downarrow>_B + \frac{1}{\sqrt{2}} |z\downarrow>_A |z\uparrow>_B$$

According to the ontic structuralist proposal, the above three wave-functions represent (or express) the entanglement structure that relates the particles A and B in 3D. Suppose we want to know the following:
1) Whether these three wavefunctions represent the same structure; and
2) Whether the particle configurations are the same.

The first thing to note is that the difference between Ψ and Φ is unobservable and undetectable. Indeed, the two wave-functions differ only by a global phase shift. This means that they will always, for the entire history of the universe, predict exactly the very same particle positions in all kinds of circumstances. Given that a change in the wave-function does not lead to any physical differences, we claimed in our discussion on the realist view that we have good grounds for rejecting the physicality of the wave-function itself. We proposed later that all the wave-functions that are related through trivial transformations such as gauge transformations should actually represent the very same entanglement structure, and we suggested taking the structure to be physically relevant. This maneuver saves the structural realist from any commitment to 'danglers' and from the problem of underdetermination. In this case, my suggestion means that the two wave-functions Ψ and Φ represent the very same structure, which is just the network of the entanglement relations among the particles.

If we want to evaluate the identity of the particle configurations given by Ψ and Φ, we said that we should take into consideration the structure. Is the structure the same but only represented by two different mathematical functions? If the answer is affirmative, as it is in this case, then the 'two' particle configurations are actually the same.

Let us now consider whether Ψ and Θ represent the same entanglement structure. If we consider all the experiments along the z-spin direction, then A and B may have exactly the very same particle configurations for all their entire history, given the same particle initial positions. But it turns out that if we performed an x-spin measurement, A and B would have very different histories depending on their wave-function. Indeed, while in the case of a z-measurement the two particles are always anti-correlated, regardless of whether they are guided by Θ or Ψ, if we perform an x-measurement, the particles of Θ will be always correlated: if A goes up, then B goes up too, and if A goes down, then B will go down as well (and vice-versa if B is the 'first' to determine the non-local correlation). But the particles A and B, which are guided by Ψ, will always be anti-correlated in the experiments. This means the two wave-functions do not share the same structure, and, consequently, that the particle configurations determined by Ψ and Θ are not identical.

7 Conclusive Remarks

7.1 The Best of Both Worlds: A Structuralist Ontology for Bohmian Mechanics

In this section, I would like to underline the advantages that the ontic structural realist view offers in the debate on the Bohmian ontology. Not only do I believe that the ontic structuralist proposes a much better methodological program than the realist and the nomological views, but I also believe that the resulting Bohmian ontology fares much better than the realist and nomological ontologies. We discussed the advantages of the OSR methodological program earlier, and given that those advantages are independent of its particular application to Bohmian mechanics, I do not want to discuss them again here. In the next section, I will only discuss the advantages concerning the Bohmian ontology, which results after applying the structuralist method. Hopefully, this will offer us more reasons to endorse a structural realist ontology.

7.1.1 The Status of the Wave-function

First of all, let us concentrate on the ontological status of the wave-function. By reifying the wave-function, the realist has three burdens. The first is to revise traditional metaphysical criteria by dropping some principles (such as reciprocity or three-dimensionality) as well as to develop a new understanding of field-entities. The second, within Valentini's kind of realism, is to account for a causation that obtains across different spaces. The third is to explain why we privilege and reify a particular formalism but not other compatible ones. By assimilating the wave-function as a law-like entity, the nomological view is forced to defend the metaphysically implausible view that the wave-function respects the criteria of lawhood. Moreover, it needs to answer the question of how laws – if they are external modal entities – act on the particles and confer them modality. The structuralist, by contrast, offers an ontology that consists entirely of three-dimensional beables, some of them are local (the particles) and some are not (the entanglement relations). Given that the physical reality is constituted only of those material matter points related through concrete relations, it is possible to regard those matter points as the primitive ontology of the theory, as defined in chapter 2. The wave-function is not an external entity that determines the bonds between the particles, but represents those bonds. In light of this, the particles and their relations constitute our raw epistemic data.

7.1.2 Balance between Parsimony and Explanatory Power

But there are more important advantages that I would like to direct attention to. First of all, the ontic structuralist view provides a good balance between the parsimonious ontology provided by the nomological view and the explanatory power provided by the realist view. We discussed previously that while the realist view presents a redundant ontology, it at least provides a powerful explanation for the motion of the Bohmian particles. At the same time, the nomological view offers a very parsimonious ontology at the cost of being explanatorily poor and unsatisfactory. I believe that the structuralist Bohmian ontology expresses the best of both of these views: on one hand, by appealing to modal and causal relations, it provides an explanation for the particle motion, and on the other hand, it is not committed to redundant entities.

Secondly, another benefit of the structuralist ontic reading of the Bohmian ontology is that it provides a causal explanation (contrary to the nomologists) without being 'mechanistic' (contrary to the realists). Causation is understood as a 'thin' notion, which simply underpins the dependent relations that a law spells out. Moreover, this new way of understanding 'causation', which avoids any appeal to forces or energy transmission, does not 'buy' the principle of back-reaction. Given that the motion of the particles is determined (physically) by (causal) relations spelled out in the guiding law, and not by an external entity exerting a force on the particles, then the particles are not supposed to react back.

7.1.3 Underdetermination

The third important advantage concerns the problem of underdetermination. We discussed the problem that the realist view could regard many different wavefunctions, all related through gauge transformations, to be 'the' universal wavefunction. Moreover, we evaluated other proposals that the realists may consider; for example, they may endorse an ontological picture where we have an infinite number of entanglement fields (Norsen, 2010) or a multi-field(s) (Hubert & Romano, 2018; Romano, 2020). The same problem of underdetermination is faced by the nomologist/dispositionalist: either each particle can have an infinite number of dispositions, or all the particles taken as a whole may have one single holistic disposition. In this respect, the structuralist presents a clear ontology that is not vulnerable to underdetermination: we have particles with one entanglement structure that relates all of them.

The following additional point, which is still related to the previous one, concerns the treatment of properties. Are scientific intrinsic properties instantiated by the wave-function or by the wave-function and the particles? The ontic structuralist cuts at the root of this problem as well: we do not have scientific intrinsic 'properties' in the fundamental ontology. And even though discussions about properties are still meaningful, they should be reduced to discussions about particle positions.

7.1.4 Compatibility with Different Mathematical Formulations

At the beginning of this book, we inferred the ontological interpretations of the realist and nomological views from their distinct mathematical formulations. We argued that it was natural to come up with their different metaphysical interpretations of the wave-function given the different formulations they rely on. The ontic structural realist ontology adopts a thin concept of causation and modest commitments, so that its ontology and dynamics are compatible with both mathematical formulations of the theory. As long as the Bohmian physicists disagree on the space-time where we live (i. e. whether it is Aristotelian or Galilean), it is not up to the metaphysicians to decide on this issue, by grounding their decision in metaphysical speculations on the wave-function. Regarding the wave-function as representing (in a non-transparent way) entanglement relations, which have only a thin-causational role, acts to secure our ontology as not being dictated by what we still do not know.

7.1.5 Experiments – Empty Trajectories

The last point I would like to draw the attention to is how well the ontic structural realist, without invoking any speculative and disrupting interpretations of the theory, can explain the problem of the 'empty trajectories' we discussed in chapter 3. There, I presented the physical effects that an empty branch of the wave-function has on an experimental device. In particular, we dealt with the case where the empty branch of a wave-function triggers the measurement device, so that it 'clicks' and reveals the presence of a physical entity in its neighborhood. That experiment, as the ontic structural realist now understands it, does not reveal that empty branches of wave-functions are physically real – on the contrary, it simply reveals that the particles have non-local entanglement relations. We thought that the fact that the measuring device is triggered even though the particle is not there reveals that the wave-function is real: indeed, only the wave-function is 'there', near the measuring device. But that thought presupposes a misleading and false assumption: the idea that the pointer of the measurement device changes only by local interaction. Given that the particles are entangled, as the ontic structural realist claims, nothing prevents us from thinking that the pointer changes its position from 'no' to 'yes' because a distant particle is entangled with it in such a way that it causes that particular interaction.

7.2 A Structuralist Reconciliation of the Realist and Nomological Views in Bohmian Mechanics

The structuralist view I am defending takes on aspects of the realist and the nomological views. Or better, I claim that we should not regard it as another competing interpretation of the ontology of Bohmian mechanics, but as a reconciliatory view. Let me show this by evaluating two main aspects: the status of the wave-function and the kind of determination that is involved between the wave-function and the particle dynamics.

7.2.1 The Status of the Wave-function

There is a first obvious way to see why the structuralist reconciles the two rival interpretations. On one hand, as in the nomological view, the structuralist claims that the wave-function is a nomological entity from which we can extract useful information about the particles. We have seen that, according to ontic structural realism, laws play a fundamental part because they show what exists in the world. The wave-function is the principal ingredient in both the Schrödinger and the guiding law of motion. For this reason, it assumes a primary nomological role. On the other hand, like the realist, the structuralist claims that the wave-function does represent something physical in the world, albeit 'in a non-transparent way'. In the ontic structuralist perspective, being 'nomological' and being 'ontologically salient' are not two incompatible aspects. In fact, from this perspective they are intrinsically connected: what is nomological must be ontologically salient. Remember that realists are also committed to the view that laws guide us to infer what exists in the world, but their mistake was to reify the mathematical entity figuring in the law. The structural realist takes on exactly the same aspect but refuses any process of reification, because they recognize that that mathematical entity is a nomological entity, which means that it does not represent the physical reality in a transparent way. To spell this out more clearly, the structural realist takes on aspects of the nomological view, since they acknowledge that the wave-function should not be reified, and for this reason it is a nomological entity. However, the fault of the nomologist was to consider nomological entities as not representing any physical entity, while the structural realist simply understands nomological entities as non-transparent representatives of the world, but still representatives of some physical features.

To conclude, we can say the ontic structural realist is a methodologically 'good' realist for a number of reasons. The realist claims that we should take the wave-function seriously because it is what the fundamental dynamical laws are about. The same goes for the structuralist, since they take the wave-function 'seriously'. But the ontic structuralist refutes any misleading reification process, and in order to eliminate the danglers and not incur in any case of underdetermination, they look at the underlying structure that the wave-function underpins and focuses their attention on the entanglement relations that it expresses.

Secondly, the ontic structural realist is a methodologically 'good' nomologist. The nomological view claims that the wave-function is a law, and so it commits to the view that it does not represent anything physical, (falsely) presupposing that if a nomological entity supervenes on another entity, then it should not be ontologically relevant. The structuralist, on the other hand, takes the wave-function seriously exactly because it appears as a central object in the laws, and the laws, according to OSR, reveal the nature of the fundamental relations of the world. In this case, the kinds of relations that the wave-function expresses are entanglement relations.

Moreover, the ontic structural realist reconciles the two views because it focuses on what the two views share: not the interpretation of the wave-function but the physical significance of the wave-function. Both the realist and the nomological views appeal to the wave-function in order to account for entanglement, and they are so obsessed with the (wrong) question of what the wave-function *is* that they forget the reason they both take the wave-function as a fundamental entity (that is, because of what it represents). It is there in the laws of motion in order to express entanglement, which should be necessarily taken into consideration in order for the theory to be empirically adequate.

In a nutshell, ontic structural realism draws the attention to what the two views have in common, and take that to be what we can be realist about. This way, it eliminates a great deal of quarreling (Pooley, 2006).

7.2.2 The Determination of the Dynamics

Regarding the wave-function as representing modal relations provides a reconciliation not only for the problem of interpretation of the status of the wave-function, but also for the question of how the wave-function determines the particle positions. While the realist insists on endorsing a causal explanation, the nomologist adopts a nomological one, according to which the wave-function, as a law-like entity, does not cause the motion but instead dictates it. But for the ontic structuralist, causal and nomological roles do not stand in rivalry. Whatever relation is spelled out in a physical theory by physical laws is a nomological-causal relation. Relations are physical and concrete, and, for this reason, they can bear a causal power. The sources of causation in a physical theory are the nomological relations that the theory presents.

7.3 A Final Defense of the Structuralist Reading of the Wave-function

There is a first criticism against the ontic structuralist view that I concede and I want to discuss. According to this criticism, all the success of the structuralist Bohmian ontology, namely the fact that it avoids embarrassing metaphysical questions on the nature of the wave-function and that it reconciles the two rival views, shows that ontic structural realism is *not* a good methodological and metaphysical program.

In particular, the fact that the OSR resulting ontology is compatible with two competing mathematical formulations of the same theory and that both the realist and the nomologist may be happy to endorse this view means that the structuralist's ontological commitments are so poor and so modest as to become plain and insignificant. In a nutshell: if the structuralist can score high it is because it uses the bad trick of reducing the ontology to a minimum.

In other words, the reason why the (successful) results of the ontic structuralist program may be regarded as an incentive for abandoning the ontic structural realist proposal is that, in order to avoid any case of underdetermination, ontic structural realism needs to keep a minimum ontological profile and it cannot specify its ontology. It presents an ontology that is not rich enough to cause any underdetermination but also not rich enough to be satisfactory. Borrowing Cao's words, which were used for a slightly different criticism against OSR, we can imagine what an anti-structuralist may want to tell us by the end of this book: "This way of reasoning may seem attractive [. . .]. But [. . .] it is not very informative. In particular, the ontological difference, which underlies a conceptual revolution, becomes invisible in this kind of structural reasoning" (Cao, 2003, p. 13).

That there may be merits in allowing unjustified and sometimes ungrounded (or 'mis-grounded') metaphysical interpretations that lead to conceptual revolutions is something that each philosophy can decide. It is clear that ontic structural realism, as I presented it here, is a meta-interpretation program. And in light of this, we should recognize its value. If we then evaluate OSR on the basis of how many conceptual revolutions it allows, obviously it will score zero. And it scores zero because it rules out all the danglers that other metaphysical interpretations may present us with, and in doing so it can defend the view that science is a cumulative progression (without disruptions), and therefore it can defend a realist attitude towards science. Then, we do not want to deny that, sometimes, accepting danglers may turn out to be a right and fruitful decision, nor do we want to deny that we may progress by committing to more than our epistemology can support. However, it seems to me if the situation of quantum mechanics is like the present one, with many theories and speculative ontologies that range from many worlds to flashes, it is because too much room has been given to what one might call 'metaphysical-revolutionary speculations'. Again, I do not want to say that metaphysics should all convert to a meta-interpretation. What I want to claim is that sometimes a 'poor' ontology based on a work of meta-interpretation is the only possible ontology if we want to endorse a good and sound methodological program. If ontic structural realism eradicates salient differences of our metaphysical interpretations eradicated is because we did not have any grounds to believe in them. They were danglers of the theory.

We saw that another merit of OSR was to have an explanatorily powerful ontology without committing to any 3ND entities. This however may be due to another trick that the ontic structural realist performs right under our eyes: the trick consists in replacing the 'explanandum' with the 'explanans'.

Let me explain this point by recalling the attitude of the realist and the nomological views. Both these views have to explain why Bohmian particles follow such strange trajectories, and both the answers they provided respectively appealed to the wave-function. But then the question at stake becomes what the wave-function can be and how it can influence the particles' motion. The realist claims that the wave-function is a field that exerts a force on the particles by determining their motion, and since the wave-function is entangled, then the dynamics of the particles is non-local. In contrast, the nomological view argues that the particles have a non-local dynamics because the wave-function is (mathematically) entangled, and being a law-like entity, it dictates a non-local dynamics. Notice that both the nomological (non-Humean) supporters and the realists are aware that the particle trajectories are due to the non-local character of the system. But *why* do the particles have a non-local dynamics? Why are they entangled? In their view, the entanglement is the *explanandum*.

But the structuralist view seems to account for the non-locality of the particles by appealing to entanglement itself: why do particles behave like this? Because they have entanglement relations. And that is the end of the story. The trick of the ontic structuralist is to take entanglement as the *explanans*. It seems that they have just reinvented the wheel!

Nevertheless, I think that the merit of OSR is exactly to 'bring back' entanglement to where it belongs: in the physical three-dimensional space. Invoking a mathematical or physical entanglement at the level of the wave-function in order to explain the 3D non-locality does not provide a true explanation in the first case and it provides a very uncomfortable explanation in the second case. An additional point worth discussing is the validity of that 'why' question that pushes the realists and the nomologists to appeal to the wave-function. The reason why particles have a non-local dynamics is that they are entangled. Is it a meaningful question to ask *why* they are entangled? Definitely not in the eyes of the structuralist. Once we acknowledge that the modal entanglement structure that connects particles is fundamental, we also change our perspective, since we do not look for an object that can explain that structure: that structure, as we said, is fundamental!

7.4 Open Questions for Future Research

Even though I argued that the structuralist view on Bohmian mechanics provides a more satisfactory account of its ontology, I have found that its ontological interpretation presents some weaknesses, which in the name of intellectual honesty I should consider and spell out. I still have not found definite resolutions to all of them, however I do not ultimately find them to be deadly threats to the structuralist proposal. Rather, I take them to be interesting sources for future research. First, I consider possible 'threats' to the structuralist view, next I consider some possible objections.

7.4.1 A Possible Threat: Circularity and Non-supervenience

First of all, I understand that my defense of the structural realist view is vulnerable to two important criticisms. The first is circularity, and the second is inconsistency.

Starting with the first objection, it may be argued that the structural realist is trapped in a vicious circular argument. Indeed, structural realists establish the identity of the entanglement structure by appealing to the identity of the particle configurations, and establish the identity of the particles by appealing to the entanglement structure. This might sound particularly problematic if individuation is taken to be a non-reciprocal determination. This is not a threat specific to Bohmian mechanics, but to moderate ontic structural realism in general.

Lowe, for example, defends a position according to which "two different individuals cannot both individuate, or help to individuate, each other. This is because individuation in the metaphysical sense is a determination relation [. . .] As such, individuation is an *explanatory* relation in the metaphysical sense of 'explanatory'" (2003, p. 93, his emphasis). He goes on: "Certainly, it seems that any satisfactory ontology will have to include self-individuating elements" (2003, p. 93).

Lowe spells this out by taking individuals into consideration; however, the same line of reasoning may be applied to relata and relations. This is for example done by Chakravartty:

> On the ontology of non-eliminative structuralism, an entity can be understood only in terms of extrinsic features, that is in terms of relations to other things. This generates a circularity or regress. (Chakravartty, 2015, p. 12)

Let me spell this worry out. Whenever we want to specify the nature of the relata, i. e. of the objects that instantiate relations, we need to appeal to the kinds of relation that object stands in, and this creates a circle.

I certainly acknowledge that this is a worry we should be concerned about. However, given that it is not specific to Bohmian mechanics but is related to the general view of MOSR, here we only refer to works in the literature where this problem has been addressed. This problem, for example, has been thoroughly discussed in Esfeld (2015), Lam (2015), French (2006, 2014). One consideration may be worth spelling out in the context of Bohmian mechanics. Let me point out the fact that, if we consider particles' spatio-temporal properties to be intrinsic, then this worry does not arise – but this would mean that one of the pillars of moderate ontic structuralism is violated. So, we are faced with two options. We can admit, in the same way the structural realists do, that the charge of circularity is not a threatening worry and that relations and relata reciprocally individuate each other. On the other hand, we can decide to reject moderate ontic structural realism tout court and endorse the claim that positions are intrinsic properties.

The second challenge is the following. If we take positions to be intrinsic properties of the particles, the uniqueness condition we introduced for the entanglement structure seems to be inconsistent with the claim that our entanglement relations do not supervene on the particles' intrinsic properties. While characterizing the structure, we said that it does not supervene on the particles' positions, but now we are claiming that the structure does supervene on the particles' positions.

If we think, in line with certain Bohmians, that positions are intrinsic properties – which, is, however, highly disputable and controversial – we may find that there is a tension between the two statements but no inconsistency.

When we discussed the uniqueness criterion, we claimed that we should commit to a uniqueness correspondence between the entanglement structure represented by the wave-function and all the possible trajectories that the particles would take. However, it is not plausible to think that the universe instantiates all of them right now. In principle, the universe will instantiate only some of them.

But this would put the structural realist in the uncomfortable position of establishing the identity of physical entities only on the basis of possible facts, which are not actualized. The only escape route is to think that the portion of time of the entire universe shows enough trajectories to reveal all the possible differences of the entanglement relations. After all, our universe is so big and so old that we have good reason to think that the entanglement structure does supervene on the particles trajectories of the entire space-time. In case the entire history of the universe did not suffice, even if we could not rule out that the two particle configurations were different, we would still not be justified in doing so.

When we claim that the entanglement relations do not supervene on the particle intrinsic properties (in this case, we are supposing that spatio-temporal properties are intrinsic), we mean that at time t_1 two indistinguishable configurations of particles may have been determined by two different entanglement structures. Hence, a change in the entanglement structure may not lead to a difference in the particle configuration at time t_1.

Taking our example of the singlet and the triplet states, in both cases, if we measure the z-spin, we may always end up with exactly the very same particle trajectories for A and B, without changing their initial positions. Suppose that 100 percent of the time A goes up and B goes down. This scenario is perfectly compatible with both different structures, the one represented by Ψ and the one represented by Θ. In this way, the entanglement structure does not supervene on the particles' positions.

The uniqueness and therefore the supervenience of the wave-function comes on the scene only when we consider the entire universe, the entire space-time. This way, we claimed, we have good reason to think that the entire history spells out the different entanglement relations of the particles. This, however, may turn out not to be the case. And we concede this possibility.

Notice that this scenario is very different from a classical scenario where, for example, the force does always supervene on the intrinsic properties of the particles for each snapshot of the history of the universe. In a classical system, we do not need to take the entire history of the whole universe to find whether a force supervenes on the particle properties. Indeed, at each moment, if there is a change of the total net force, then there must be a change in the momentum of the particles. The supervenience is supposed to be valid for each instant; hence, the uniqueness of the force is definitely much stronger than the one of the Bohmian structure. In fact, in the Bohmian case, the uniqueness of the structure is valid only for the entire space-time, and this is because we need the entire space-time to allow all the possible entanglement differences to be spelled out.

7.4.2 A Possible Threat: The Wave-function as a Background Structure – A Case of Underdetermination?

There is a possible threat that may undermine all our structuralist discussion of the wave-function. The threat is that there may be another possible interpretation of the structure represented by the wave-function – if this is true, and if it is true that there is another viable metaphysical interpretation, then we fall into a case of underdetermination. And given that the problem of underdetermination is the main reason to support ontic structural realism, then if even an ontic structuralist interpretation can be charged with being underdetermined, there is no reason to endorse ontic structural realism. Therefore, if this threat is real, we are not justified in endorsing an OSR methodological program and any OSR metaphysical commitment. As such, it is better for us to consider this threat seriously.

In order to understand this possible metaphysical interpretation of the structure represented by the wave-function, we should go back to our discussion of the nomological view. According to the Rutgers-Munich-Geneva group, the wave-function should be regarded as a law-like entity that dictates the motion of the particles without being physically involved in the ontology (chapter 3). One of the main criticisms was that while laws do not evolve in time, the wave-function does, so it seems wrong to categorize it as a law. The DGZ answer was to regard the wave-function as a rigid and fixed time-independent entity, following the Wheeler-DeWitt proposal. In this scenario, the wave-function becomes an entity that is not involved in the physical dynamics of the theory, one that is not subjected to any temporal development but dictates or fixes it.

We also pointed out a problem that the nomological view has to face, namely the problem of inertial trajectory. If we do not regard the wave-function as perturbing the natural motion of the particles, then we have to interpret the guiding law as a kinematic equation, expressing the inertial trajectories of the particles. But if the inertial trajectories of the particles are those generated by the wave-function through the guiding law of motion, then this inertial system violates the nature of the Galilean space-time, which is stipulated to be the right space-time for the Bohmian system by the guiding law of motion! Indeed, in the Galilean space-time, the affine structure is identified with the inertial structure, so the inertial trajectories are straight lines. In contrast, if the trajectories specified by the wave-function are the ones generated through the guiding law, then they are not straight lines.

A solution to the problem would be to take the wave-function as determining the structure of space-time by specifying the geodesic space-time curvatures, so that Bohmian mechanics has a new space-time determined by the wave-function through the guiding law. This way, the wave-function is not involved in the dynamics of the particles; rather, it determines the kinematic of the particles by shaping the Galilean space-time. In this scenario, which the nomological view proposes, the wave-function does not represent any features of the particle system – on the contrary, it represents a background structure. Therefore, according to this interpretation, the wave-function should not be regarded as a network of entanglement relations, but just as a fixed structure that determines the shape of inertial trajectories. In this new framework, particles follow certain non-Newtonian trajectories not because the particles are entangled but because those trajectories are their inertial. The background structure that the wave-function represents can be characterized as follows. First of all, it is insensitive to any dynamical aspects of the theory (the particle motion) but it determines it. Secondly, by geometrizing the wave-function, we can say that this structure is a persistent geometrical object that does not evolve (indeed, the wave-function does not evolve). Finally, it is a modal structure insofar as it is nomically necessary, which simply means that it is a necessary element for the theory. We can identify an entity as nomically necessary (Vassallo, 2016) whenever the question "Why is it so and not otherwise?" is not applicable. While this very same question is meaningful when it concerns the particle configuration – we know why the particle configuration is like this and not otherwise, and the answer relies on the wave-function – it is meaningless when it concerns the wave-function.

There is an additional motivation to regard the wave-function as a background structure. One of the necessary criteria for an entity to be defined as a background structure is that it should not be possible to describe its dynamical influences in terms of physical interactions between objects; hence, it should be impossible to describe its influence as forces *between* objects. Bohmian mechanics presents us with the exactly this scenario. We know that it would be impossible to describe the dynamics of the particles as a direct interaction obtaining between one particle and the other (Esfeld et al., 2014). Particles do not interact on each other through forces; instead, their interaction is always mediated through the wave-function. Therefore, the wave-function is essential in determining the dynamics of the particles. However, Norsen's (2010) theory comes to our aid. Indeed, he shows that it is at least possible to construct a theory based on fields interacting with each other through entanglement fields. This would be already enough to crumble the proposal of regarding the wave-function as a background structure. But another reason pushes me to rule out this threat. As we know, the ontic structural realist starts from the laws, and from them they infer the ontology. But, unfortunately, if we want to take the wave-function as a background structure, then the laws should not be spelled out as we see them now. And there seems to be no way to formulate them in a straightforward manner. This interpretation, indeed, is very speculative and departs from a faithful reading of the laws. Pitowski (1991), for example, did reformulate Bohmian mechanics along these lines by taking the wave-function as a background structure; however, according to his theory, trajectories are not defined but are 'spread out', violating in this way the very true nature of Bohmian mechanics. Up to now, there has not been any successful reformulation of Bohmian mechanics with a background structure defined by the wave-function. Hence, it seems to me that appealing to a speculative interpretation of the wave-function, which should be supported by a non-existing theory, does not constitute a true threat for the ontic structural realist, who relies on totally different methodological criteria (i. e. taking physics as informing metaphysics and not vice-versa). Obviously, the nomological interpretation may push us to investigate the possibility of regarding the wave-function as a background structure and to develop a new theory accordingly, and we find that this proposal is particularly appealing. But as the theory stands now, it does not allow this interpretation.

7.4.3 A Possible Threat: The Single Particle Case

There is another threat that may undermine not the OSR program as presented before, but OSR's resulting ontological interpretation. We claimed that the wave-function represents (non-uniquely) a network of entanglement relations between the particles. Still, we do not use the wave-function only to determine the motion of a many-particle configuration – we also use it to determine the motion of one single particle, and in this case it is clear that the wave-function cannot represent entanglement relations, given that we have only one particle! In a nutshell, this is the problem: if the wave-function 'represents' entanglement correlations, what about the case of one single particle?

The first thing that we should note is that for the mathematical construction of the wave-function, it does not matter whether we are computing the particles' trajectories of one particle in an N dimensional space where N>2 or many particles in a one-dimensional space. That the wave-function represents the entanglement relations is a natural consequence of the mathematical structure of the wave-function if we have more than one particle in our system, but the same 'entanglement' structure remains in one 3D particle wave-function. The role of the wave-function is to entangle all the different degrees of freedom of the system, regardless of what degrees of freedom refer to the number of particles and what degrees of freedom refer to their spatial dimensions (whether they live in one-, two- or three-dimensional space). We should recall that the wave-function, as a mathematical entity, lives in the configuration space, where all the axes are democratically regarded as equal. So, in the case of one single particle in three-dimensional space, the wave-function will 'entangle' its degrees of freedom in the same way it entangles the positions of three particles in one-dimensional space. So, in the hypothetical case where we have only one particle in a 3D universe, the wave-function would represent entanglement relations not between particles but between degrees of freedom.

However, I have not touched on the most problematic case, which is of one particle in one-dimensional space. This case presents a system with only one degree of freedom. In this case, the answer would be to stress that in this work we have inquired into the ontological status of the universal wave-function of a multi-particle system. What we did was to point out the ontological significance of that particular mathematical object. Pointing to a case where there are no particles but one does not hinder our metaphysical discussion, simply because we are not considering the very same mathematical object.

7.4.4 A Possible Threat: Is Bohmian Mechanics with Property-less Particles Possible?

The other threat comes from an ontology of particles purged of properties. We defended an ontology where particles do not instantiate scientific monadic properties such as mass, charge, angular momentum and so on. We argued this on the basis of experiments, formalism, and metaphysical principles such as parsimony and epistemic access. For this reason, we take this metaphysical commitment as valid, and not only dictated by metaphysical caprice. However, the theory itself is formulated as if properties were instantiated by particles. If we take the law of motion for the particles, for example, the mass that figures in the first component of the equation is normally attributed to a particular particle and the value chosen depends on the natural kind to which the particle we are describing belongs.

If we claim that our system consists of property-less particles, then our laws and the whole mathematical structure describing the system should respect and reflect this ontological commitment. For example, the dynamics a property-less ontology of bare particulars should be governed by permutation invariant laws. Indeed, in a property-less system, it does not matter which property is where, which means that if we permute the position of two particles, the dynamics of the system will remain invariant. A reformulation, however, should not involve only the laws but also the space where the theory is set, in particular the space where the wave-function is (we will see why in a while). The question we want to ask in this section is whether such a reformulation of Bohmian mechanics is possible. Fortunately, this is not only possible, but it has been already accomplished by Goldstein et al. (2005). This new formulation of Bohmian mechanics is called "identity-based Bohmian mechanics" so that we can distinguish it from the standard one. I will present the main important steps of constructing the identity-based Bohmian mechanics,[170] and I will conclude with some considerations that may threaten the commitment to a property-less ontology.

First of all, we need to look at the way we represented the Bohmian particle configuration. In chapter 1, we represented the particle configuration as an N-tuple of this form:

$$Q = (q_1, q_2, q_3 \ldots q_N)$$

This mathematical representation tells you that while particle 1 is at position q_1, particle 2 is at position q_2. Given this, in this representation the order of the particles matters. If I permute particle 1 with particle 2, then the particle configuration should be written instead as:

$$Q = (q_2, q_1, q_3 \ldots q_N)$$

However, in an ontology with property-less and indistinguishable particles, we know that the order does not and should not count. What counts is whether particular spatial points are occupied or not, and it is not relevant to know which particle occupies which spatial point. It does not matter which particle occupies which point since a permutation of particles does not lead to any new physically meaningful scenario. For this reason, when we represent the particle configuration, we should adopt a set instead of a tuple. In a set, indeed, the order of its elements is not significant.

$$Q = \{q_1, q_2, q_3 \ldots q_N\}$$

This way of representing the particle configuration simply tells that there is 'one particle' occupying position q_1 and another occupying position q_2 and so on, without specifying which particle.

This obviously does not mean that we cannot label and distinguish the particles. We can, but only through the position. However, this means that it does not make any sense to think that a state is different if we change the positions of the particles. If we changed the positions of the particles, the entanglement relations would be the same, which means that the particles' identity would be the same.

If we wanted to insist that, despite the apparent invariance, permutation does lead to the constitution of a different state, then our claim would amount to introducing a primitive this-ness of particles, which would be redundant and inaccessible. Certainly, introducing this this-ness would be against the criteria set up by ontic structural realism.

---

[170] For technical details, see Goldstein et al., 2005a, 2005b; and Esfeld et al., 2015.

Now that we have inquired into the representation of particle configuration, the next question is how we should represent the configuration space. Given the change from tuples to sets, we can say that the new configuration space for property-less particles should be constructed out of sets instead of tuples. The normal full configuration space contains too much information that is both irrelevant and redundant. Recall that in the normal configuration space, each axis represents a particular particle degree of freedom (or more specifically, one particle possible position along one three-dimensional dimension). Therefore, the full configuration space tells us which particle occupies which position, a piece of information that is no longer meaningful given that the particles are indistinguishable. The new space formed with sets instead of tuples is denoted by $^3R^N$, and it is isomorphic to a space where we delete the configuration space middle axis and all the coincident points. The information we need is simply that contained under the middle axis of the configuration space (Figure 12).

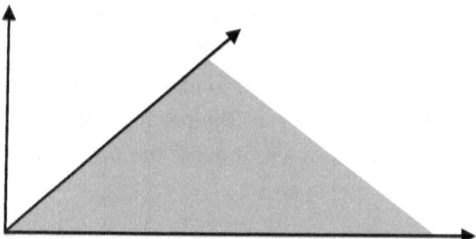

Figure 12: The reduced configuration space.

To sum up, given the reduced configuration $^3R^N$, there is no way to distinguish which particle is at one particular point. What we know is just that one point is occupied: particles may be distinguished only by their position. In contrast, a normal configuration in R^{3N} has a structure that indicates that a particular particle is at one particular point. Moreover, the reduced configuration space has the advantage that it perfectly reflects the permutation invariance of the theory – changing the positions of the particles would not affect the dynamics of the theory, since it is completely irrelevant which particle is at which point.

We successfully constructed a new way to represent the particle configuration and the configuration space given the property-less character of particles. Now we need to formulate a new law of motion for the particle. In particular, we need to formulate a permutation invariant law, as we have seen at the beginning of this section. The dynamics developed by the laws should not change depending on the permutation of particles.

In order to understand the formulation of the new invariant laws better, let us imagine an entangled system of two particles governed by one wave-function (Goldstein et al., 2005). Here we have three elements: one particle (in order to identify the particle let us suppose that in any standard quantum theory it would be classified as an electron, and let us call it q_1), another particle (q_2, a muon in a standard quantum theory), and a scalar valued wave-function $\psi(q_1, q_2)$. Let us also suppose that the wave-function is factorizable in this way: $\psi(q_1, q_2) = \chi(q_1)\varphi(q_2)$. Then, according to identity-based Bohmian mechanics, the dynamics of the two particles should be calculated in this way:

$$\frac{dQ_1}{dt} = \frac{\frac{\hbar}{m_e}|\chi(Q_2)|^2 \, Im\left[\varphi(Q_1)^*(\nabla\varphi)(Q_1)\right] + \frac{\hbar}{m_\mu}|\varphi(Q_2)|^2 \, Im\left[\chi(Q_1)^*(\nabla\chi)(Q_1)\right]}{|\varphi(Q_1)|^2 |\chi(Q_2)|^2 + |\varphi(Q_2)|^2 |\chi(Q_1)|^2}$$

$$\frac{dQ_2}{dt} = \frac{\frac{\hbar}{m_\mu}|\varphi(Q_1)|^2 \, Im\left[\chi(Q_2)^*(\nabla\chi)(Q_2)\right] + \frac{\hbar}{m_e}|\chi(Q_1)|^2 \, Im\left[\varphi(Q_2)^*(\nabla\varphi)(Q_2)\right]}{|\varphi(Q_1)|^2 |\chi(Q_2)|^2 + |\varphi(Q_2)|^2 |\chi(Q_1)|^2}$$

where m_e and m_μ are the mass of the electron and the mass of the muon respectively.

In this formulation, it is impossible to distinguish one particle from the other except for their positions: what we know is that whichever particle is on the left will behave like an electron, and whichever particle is on the right will behave like a muon (given that the supporters of the two wave-functions are disjoint). In a nutshell, if we have in one configuration one 'electron' at the space point P_1 and a 'muon' at P_2, and in another configuration one 'muon' at P_1 and an 'electron' at P_2, then in both scenarios the particle at P_1 would behave in the same way, and the particles at P_2 would behave in the same way, regardless of what 'kind' of particles they are. That one particle will have a particular trajectory and that the other will follow another trajectory does not depend on the nature of the particles; rather, it depends on the law and on the initial conditions of the system (the particle positions). For this reason, we can clearly state that the particles are identical: they do not bear any properties in virtue of which they belong to a particular natural kind. We can distinguish particles only through their position and through their trajectories: their difference is only due to how the guiding law of motion directs them and on the contingent initial conditions. To appreciate this proposal, we should keep in mind that although none of the properties normally attributed to the particles are directly observable, they are all deduced from their motion. Thus we know that two particles are different in some respect not because we see that their properties are different, but because their motions are different in the same empirical situation.

At this point, it might be very interesting to inquire into how the dynamics arises in a context where the particles do not have any properties. In particular, what we would like to know is the reason why one particle moves towards one direction and another identical particle moves towards another direction: since the two particles are exactly the same, it seems hard to explain the difference of motion without appealing to any intrinsic difference. In this theory, the explanation of the dynamics is a burden for the universal wave-function. The wave-function is indeed thought to be multi-component, so that it has all the components corresponding to all the possible motions that the particle could take. As we can see, both the components of the wave-function, the one for the electron and the one for the muon, determine the motion of each of the two particles. However, the two components do not determine the two particle trajectories in the same way. Depending on the position of the particle, one component influences the motion more than the other one, so that they determine a mixed trajectory (which, however, is unobservable). The most interesting case is when the two wave-functions have disjoint supporters: in such a case, each component influences only one particle, since the other one vanishes. This way, we would get an observable and a 'pure' trajectory, one that is either proper of an electron or proper of a muon. However, this way of characterizing the trajectory is improper in this theory. As we have seen, the theory postulates only the existence of one single species, since the particles are all identical and not label-able in any way except for their spatio-temporal properties.

It seems that this program is entirely successful. In light of this, we could claim that it is legitimate to postulate a property-less ontology given that the laws of Bohmian mechanics can be reformulated as permutation invariant. In particular, we could claim that while the standard formulation of Bohmian mechanics is much more convenient and efficient, and, for this reason, it should be kept, the identity-based formulation of Bohmian mechanics is more faithful to the ontology. And this is certainly not a problem for the structural realist since they do not reify the mathematical structure of the theory. However, this is not the right conclusion to draw. Indeed, a major problem comes from the predictions determined by the identity-based Bohmian mechanics. Even though both Bohmian mechanics and the identity-based Bohmian mechanics are equally empirically adequate since their predictions match experimental results, they determine different trajectories. Practically speaking, given that we cannot see trajectories (all the knowledge we get about the system is filtered through the wave-function), this does not raise any problem. But the real issue at stake is that Bohmian mechanics and identity-based Bohmian mechanics are not the same theory – they are two different theories, generating two different kinds of evolution for the system. This means that, strictly speaking, we have not actually proved that we can reformulate Bohmian mechanics as a theory faithful to a property-less ontology. Rather, we created a new one. More strikingly, it seems that it is not possible to build Bohmian mechanics with permutation invariant laws without changing the particle trajectories.

This leaves us with a dilemma. The first option would be to endorse the identity-based Bohmian mechanics from the beginning and leave aside the formulation of standard Bohmian mechanics. This way, our laws are extremely complicated but they are faithful to the underlying ontology. The second option would be to keep Bohmian mechanics and admit a gap between the laws and the ontology. This is certainly a viable option for the structuralists given that, as we have just seen, they do not reify the mathematical structure of the theory. However, it would be a very uncomfortable situation, given that a pillar of their methodology is to infer the ontology from the laws. For this reason, we are inclined to choose the first option.

7.5 Possible Objections

Now that I have discussed potential threats for my accounts, let me turn to address possible objections.

7.5.1 The Unobservability and Underdetermination of the Dynamical Structure

A criticism that may be raised, and which I want to address now, concerns the unobservability and underdetermination of the dynamical relations represented by the wave-function. In section 5.3, we set some desiderata that the methodological program of OSR ought to achieve. One of those desiderata is the elimination of the gap between epistemic access and ontology in order to reduce cases of underdetermination to a minimum. The fact that many entities postulated by a theory are unobservable is not a problem in itself – for sure it is impossible to eliminate all unobservable entities and keep only the observable ones. However, the problem comes whenever those unobservable entities are redundant and whenever they generate a serious case of underdetermination. For this reason, according to OSR, it is better to opt for a more parsimonious and modest ontology and to commit to the existence only of those entities that are necessary and essential for the theory. In the case of Bohmian mechanics, we claimed that the necessary and essential entity that wave-function represents is not a field in 3ND, but an entanglement structure in 3D, which relates all the particles. The question that should be seriously addressed is whether this structure generates a case of underdetermination. We have already touched upon this question when we were examining whether the wave-function could represent a background structure, but our primary aim was to show that the interpretation of the wave-function as a background structure is not feasible; now, by contrast, our aim is more ambitious and consists in showing that it is not the case that there are different interpretations of the structure represented by the wave-function, which are ontologically different but empirically equivalent with a body of observation O.

As I stressed earlier, the notion of structure adopted by OSR is certainly vague and lacks a precise definition. For this reason, it may be easy to cook up another metaphysical description of the structure represented by the wave-function. However, the methodology we developed in order to depict that structure does not allow much room for discordance. We want the structure to be invariant under 3D coordinate transformations, we want it to be modal and non-local in order to be explanatorily powerful. I do not see how, once we put the methodology in practice, we could have a different metaphysical interpretation of the structure. If the reader has followed step by step the process of applying the methodology to the case of the Bohmian wave-function, then she can only accept the result. The reader may refuse the methodology in the first place, and that may certainly lead to the identification of another physical structure as the one represented by the wave-function. But this does not threaten the scope of my work, which was to show that the kind of ontology results from applying a certain structuralist methodology to Bohmian mechanics does not fall into the problem of underdetermination.

7.5.2 It Is Not a Structuralist 'Reconciliation', Rather It Is a Structuralist 'Rejection'

Another criticism is that even though the reconciliation between realism and nomologicalism seems like a noble aim, the structuralist view denies central theses of both camps. Indeed, according to the structuralist interpretation, the wave-function is not a law, and is not a physical field. For this reason, the criticism concludes that more fundamentally, the structuralist view is a rejection of both camps, and not a reconciliation.

It may be only an issue of seeing the glass as half empty or as half full, but I actually do not agree with the above conclusion for the following. We saw that, according to the structuralist view, the wave-function is a nomological entity and we also saw that, according to the structuralist view, the wave-function does represent a physical entity (so we should be 'realist' about the wave-function). Both the claims are the core claims of the nomological and realist view respectively. However, the structuralist view develops those two claims in a different way, by adopting a good methodology. On the one hand, the structuralist rejects any process of reification and distinguishes the ontologically complete representation of the system from the informationally complete representation of the system. On the other hand, she takes the nomological entity seriously and recognizes their ontological salience. In this regard, what the structural realist achieves is a reconciliation of the two views.

Conclusion

At the end of the last chapter, we evaluated the structuralist ontological interpretation of Bohmian mechanics by comparing and contrasting it to the interpretations endorsed by the realist view and the nomological view respectively. To summarize the specific conclusions of the chapter, I claimed not only that the structuralist view provides the best ontology, but also that it should be regarded as a reconciliatory view between the realist stance, which considers the wave-function as a physical entity, and the nomological stance, according to which the wave-function is a law-like entity. Indeed, the structuralist interpretation takes on aspects of both views. We also discussed some pressing questions that ought to be explored further and that will provide a foundation for future research.

In these final pages, I would like to present some more general considerations about my book.

When it is time to conclude a work on which so much time has been spent, I believe it is always a good practice not to look for its merits and achievements – which, I hope, are not absent – but rather to take a more critical stance. This is certainly a good *modus operandi* that can help us to improve future research and assist us in drawing more interesting conclusions. For this reason, in what follows I will evaluate three different limitations of my book that I think are worth considering.

The first weakness of my work is that my investigation very often failed to navigate between the 'Scylla' of formalism and the 'Charybdis' of metaphysics (borrowing an expression used in the very first pages of this book). In my introduction, I claimed that the aim of this book is to develop a good ontological interpretation of Bohmian mechanics, and that the methodology adopted should let neither formalism nor metaphysical speculations take over and completely dictate the ontology. I argued that both aspects are equally needed, and the process of inferring the best ontology should involve a back-and-forth approach between mathematical and metaphysical considerations.

In my book, I always tried to evaluate and consider both the metaphysical and formal aspects. However, at several points, I had to definitively choose between the two. On many occasions, when evaluating the realist and nomological views, I already had in mind some metaphysical criteria for evaluation (for example, that laws cannot be temporal or that physical fields should respect some metaphysical characterizations). Other times, I decided to let the formulation of the theory dictate the ontology, without leaving space for any other options. This occurred, for example, when I ruled out the relational view of Bohmian mechanics. A further example can be found in the case of particle impenetrability (chapter 2), which presented an 'out-out' option between the formalism and the metaphysical presuppositions:

either we presuppose the impenetrability conditions of the particles on the basis of purely metaphysical criteria, or, following the formalism of the theory, we accept the possibility that different particles can share the same positions. It was not always possible to engage in a dialogue between metaphysics and formalism and to take both into consideration in my final decisions. In my discussions, whenever I failed to find a good compromise between formalism and metaphysics as a result of the fact that the two were pulling in completely opposite directions, I spelled out my presuppositions explicitly and tried to motivate my position as much as I could. However, there was always an element of arbitrariness that was difficult to eliminate completely. This showed me that sometimes pursuing and applying a good methodology is simply impossible. As philosophers of physics, we are forced at times to decide between formal or metaphysical considerations and to acknowledge that it is impossible to take into account both while drawing some conclusions. What we can do is only to evaluate the two and decide which aspects are more compelling.

The second weakness of my work is that, on several occasions, I left the discussion incomplete. This happened whenever I touched upon but did not spell out certain metaphysical problems inherent in general metaphysical conceptions that were not specifically related to the Bohmian ontology. While I did deal with such metaphysical questions within the particular framework under consideration (i. e. Bohmian mechanics), they definitely deserve a much broader and deeper discussion than I have offered. Engaging in such discussions would have risked going beyond the scope of this book; however, not digging into those questions also meant that related discussions remained limited and unsatisfactory. The case of structural realism is emblematic in this regard. In the chapter on the structuralist interpretation of the Bohmian ontology (chapter 6), I had to face several problems, such as how to formulate the definition of structure according to OSR, and how OSR faces the threat of circularity concerning the identity conditions for the relata. These are problems that the structuralist view has not successfully tackled yet. And it may be argued that these problems seem to be of such great importance that it is useless to endorse this view at all until it solves them. More generally, it may be argued that if a metaphysical view is not robust and cannot stand on its own, it is useless to discuss it in its application to specific cases. However, in this respect, I should underline that it was not my intention to take this view as metaphysically robust and then to argue that the Bohmian ontology can be interpreted according to its metaphysical commitments. Rather, I took the ontic structural realist methodological program, which, I argued, is the best, and showed how it can provide the best ontological interpretations we have so far. This should encourage us to regard the structuralist view as promising and worthy of discussion despite the difficulties it faces.

The third weakness of my book concerns the structuralist ontological interpretation of Bohmian mechanics I am proposing. I started my book by distinguishing between formalism and metaphysics. I argued that, while developing a good ontological interpretation of the theory, we should engage in a dialogue between the two and treat them equally. During the writing of my book, I acquired the clear understanding that for an ontological interpretation to be successful, it must realize a sentence by Enriques: "Science et philosophie ne se laissent séparer qu'à un point de vue abstrait" (science and philosophy may separate only on an abstract level) (Enriques, 1937, p. 221). Whenever the dialogue between formalism and metaphysics is truly successful, it should be almost impossible to separate the two aspects of the theory in the ontological interpretation. This means that it should be almost impossible to rigidly adduce a particular ontological interpretation to the kind of formalism adopted or the kind of metaphysical view we endorse. I believe that the structuralist interpretation provides the ontology where formalism and metaphysics are best intermixed. In the nomological and realist views, on the other hand, the two aspects of the theory are not equally evaluated and one is mainly preferred over the other, and this affects the resulting ontology. However, it is also true that the structuralist interpretation I am defending is still not completely satisfactory. This was clearly visible when we looked at what the formalism would be like if the theory were really about property-less particles. In this case, it is right to admit that our ontological characterization of particles is given by metaphysical concerns rather than an evaluation of the formalism.

Now, to this paragraph I dedicate the dearest conclusive remark of my book. The discussion of the ontological interpretation of Bohmian mechanics has recently taken the form of a harsh debate between the realist and nomological camps. In this book, I wanted to offer the reader a fair interpretation of the Bohmian ontology that could be considered equally appealing to both the realists and the nomologists. Moreover, I tried to spell out all the commitments and implications of the two views in order to show the merits and disadvantages of both, as well as to demonstrate why they should not be considered as two out-out alternatives. I hope to have shown that the debate surrounding the Bohmian ontology need not revolve solely around these two views. In particular, I hope to have shown that questions about the Bohmian ontology should not die out, because it is incorrect to suppose that we already know all the possible answers and that it is only a matter of which one we should choose. On the contrary, we still do not know all the possible answers, and so we are still entitled to ask the same questions again and to find new ways to tackle them. Careful philosophical thinking should not be relegated to the frameworks provided by those two camps; rather, it is time for us to apply this kind of thinking in order to come up with new interpretations.

Bibliography

Aharonov, Y. & Vaidman, L. (1996). "About Position Measurements which Do Not Show the Bohmian Particle Position". In J. T. Cushing, A. Fine & S. Goldstein (Eds.), *Bohmian Mechanics and Quantum Theory: An Appraisal* (pp. 141–154). Dordrecht: Springer.

Ainsworth, P. M. (2009). "What Is Ontic Structural Realism?" *Studies in History and Philosophy of Modern Physics* 41(1): 50–57.

Albert, D. Z. (1996). "Elementary Quantum Metaphysics". In J. T. Cushing, A. Fine & S. Goldstein (Eds.), *Bohmian Mechanics and Quantum Theory: An Appraisal* (pp. 277–284). Dordrecht: Springer.

Albert, D. Z. (2009). *Quantum Mechanics and Experience*. Cambridge: Harvard University Press.

Albert, D. Z. (2013). "Wave Function Realism". In A. Ney & D. Albert (Eds.), *The Wave Function: Essays on the Metaphysics of Quantum Mechanics* (pp. 52–57). Oxford/New York: Oxford University Press.

Allori, V. (2013). "Primitive Ontology and the Structure of Fundamental Physical Theories". In A. Ney & D. Albert (Eds.), *The Wave Function: Essays on the Metaphysics of Quantum Mechanics* (pp. 58–75). Oxford/New York: Oxford University Press.

Allori, V. (2015). "Primitive Ontology in a Nutshell". URL: http://commons.lib.niu.edu/handle/10843/16041 (last accessed 17. 10.2022).

Allori, V. (2017). "Primitive Ontology and the Classical World". In R. Kastner, J. Jeknic-Dugic & G. Jaroszkiewicz (Eds.), *Quantum Structural Studies: Classical Emergence from the Quantum Level* (pp. 175–199). London/Hackensack,NJ: World Scientific.

Allori, V., Dorato, M., Laudisa, F. & Zanghì, N. (2005). *La natura delle cose*. Rome: Carocci.

Anandan, J. & Brown, H. R. (1995). "On the Reality of Space-time Geometry and the Wavefunction". *Foundations of Physics* 25(2): 349–360.

Anderson, J. (1964). "Relativity Principles and the Role of Coordinates in Physics". In H. Chiu & W. Hoffmann (Eds.), *Gravitation and Relativity* (pp. 175–194). New York: Benjamin.

Anderson, J. (1967). *Principles of Relativity Physics*. New York: Academic Press.

Arenhart, J. R. B. & Bueno, O. (2015). "Structural Realism and the Nature of Structure". *European Journal for Philosophy of Science* 5(1): 111–139.

Bacciagaluppi, G. (1999). "Nelsonian Mechanics Revisited". *Foundations of Physics Letters* 12(1): 1–16.

Bacciagaluppi, G. (2012). "Non-equilibrium in Stochastic Mechanics". *Journal of Physics: Conference Series* 361(1): 1–11.

Bacciagaluppi, G. & Valentini, A. (2009). *Quantum Theory at the Crossroads: Reconsidering the 1927 Solvay Conference*. Cambridge: Cambridge University Press.

Bain, J. (2013). "Category-theoretic Structure and Radical Ontic Structural Realism". *Synthese* 190(9): 1621–1635.

Bedard, K. (1999). "Material Objects in Bohm's Interpretation". *Philosophy of Science* 66(2): 221–242.

Bell, J. S. (1987). *Speakable and Unspeakable in Quantum Mechanics*. Cambridge: Cambridge University Press.

Belot, G. (2012). "Quantum States for Primitive Ontologists". *European Journal for Philosophy of Science* 2(1): 67–83.

Belousek, D. W. (2003). "Formalism, Ontology and Methodology in Bohmian Mechanics". *Foundations of Science* 8(2): 109–172.

Berenstain, N. & Ladyman, J. (2012). "Ontic Structural Realism and Modality". In E. Landry & D. Rickles (Eds.), *Structural Realism: Structure, Object, and Causality* (pp. 149–168). Dordrecht: Springer.

Bigaj, T. (2014). "In Defense of an Essentialist Approach to Ontic Structural Realism". *Methode: Analytic Perspective* 3(4): 1–24.
Bigaj, T. & Wüthrich, C. (Eds.) (2015). *Metaphysics in Contemporary Physics*. Leiden: Brill, Rodopi.
Bigelow, J., Ellis, B. & Pargetter, R. (1988). "Forces". *Philosophy of Science* 55(4): 614–630.
Bowman, G. E. (2008). *Essential Quantum Mechanics*. Oxford/New York: Oxford University Press.
Brading, K. (2010). "Structuralist Approaches to Physics: Objects, Models and Modality" In A. Bokulich & P. Bokulich (Eds.), *Scientific Structuralism* (pp. 43–65). Dordrecht: Springer.
Brading, K. & Skiles, A. (2012). "Underdetermination as a Path to Structural Realism". In E. Landry & D. Rickles (Eds.), *Structural Realism: Structure, Object, and Causality* (pp. 99–115)). Dordrecht: Springer.
Brown, H. R., Dewdney, C. & Horton, G. (1995). "Bohm Particles and Their Detection in the Light of Neutron Interferometry". *Foundations of Physics* 25(2): 329–347.
Brown, H. R., Elby, A. & Weingard, R. (1996). "Cause and Effect in the Pilot-wave Interpretation of Quantum Mechanics". In J. T. Cushing, A. Fine & S. Goldstein (Eds.), *Bohmian Mechanics and Quantum Theory: An Appraisal* (pp. 309–319). Dordrecht: Springer.
Brown, H. R. & Wallace, D. (2005). "Solving the Measurement Problem: De Broglie--Bohm Loses Out to Everett". *Foundations of Physics* 35(4): 517–540.
Brown, H. R. & Pooley, O. (2006). "Minkowski Space-time: A Glorious Non-entity". *Philosophy and Foundations of Physics* 1: 67–89.
Brown, H. R. & Lehmkuhl, D. (2013). "Einstein, the Reality of Space, and the Action-reaction Principle". In P. Ghose (Ed.), *Einstein, Tagore, and the Nature of Reality* (pp. 9–36). London/New York: Routledge.
Callender, C. (2015). "One World, One Beable". *Synthese* 192(10): 3153–3177.
Cao, T. Y. (2003). "Structural Realism and the Interpretation of Quantum Field Theory". *Synthese* 136(1): 3–24.
Cassirer, E. (1957). *Zur modern Physik*. Darmstadt: Wissenschaftliche Buchgesellschaft.
Cei, A. & French, S. (2014). "Getting Away from Governance: A Structuralist Approach to Laws and Symmetries". *Methode* 3(4): 25–48.
Chakravartty, A. (2003). "The Structuralist Conception of Objects". *Philosophy of Science* 70(5): 867–878.
Chakravartty, A. (2004). "Structuralism as a Form of Scientific Realism". *International Studies in the Philosophy of Science* 18(2 & 3): 151–171.
Chakravartty, A. (2005). "Causal Realism: Events and Processes". *Erkenntnis* 63(1): 7–31.
Chakravartty, A. (2013). "Scientific Realism". *The Stanford Encyclopedia of Philosophy*. URL: https://plato.stanford.edu/entries/scientific-realism/ (last accessed 17. 10.2022).
Chakravartty, A. (2017). "Particles, causation, and the metaphysics of structure". *Synthese*, 194(7),2273–2289.
Chen, E. K. (2017). "Our fundamental physical space: An essay on the metaphysics of the wave function". *The Journal of Philosophy*, 114(7),333–365.
Chen, E. K. (2019). "Realism about the wave function". *Philosophy compass, 14*(7), e12611.
Cohen, J. & Callender, C. (2009). "A Better Best System Account of Lawhood". *Philosophical Studies* 145(1): 1–34.
Cushing, J. T. (1994). *Quantum Mechanics: Historical Contingency and the Copenhagen Hegemony*. Chicago: University of Chicago Press.
Cushing, J. T., Fine, A. & Goldstein, S. (1996). *Bohmian Mechanics and Quantum Theory: An Appraisal*. Dordrecht: Springer.
Dainton, B. (2016). *Time and Space*. Durham: Routledge.

Dasgupta, S. (2009). "Individuals: An Essay in Revisionary Metaphysics". *Philosophical Studies* 145(1): 35–67.
Dasgupta, S. (2014). "On the Plurality of Grounds". *Philosophers' Imprint* 14(20): 1–28.
Daumer, M., Dürr, D., Goldstein, S. & Zanghì, N. (1996). "Naive Realism about Operators". *Erkenntnis* 45(2–3): 379–397.
Dewdney, C., Hardy, L. & Squires, E. J. (1993). "How Late Measurements of Quantum Trajectories Can Fool a Detector". *Physics Letters A* 184(1): 6–11.
Dickson, M. (2000). "Are There Material Objects in Bohm's Theory?" *Philosophy of Science* 67(4): 704–710.
Dieks, D. (2006). *The Ontology of Spacetime*. Vol. 1. Elsevier.
Dieks, D. (2008). *The Ontology of Spacetime II*. Vol. 2. Elsevier.
Dorato, M. (2006). "Properties and Dispositions: Some Metaphysical Remarks on Quantum Ontology". In A. Bassi, D. Dürr, T. Weber & N. Zanghi (Eds.), *AIP Conference Proceedings* (Vol. 844, No. 1, pp. 139–157). New York: American Institute of Physics.
Dorato, M. & Morganti, M. (2013). "Grades of Individuality. A Pluralistic View of Identity in Quantum Mechanics and in the Sciences". *Philosophical Studies* 163(3): 591–610.
Dorato, M. & Laudisa F. (2014). "Realism and Instrumentalism about the Wave Function. How Should We Choose?" In Shan Gao (Ed.), *Protective Measurements and Quantum Reality: Toward a New Understanding of Quantum Mechanics* (pp. 119–134). Cambridge: Cambridge University Press.
Dorato, M. & Esfeld, M. (2015). "The Metaphysics of Laws: Dispositionalism vs. Primitivism". In T. Bigaj & C. Wüthrich (Eds.), *Metaphysics in Contemporary Physics* (pp. 403–424). Amsterdam: Rodopi.
Dorr, C. (2009). *Finding Ordinary Objects in Some Quantum Worlds*. URL: https://pages.nyu.edu/dorr/papers/Finding.pdf (last accessed 17.10.2022).
Dürr, D., Goldstein, S. & Zanghì, N. (1992). "Quantum Equilibrium and the Origin of Absolute Uncertainty". *Journal of Statistical Physics* 67(5–6): 843–907.
Dürr, D., Goldstein, S. & Zanghì, N. (1995). "Bohmian Mechanics and Quantum Equilibrium". *Stochastic Processes, Physics and Geometry* 2: 221–232.
Dürr, D., Goldstein, S. & Zanghì, N. (1996b). "Bohmian Mechanics as the Foundation of Quantum Mechanics". In J. T. Cushing, A. Fine & S. Goldstein (Eds.), *Bohmian Mechanics and Quantum Theory: An Appraisal* (pp. 21–44). Dordrecht: Springer.
Dürr, D., Goldstein, S. & Zangh, N. (1997). "Bohmian Mechanics and the Meaning of the Wave Function". In R. S. Cohen, M. Horne & J. J. Stacher (Eds.), *Experimental Metaphysics: Quantum Mechanical Studies in honor of Abner Shimony* (25–38). Dordrecht: Springer.
Dürr, D. & Teufel, S. (2009). *Bohmian Mechanics: The Physics and Mathematics of Quantum Theory*. Berlin: Springer.
Dürr, D., Goldstein, S. & Zanghì, N. (2012). *Quantum Physics without Quantum Philosophy*. Berlin: Springer.
Dürr, D., & Lazarovici, D. (2020). Bohmian Mechanics. In *Understanding Quantum Mechanics* (pp. 75–103). Springer, Cham.
Earman, J. (1989). *World Enough and Spacetime: Absolute versus Relational Theories of Space and Time*. Cambridge, MA: MIT Press.
Egg, M. & Esfeld, M. (2015). "Primitive Ontology and Quantum State in the GRW Matter Density Theory". *Synthese* 192(10): 3229–3245.
Einstein, A. (1922). *The Meaning of Relativity*. Princeton: Princeton University Press.

Einstein, A. (1924). "Über den Äther" *Verhandlungen der Schweizerischen Naturforschenden Gesellschaft* 104: 85-93 English translation in S. W. Saunders & H. R. Brown (Eds.) (1991), *The Philosophy of Vacuum* (pp. 13-20). Oxford/New York: Oxford University Press.

Einstein, A. (1961). *The Special and the General Theory*. New York: Crown.

Einstein, A. (1969). "Autobiographical Notes". In P. A. Schilpp (Ed.), *Albert Einstein: Philosopherscientist*. Vol. 1 (pp. 1-94). La Salle, IL: Open Court.

Einstein, A., Podolsky, B. & Rosen, N. (1935). "Can Quantum-mechanical Description of Physical Reality Be Considered Complete?" *Physical Review* 47(10): 777-784.

Enriques, F. (1937). "Descartes et Galilée". *Revue De Métaphysique Et De Morale* 44(1): 221-235.

Esfeld, M. (2001). *Holism in Philosophy of Mind and Philosophy of Physics*. Berlin: Springer.

Esfeld, M. (2003). "Do Relations Require Underlying Intrinsic Properties? A Physical Argument for a Metaphysics of Relations". *Metaphysica: International Journal for Ontology and Metaphysics* 4(1): 5-25.

Esfeld, M. (2004). "Quantum Entanglement and a Metaphysics of Relations". *Studies in History and Philosophy of Science Part B: Studies in History and Philosophy of Modern Physics* 35(4): 601-617.

Esfeld, M. (2009). "The Modal Nature of Structures in Ontic Structural Realism". *International Studies in the Philosophy of Science* 23(2): 179-194.

Esfeld, M. (2013). "Ontic Structural Realism and the Interpretation of Quantum Mechanics". *European Journal for Philosophy of Science* 3(1): 19-32.

Esfeld, M. (2014a). "Quantum Humeanism, or: Physicalism without Properties". *The Philosophical Quarterly* 64(256): 453-470.

Esfeld, M. (2014b). "The Primitive Ontology of Quantum Physics: Guidelines for an Assessment of the Proposals". *Studies in History and Philosophy of Science Part B: Studies in History and Philosophy of Modern Physics* 47: 99-106.

Esfeld, M. (2015). "The Structural Individuation of Quantum Objects". *Methode* 3(4): 49-63.

Esfeld, M. (2017). "How to Account for Quantum Non-locality: Ontic Structural Realism and the Primitive Ontology of Quantum Physics". *Synthese*. DOI: 10.1007/s11229-014-0549-4.

Esfeld, M. (2020). "A Proposal for a Minimalist Ontology". *Synthese* 197(5): 1889-1905.

Esfeld, M. & Lam, V. (2008). "Moderate Structural Realism about Space-time". *Synthese* 160(1): 27-46.

Esfeld, M. & Lam, V. (2010). "Ontic Structural Realism as a Metaphysics of Objects". In A. Bokulich & P. Bokulich (Eds.), *Scientific Structuralism* (pp. 143-159). Dordrecht: Springer.

Esfeld, M., Hubert, M., Lazarovici, D. & Dürr, D. (2014). "The Ontology of Bohmian Mechanics". *The British Journal for the Philosophy of Science* 65(4): 773-796.

Esfeld, M., Lazarovici, D., Lam, V. & Hubert, M. (2015). "The Physics and Metaphysics of Primitive Stuff". *The British Journal for the Philosophy of Science* 68(1): 133-161.

Esfeld, M., Deckert, D. A., Lazarovici, D., Oldofredi, A., & Vassallo, A. (2017). *A minimalist ontology of the natural world*. New York: Routledge.

Faraday, M. (1844). "A Speculation Touching Electric Conduction, and the Nature of Matter". *Journal of the Franklin Institute* 37(6): 392-399.

Feynman, R. P. (1964). *Feynman Lectures on Physics*. Vol. 2: *Mainly Electromagnetism and Matter*. Edited by R. P. Feynman, R. B. Leighton & M. Sands. Reading, MA: Addison-Wesley.

Feynman, R. P., Leighton, R. B. & Sands, M. (1963). *The Feynman Lectures on Physics*. Vol. 1. Reading, MA: Addison-Wesley.

Field, H. (1980). *Science without Numbers*. Oxford: Blackbell.

Field, H. (1982). "Realism and Anti-realism about Mathematics". *Philosophical Topics* 13(1): 45-69.

Field, H. (1984). "Can we dispense with space-time?". In *PSA: Proceedings of the Biennial meeting of the philosophy of science association*, vol. 2, pp. 32-90. Cambridge University Press.

French, S. (2014). *The Structure of the World: Metaphysics and Representation*. Oxford/New York: Oxford University Press.
French, S. & Ladyman, J. (2003). "Remodelling Structural Realism: Quantum Physics and the Metaphysics of Structure". *Synthese* 136(1): 31–56.
French, S. & Rickles, D. (2003). "Understanding Permutation Symmetry". Brading, K., & Castellani, E. (Eds.). *Symmetries in Physics: Philosophical Reflections* (pp. 212–238). Cambridge: Cambridge University Press.
French, S. & Krause, D. (2006). *Identity in Physics: A Historical, Philosophical, and Formal Analysis*. Oxford/New York: Oxford University Press.
Frigg, R. & Votsis, I. (2011). "Everything You Always Wanted to Know about Structural Realism But Were Afraid to Ask". *European Journal for Philosophy of Science* 1(2): 227–276.
Goldstein, S. (1996). "Review Essay: Bohmian Mechanics and the Quantum Revolution". *Synthese* 107(1): 145–165.
Goldstein, S., Taylor, J., Tumulka, R. & Zanghì N. (2005). "Are All Particles Identical?" *Journal of Physics A: Mathematical and General* 38(7): 1567–1576.
Goldstein, S. & Struyve, W. (2007). "On the Uniqueness of Quantum Equilibrium in Bohmian Mechanics". *Journal of Statistical Physics* 128(5): 1197–1209.
Goldstein, S. & Zanghì, N. (2013). "Reality and the Role of the Wave Function in Quantum Theory". In A. Ney & D. Albert (Eds.), *The Wave Function: Essays on the Metaphysics of Quantum Mechanics* (pp. 91–109). Oxford/New York: Oxford University Press.
Greaves, H. (2011). "In Search of (Spacetime) Structuralism". *Philosophical Perspectives* 25(1): 189–204.
Guay, A. & Pradeu, T. (2015). *Individuals Across the Sciences*. Oxford/New York: Oxford University Press.
Hale, S. C. (1988). "Spacetime and the Abstract/Concrete Distinction". *Philosophical Studies* 53(1): 85–102.
Healey, R. (2001). "On the Reality of Gauge Potentials". *Philosophy of Science* 68(4): 432–455.
Healey, R. (2004). "Gauge Theories and Holisms". *Studies in History and Philosophy of Science Part B: Studies in History and Philosophy of Modern Physics* 35(4): 619–642.
Healey, R. (2007). *Gauging What's Real: The Conceptual Foundations of Contemporary Gauge Theories*. Oxford/New York: Oxford University Press.
Hildebrand, T. (2013). "Can Primitive Laws Explain?" *Philosophers' Imprint* 13(15): 1–15.
Holland, P. R. (1995). *The Quantum Theory of Motion: An Account of the De Broglie-Bohm Causal Interpretation of Quantum Mechanics*. Cambridge: Cambridge University Press.
Holland, P. (2001). "Hamiltonian Theory of Wave and Particle in Quantum Mechanics II: Hamilton-Jacobi Theory and Particle Back-reaction". *Nuovo Cimento-Societa' Italiana di Fisica Sezione B* 116(10): 1143–1172.
Horgan, T. & Potrč, M. (2000). "Blobjectivism and Indirect Correspondence". *Facta Philosophica* 2(2): 249–270.
Howard, D. (1985). "Einstein on locality and separability". *Studies in History and Philosophy of Science Part A*, 16(3),171–201.
Hubert, M. (2014). "Quantity of Matter or Intrinsic Property: Why Mass Cannot Be Both". In L. Felline, A. Ledda, F. Paoli & E. Rossanese (Eds.), *New Directions in Logic and the Philosophy of Science* (The SILFS Series 3) (pp. 267–277). London: College Publications.
Hubert, M. (2016). *Particles and Laws of Nature in Classical and Quantum Physics*. PhD dissertation. URL: https://serval.unil.ch/resource/serval:BIB_DCCBD627C57C.P002/REF (last accessed 17. 10.2022).
Hubert, M. & Romano, D. (2018). "The Wave-function as a Multi-field". *European Journal for Philosophy of Science* 8(3): 521–537.

Jackson, F. (1994). "Armchair Metaphysics". In J. O'Leary-Hawthorne & M. Michaelis (Eds.), *Philosophy in Mind* (pp. 23–42). Boston: Kluwer.

Jackson, F. (1998). *From Metaphysics to Ethics: A Defence of Conceptual Analysis*. Oxford/New York: Oxford University Press.

Ladyman, J. (1998). "What Is Structural Realism?" *Studies in History and Philosophy of Science Part A* 29(3): 409–424.

Ladyman, J. (2011). "Structural Realism versus Standard Scientific Realism: The Case of Phlogiston and Dephlogisticated Air". *Synthese* 180(2): 87–101.

Ladyman, J. & Ross, D. (2007). *Every Thing Must Go: Metaphysics Naturalized*. Oxford/New York: Oxford University Press.

Lam, V. (2014). "Protective Measurements and the Status of the Wave Function within the Primitive Ontology Approach". In S. Gao (Ed.), *Protective Measurement and Quantum Realit: Toward a New Understanding of Quantum Mechanics* (pp. 195–210). Cambridge: Cambridge University Press.

Lam, V. (2015). "Quantum Structure and Spacetime". In T. Bigaj & C. Wüthrich (Eds.), *Metaphysics in Contemporary Physics* (pp. 209–228). Leiden: Brill, Rodopi.

Lange, M. (2002). *An Introduction to the Philosophy of Physics Locality, Fields, Energy, and Mass*. Oxford: Blackwell.

Laudan, L. (1981). "A Confutation of Convergent Realism". *Philosophy of Science* 48: 19–49.

Leibniz, G.W. (1989). Specimen Dynamicum. In: Loemker, L.E. (eds) Philosophical Papers and Letters. The New Synthese Historical Library, vol 2. Springer, Dordrecht.

Leibniz, G. W. (2000). *Correspondence*. Indianapolis, IN: Hackett.

Lewis, D. (1986). *On the Plurality of Worlds*. Oxford: Blackwell.

Lewis, D. (1994). "Humean Supervenience Debugged". *Mind* 103(412): 473–490.

Lewis, P. J. (2004). "Life in Configuration Space". *The British Journal for the Philosophy of Science* 55(4): 713–729.

Lewis, P. J. (2007). "Empty Waves in Bohmian Quantum Mechanics". *The British Journal for the Philosophy of Science* 58(4): 787–803.

Lewis, P. J. (2013). "Dimension and Illusion". In A. Ney & D. Albert (Eds.), *The Wave Function: Essays on the Metaphysics of Quantum Mechanics* (pp.110–125). Oxford/New York: Oxford University Press.

Lewis, P. J. (2014). "Measurement and Metaphysics". In S. Gao, *Protective Measurement and Quantum Reality. Towards a New Understanding of Quantum Mechanics* (pp. 93–107). Cambridge: Cambridge University Press.

Lyre, H. (2004). "Holism and Structuralism in U (1) Gauge Theory". *Studies in History and Philosophy of Science Part B: Studies in History and Philosophy of Modern Physics* 35(4): 643–670.

Maudlin, T. (1998). "Healey on the Aharonov-Bohm Effect". *Philosophy of Science* 65(2): 361–368.

Maudlin, T. W. (2007a). "Completeness, Supervenience and Ontology". *Journal of Physics A: Mathematical and Theoretical* 40(12): 3151.

Maudlin, T. (2007b). *The Metaphysics within Physics*. Oxford/New York: Oxford University Press.

Maudlin, T. (2011). *Quantum Non-locality and Relativity: Metaphysical Intimations of Modern Physics*. Malden, MA: Wiley-Blackwell.

Maudlin, T. (2013). "The Nature of the Quantum State". In A. Ney & D. Albert (Eds.), *The Wave Function: Essays on the Metaphysics of Quantum Mechanics* (pp.126–153). Oxford/New York: Oxford University Press.

Maxwell, G. (1962). "The Ontological Status of Theoretical Entities". In H. Feigl & G. Maxwell (Eds.), *Scientific Explanation, Space, and Time* (Minnesota Studies in the Philosophy of Science 3) (pp. 181–192). Minneapolis, MN: University of Minnesota Press.

Maxwell, G. (1968). "Scientific Methodology and the Causal Theory of Perception". In I. Lakatos & A. Musgrave (Eds.), *Problems in the Philosophy of Science* (pp. 289–314). Amsterdam: North-Holland.

Maxwell, G. (1970). "Structural Realism and the Meaning of Theoretical Terms". In S. Winokur & M. Radner (Eds.), *Analyses of Theories, and Methods of Physics and Psychology* (pp. 181–192). Minneapolis: University of Minnesota Press.

Maxwell, G. (1971). "Theories, Perception and Structural Realism". In R. Colodny (Ed.), *Nature and Function of Scientific Theories* (pp. 3–34). Pittsburgh: University of Pittsburgh Press.

Maxwell, J. C. (1954). *Electricity and Magnetism*. New York: Dover.

Miller, E. (2014). "Quantum Entanglement, Bohmian Mechanics, and Humean Supervenience". *Australasian Journal of Philosophy* 92(3): 567–583.

Mompart, J. (Ed.) (2012). *Applied Bohmian Mechanics: From Nanoscale Systems to Cosmology*. Singapore: Pan Stanford.

Monton, B. (2006). "Quantum Mechanics and 3 N-dimensional Space". *Philosophy of Science* 73(5): 778–789.

Morganti, M. (2004). "On the Preferability of Epistemic Structural Realism". *Synthese* 142(1): 81–107.

Morganti, M. (2011). "Is There a Compelling Argument for Ontic Structural Realism?" *Philosophy of Science* 78(5): 1165–1176.

Myrvold, W. C. (2015). "What Is a Wavefunction?" *Synthese* 192(10): 3247–3274.

Nelson, E. (1966). "Derivation of the Schrödinger Equation from Newtonian Mechanics". *Physical Review* 150(4): 1079.

Newton, I. (1704/1952). *Opticks, or, a treatise of the reflections, refractions, inflections & colours of light*. Courier Corporation.

Newton, I. (1687/1999). *The Principia: Mathematical Principles of Natural Philosophy*. Berkeley/Los Angeles/London: University of California Press.

Ney, A. (2010). "Are There Fundamental Intrinsic Properties?" In A. Hazlett (Ed.), *New Waves in Metaphysics* (pp. 219–239). Basingstoke: Palgrave-Macmillan.

Ney, A. (2020). "Finding the world in the wave function: Some strategies for solving the macro-object problem". *Synthese*, 197(10),4227–4249.

Ney, A. & Albert, D. Z. (Eds.) (2013). *The Wave Function: Essays on the Metaphysics of Quantum Mechanics*. Oxford/New York: Oxford University Press.

Norsen, T. (2010). "The Theory of (Exclusively) Local Beables". *Foundations of Physics* 40(12): 1858–1884.

North, J. (2009). "The 'Structure' of Physics: A Case Study". *The Journal of Philosophy* 106(2): 57–88.

North, J. (2013). "The Structure of a Quantum World". In A. Ney & D. Albert: *The Wave Function: Essays on the Metaphysics of Quantum Mechanics* (pp. 184–202). Oxford/New York: Oxford University Press.

Oldofredi, A., Lazarovici, D., Deckert, D. & Esfeld, M. (forthcoming). "From the Universe to Subsystems: Why Quantum Mechanics Appears More Stochastic than Classical Mechanics". *Fluctuations and Noise Letters*, Special issue: *Quantum and Classical Frontiers of Noise*.

Oriolis, X. & Mompart, J. (Ed.) (2012). *Applied Bohmian Mechanics: From Nanoscale Systems to Cosmology*. New York: Jenny Stanford.

Pitowski, L. (1991). "Bohm's Quantum Potential and Quantum Gravity". *Foundations of Physics* 21: 343–352.

Poincaré, H. (1958). *The Value of Science*. New York: Dover.

Pooley, O. (2006). "Points, Particles and Structural Realism". In D. Rickles, S. French & J. Saatsi (Eds.), *The Structural Foundations of Quantum Gravity* (pp. 83–120). Oxford/New York: Oxford University Press.
Psillos, S. (1995). "Is Structural Realism the Best of Both Worlds?" *Dialectica* 49(1): 15–46.
Psillos, S. (1996). "Scientific Realism and the Pessimistic Induction". *Philosophy of Science* 63: S306–S314.
Psillos, S. (1999). *Scientific Realism: How Science Tracks Truth*. London: Routledge.
Psillos, S. (2001). "Is Structural Realism Possible?" *Proceedings of the Philosophy of Science Association* 3: S13–S24.
Psillos, S. (2006). "The Structure, the Whole Structure, and Nothing But the Structure?" *Philosophy of Science* 73(5): 560–570.
Putnam, H. (1975). *Mathematics, Matter, and Method*. Vol. 1. Cambridge: Cambridge University Press.
Pylkkänen, P., Hiley, B. J. & Pättiniemi, I. (2014). "Bohm's Approach and Individuality". In T. Pradeau & A. Guay (Eds.), *Individuals across the Sciences. A Revisionary Metaphyscs?* (226–246). Oxford/New York: Oxford University Press.
Ramírez, S. M. (2020). "Separating Einstein's separability". *Studies in History and Philosophy of Science Part B: Studies in History and Philosophy of Modern Physics*, 72, 138–149.
Rickles, D., French, S. & Saatsi, J. (Eds.) (2006). *The Structural Foundations of Quantum Gravity*. Oxford/New York: Oxford University Press.
Rickles, D. (2008). "Who's afraid of background independence?". In Dieks, D. (2008). *The ontology of spacetime II. Philosophy and Foundations of Physics*, 4 (pp. 133–152). Amsterdam: Elsevier.
Romano, D. (2021). "Multi-field and Bohm's Theory". *Synthese* 198(11): 10587–10609.
Russell, B. (1912). *The Problems of Philosophy*. New York: Barnes & Noble.
Russell, B. (1927). *The Analysis of Matter*. London: Kegan Paul.
Sanz, Á. S. & Miret-Artés, S. (2013). *A Trajectory Description of Quantum Processes. II. Applications: A Bohmian Perspective*. Dordrecht: Springer.
Scully, M. O., Englert, B. G. & Walther, H. (1998). "Do Bohm Trajectories Always Provide a Trustworthy Physical Picture of Particle Motion?" *Physica Scripta-Topical Volumes* 76: 41–46.
Shapiro, S. (1997). *Philosophy of Mathematics: Structure and Ontology*. Oxford/New York: Oxford University Press.
Skow, B. (2010). "On a Symmetry Argument for the Guidance Equation in Bohmian Mechanics". *International Studies in the Philosophy of Science* 24(4): 393–410.
Slowik, E. (2005). "Spacetime, Ontology, and Structural Realism". *International Studies in the Philosophy of Science* 19(2): 147–166.
Smolin, L. (2006). "The Case for Background Independence". In D. Rickles, S. French & J. T. Saatsi (Eds.), *The Structural Foundations of Quantum Gravity* (pp. 196–240). Oxford/New York: Oxford University Press.
Solé, A. (2013). "Bohmian Mechanics without Wave Function Ontology". *Studies in History and Philosophy of Science Part B: Studies in History and Philosophy of Modern Physics* 44(4): 365–378.
Suárez, M. (2015). "Bohmian Dispositions". *Synthese* 192(10): 3203–3228.
Thompson-Jones, M. (2005). "Dispositions and Quantum Mechanics". Unpublished.
Vaidman, L. (2005). "The Reality in Bohmian Quantum Mechanics or Can You Kill with an Empty Wave Vullet?" *Foundations of Physics* 35(2): 299–312.
Valentini, A. (1991). "Signal-locality, Uncertainty, and the Subquantum H-theorem. I". *Physics Letters A* 156(1–2): 5–11.
Valentini, A. (1992). *On the Pilot-wave Theory of Classical, Quantum and Subquantum Physics*. PhD thesis.

Valentini, A. (1996). "Pilot-wave Theory of Fields, Gravitation and Cosmology". In J. T. Cushing, A. Fine & S. Goldstein (Eds.), *Bohmian Mechanics and Quantum Theory: An Appraisal* (pp. 45–66). Dordrecht: Springer.

Valentini, A. (1997). "On Galilean and Lorentz Invariance in Pilot-wave Dynamics". *Physics Letters A* 228(4–5): 215–222.

Valentini, A. (2001). "Hidden Variables, Statistical Mechanics and the Early Universe". In J. Bricmont, D. Dürr, G. Ghirardi & N. Zanghì (Eds.), *Chance in Physics* (pp. 165–181). Berlin: Springer.

Valentini, A. (2002). "Signal-locality in Hidden-variables Theories". *Physics Letters A* 297(5): 273–278.

Valentini, A. (2009). "The Nature of the Wave Function in De Broglie's Pilot-wave Theory". PIAF 09' New Perspectives on the Quantum State, Perimeter Institute. PIRSA Number: 09090094. URL: https://pirsa.org/09090094 (last accessed 17. 12.2022).

Valentini, A. (2012). "De Broglie-Bohm Pilot-wave Theory: Many Worlds in Denial?" In S. W. Saunders, et al. (Eds.), *Many worlds? Everett, quantum theory and reality* (pp. 476–509). Oxford: Oxford University Press.

Valentini, A. & Westman, H. (2005). "Dynamical Origin of Quantum Probabilities". *Proceedings of the Royal Society of London A: Mathematical, Physical and Engineering Sciences* 461(2053): 253–272.

Van Fraassen, B. C. (1997). "Structure and Perspective: Philosophical Perplexity and Paradox". In M. L. Dalla Chiara et al. (Eds.), *Logic and Scientific Methods* (pp. 511–530). Dordrecht: Springer.

Vassallo, A. (2015). "Can Bohmian Mechanics Be Made Background Independent?" *Studies in History and Philosophy of Science Part B: Studies in History and Philosophy of Modern Physics* 52: 242–250.

Vassallo, A. (2016). "A Metaphysical Reflection on the Notion of Background in Modern Spacetime Physics" In L. Felline, F. Paoli, E. Rossanese & A. Ledda (eds.), *New Developments in Logic and Philosophy of Science*. College Publications. pp. 349–365.

Vassallo, A. & Ip, P. H. (2016). "On the Conceptual Issues Surrounding the Notion of Relational Bohmian Dynamics". *Foundations of Physics* 46(8): 943–972.

Votsis, I. (2005). "The Upward Path to Structural Realism". *Philosophy of Science* 72(5): 1361–1372.

Wolff, J. (2012). "Do Objects Depend on Structures?" *British Journal for the Philosophy of Science* 63(3): 607–625.

Wolff, J. (2013). "Are Conservation Laws Metaphysically Necessary?" *Philosophy of Science* 80(5): 898–906.

Wolff, J. (2015). "Spin as a Determinable". *Topoi* 34(2): 379–386.

Worrall, J. (1989). "Structural Realism: The Best of Both Worlds?" *Dialectica* 43(1–2): 99–124.

Worrall, J. (1994). "How to Remain (Reasonably) Optimistic: Scientific Realism and the 'Luminiferous Ether'". In D. Hull, M. Forbes, & R. M. Burian (Eds.) *PSA: Proceedings of the Biennial Meeting of the Philosophy of Science Association 1994* (pp. 334–342). Cambridge: Cambridge University Press.

Worrall, J. (2007). "Miracles and Models: Why Reports of the Death of Structural Realism May Be Exaggerated". In A. O'Hare (Ed.), *Philosophy of science (Royal Institute of Philosophy 61)* (pp. 125–154). Cambridge: Cambridge University Press.

Worrall, J. (2012). "Miracles and Structural Realism". In E. Landry & D. Rickles (Eds.), *Structural Realism* (pp. 77–95). Dordrecht: Springer.

Index

Aristotelian kinematics 69

blobjectivism 72

causality 72, 86, 92
configuration space 9–11, 94
contextual properties 45–47
criterion of back-action 86, 89, 95, 161

danglers 191–193, 197
determinism 23–24
dispositional interpretation 142–145

energy 13–15
equivariance 25–27
explanation 54, 56–57

field theory 71–72
fundamentality 103–104

guiding equation 15, 64, 103–104, 114

Hamiltonian 13–15, 64, 87
Humean view 103, 124, 134
hydrogen atom 87–88

identity-based Bohmian Mechanics 223
individuality 193–194

Lausanne school 53, 57–59
Leibnizian Principle of reciprocity 85

modality 186–190

Newtonian mechanics 67
no-intersection theorem 23–24
nomological view 114, 122
non-locality 138–139

ontic structural realism 161–163

particles 35–59
primitive ontology 53–57
probabilities 24–25
properties 35, 50–52

quantum equilibrium hypothesis 25–27

reciprocity 82–86
reification 94–97

Schrödinger equation 13–15
simplicity 104–106
structural realism 163–164
super-humeanism 149–150
supervenience 136–137, 214

the principle of generosity 49
the principle of parsimony 50

underdetermination 52, 150, 178, 208, 217, 225

wave-function 11, 210
wave-function realism 63–111

www.ingramcontent.com/pod-product-compliance
Lightning Source LLC
Chambersburg PA
CBHW020227170426
43201CB00007B/338